LETTERS FROM IRELAND

Harriet Martineau

1833

Engraving of Harriet Martineau, 1833, by George Richmond, R.A.
The Armitt Trust

Letters from Ireland
Harriet Martineau

GLENN HOOPER

Editor

IRISH ACADEMIC PRESS
DUBLIN • PORTLAND, OR

First published in 2001 by
IRISH ACADEMIC PRESS
44, Northumberland Road, Dublin 4, Ireland
and in the United States of America by
IRISH ACADEMIC PRESS
c/o ISBS, 5824 NE Hassalo Street,
Portland, OR 97213–3644

Website: www.iap.ie

British Library Cataloguing in Publication Data
Martineau, Harriet, 1802–1876
   Letters from Ireland. – (Women in Irish history)
   1. Martineau, Harriet, 1802–1876 – Correspondence   2. Martineau, Harriet,
   1802–1876 – Journeys – Ireland.   3. Ireland – Social conditions – 19th century
   4. Ireland – Description and travel.
   I. Title   II. Hooper, Glenn
   941.5'081
   ISBN 0–7165–2653–0

Library of Congress Cataloging-in-Publication Data
Martineau Harriet, 1802–1876.
   Letters from Ireland / Harriet Martineau; edited by Glenn Hooper.
      p. cm.
   Originally published: London: Chapman, 1852.
   Includes index.
   ISBN 0–7165–2653–0
   1. Ireland—Description and travel.   2. Martineau, Harriet, 1802–1876—
Journeys—Ireland.   I. Hooper, Glenn, 1959–   II. Title.

DA975.M38 2000
941.5081—dc21   00–025122

Typeset in 11 pt on 13 pt Sabon
by Carrigboy Typesetting Services, County Cork
Printed by Creative Print and Design (Wales) Ebbw Vale

Contents

Acknowledgements

VERY FEW editorial changes have been made to Martineau's text, as I believe little is to be gained from modernising the original. Besides, Martineau's voice is so clear, and so emphatic at times that it is difficult to determine what could have constituted safe editorial intervention. A few minor misspellings have been corrected, and a small number of alternations in layout have been necessarily incorporated, but a misdated letter has been retained because Martineau's intentions remain clear. Indeed, in only one or two instances did I really feel an alteration necessary, believing that even the rather long paragraphs, quirky phraseology, and sometimes stilted punctuation favoured by Martineau, should be faithfully reproduced. *Letters,* published almost exactly as it was by John Chapman in 1852, carries therefore some of the flaws, but also the originality and interest of its first printing.

I am grateful to a number of individuals who assisted me in editing this text, either directly or by example. My thanks, firstly, to Declan Kiberd, who patiently supervised my earlier encounters with Harriet, and who provided much needed encouragement along the way. Margaret Kelleher and Valerie Sanders read an early draft of the work, and offered particularly useful advice on a number of points. Christine Kinealy and Kevin Whelan took time out of their busy schedules to comment at a later stage, and helped keep the project alive. Hilary Bell proved an invaluable and courteous reader, while Brenda Collins and Kathleen Villiers-Tuthill provided much needed information about the linen industry and Mayo local history respectively. My thanks, finally, to the staff of the Linenhall Library Belfast, particularly Gerry Healey, to the staff of the University of Aberdeen Library, and to Nancy Riggs-Miller for allowing permission to use Moynan's fine painting as a cover illustration. Figures one to eighteen are reproduced courtesy of the National Library of Ireland.

List of Illustrations

Illustrations appear between pages 56 & 57 and 120 & 121

Editor's Introduction

FOR ALMOST forty years – from 1830 until 1869 – few writers were more prolific, or more attuned to the rhythms of Victorian Britain, than Harriet Martineau. Quite apart from the breadth of subjects upon which she wrote – biography, political economy, theology, literary criticism – Martineau's output was staggering. She published *Illustrations of Political Economy* (24 volumes, 1832–4), *Society in America* (3 volumes, 1837), *How to Observe: Morals and Manners* (1838), *Retrospect of Western Travel* (3 volumes, 1838), the novel *Deerbrook* (1839), *Life in the Sickroom* (1843), *Letters on Mesmerism* (1845), *Eastern Life, Present and Past* (3 volumes, 1848), a translation of *The Philosophy of Comte* (2 volumes, 1853), and many others. *British Rule in India* was published in 1857, followed by *Suggestions towards the Future Government of India*, in 1858. Her *Autobiography*, written twenty-one years earlier when the writer considered her health poor enough to warrant it, was posthumously published in 1877. She was a remarkable figure: industrious, self-reliant, and driven by a desire to see to press texts that she felt would significantly improve society.[1] In 1852 she travelled to Ireland, not for the first time, but at an important period in Irish history. *Letters from Ireland*, originally written as a series of leaders for the *Daily News*, was published in 1852. This is the first republication of the text since that date.

EARLY YEARS

Harriet Martineau was born in Norwich on 12 June 1802 to Thomas and Elizabeth Martineau. Her father was a wealthy manufacturer who belonged 'to an old and distinguished Norwich family'; her mother, Elizabeth Rankin, came from a Newcastle business family involved in sugar-refining and wholesale grocery.[2] Elizabeth and Thomas Martineau maintained a largely supportive household, and emphasized the benefits of education for all their children, girls and boys. Her mother, who had had a modest education, continued to educate herself, while her father, 'a mild man, comforting, generous, and sound', provided a relatively stable background for the young Harriet.[3] She had seven brothers and sisters (she being the sixth

1

child), and although she records generally happy memories of her siblings, she is reputed to have been a difficult child. She developed problems with her hearing at an early age, took particular exception to dreams and other anxieties, and lived in a state of agitation for most of her childhood, and well into adolescence. Indeed, illness was an important element in Martineau's early years, particularly the medication, lengthy recuperation, and predictions about the future that frequently accompanied it. In her *Autobiography*, a useful contextualising source,[4] Martineau related the efforts that her parents made to deal with her various sicknesses, but she also emphasized the feelings of insecurity that accompanied these crises. At eighteen she was practically deaf, mortified by its social implications, and unsure how to best cope with it in public. The difficulties for a woman with literary ambitions at the beginning of the nineteenth century, with the additional burden of a physical handicap, should not be under-estimated.[5]

While Martineau was troubled by a variety of illnesses throughout her life, she describes her adolescence as particularly intolerable: 'My health was bad, however, and my mind ill at ease. It was a depressed and wrangling life; and I have no doubt I was as disagreeable as possible.'[6] Not surprisingly, such health-related problems were seriously to affect her self-development, and encouraged an uneasy set of relations towards those around her: 'I had no self-respect, and an unbounded need of approbation and affection. My capacity for jealousy was something frightful.'[7] Nevertheless, she developed intellectually, went through a particularly intense religious phase, and became increasingly focused and single-minded in her literary ambitions. She was especially close to her younger brother, James, trusting his instincts, and taking his advice on everything from literary and spiritual matters to questions of a more personal nature. James was the mediator between herself and John Worthington, for example, a young minister who asked for Harriet's hand in marriage in 1826, but who went insane during a pre-nuptial trial period and died at the age of twenty-seven. Harriet saw James as the natural figure to whom she could turn for religious and philosophical clarification. And it was James, based in Dublin, who ultimately encouraged her to write for the benefit of political economy in more extended and lasting forms. Unfortunately, the relationship between the two ended unhappily when Harriet wrote favourably about her experiences with mesmerism in *Letters on the Laws of Man's Social Nature and Development* (1851), which James publicly denounced in the *Prospective Review*. Their break was total: they never spoke nor met again. Harriet died in 1876; James in 1900.

Although the Martineaus had arrived in Norwich as Huguenots in the seventeenth century, their eventual conversion to Unitarianism was to provide Harriet with the opportunity for as much literary as spiritual development, even if she was to reject Unitarianism in later years. When she was sent to Bristol at the age of fifteen, for example, to a school run by her aunt, her interests were kindled by the visit of Lant Carpenter, the formidable Unitarian preacher and teacher who had recently arrived in the city from Exeter. After winning a prize from the Unitarian Society for a number of theological essays (1830), she travelled to Ireland to visit her brother James (who had taken up a ministry), to conduct research, and to sketch out the plan of her *Political Economy* series. Martineau resided in Dublin from May until September 1831, noting in her autobiography that she was

> writing all the time, and pondering the scheme of my Political Economy Series. My own idea was that my stories should appear quarterly. My brother and the publishers urged their being monthly. The idea was overwhelming at first: and there were times when truly I was scared at other parts of the scheme than that. The whole business was the strongest act of will that I ever committed myself to; and my will was always a pretty strong one.[8]

Not surprisingly, the series proved to be much less of a risk than was originally thought, as the author produced narratives that illustrated the benefits of political economy in relatively direct and simple terms.

While little interest is shown in the series today, volume IX, *Ireland: A Tale*, is a topical one. Among other things, Martineau presents emigration as a possible solution to Ireland's ongoing economic difficulties, an argument which would resurface twenty years later in *Letters*, when the rage for political economy was gathering force. Political economy, explains Robert Lee Wolff in the 1979 republication of *Ireland: A Tale*, took a firm position 'on the side of laissez-faire, free trade, and the interests of the manufacturer'.[9] However, in a recent article by Timothy Foley, a more emphatic interpretation, which points to the potentially ruthless, pseudo-scientific danger of such a philosophy, is also declared:

> In the nineteenth century, political economy was undoubtedly the sovereign discourse of the public sphere, the quintessentially male space, in the modern industrial Great Britain. It was perceived as a

natural science, its laws the laws of nature, which were not only seen as given and unchanging, but as virtually unchangeable. Like the laws of nature, they were seen as stern and unbending and utterly ruthless in their application. In the harsh climate of the competitive public sphere in modern industrial society, only the fittest survived.[10]

Although critics of political economy are correct to point to its divisive nature, to the components of a doctrine that advocated efficiency above all else, Martineau regarded it as a solution to the economic difficulties of the day, and one that should have a practical application in particular.[11] In the preface to her first volume, for example, she suggests that 'Political Economy treats of the Production, Distribution and Consumption of Wealth; by which term is meant whatever material objects contribute to the support and enjoyment of life.' But some pages later, by way of explaining the necessity for an everyday form of instruction, she writes:

> The works already written on Political Economy almost all bear a reference to books which have preceded, or consist in part of the discussions of disputed points. Such references and such discussions are very interesting to those whom they concern, but offer a poor introduction to those to whom the subject is new. There are a few, a very few, which teach the science systematically as far as it is yet understood. These too are very valuable: but they do not give us what we want – the science in a familiar, practical form. They give us its history; they give us its philosophy; but we want its *picture*. They give us truths, and leave us to look about us, and go hither and thither in search of illustrations of those truths.

This belief in the benefits of political economy, on how it should be conveyed and taught to others, permeates much of Martineau's work.[12] But even the *Edinburgh Review* thought *Ireland: A Tale* flawed in at least one major area:

> Miss Martineau states in her Preface, that 'she considers it her business to treat rather of Irish economy than of Irish politics.' Alas! she lays down a rule to which it would be difficult, if not impossible, to adhere. No surgeon's knife has so fine an edge as to be capable of separating these two elements; and the politics and the political economy of Ireland, as, perhaps, of most other countries, are so blended and intermixed, they act and react upon each other in such a perpetual chain of cause and effect, that there is no analysis so subtle as to make the distinction.

Despite the fact that Martineau tackles a different set of principles in each of her volumes, a remarkably high level of consistency is maintained, even between the apparently naive position adopted in *Ireland: A Tale* and her other volumes. For example, the first volume, *Life in the Wilds*, is set in South Africa; the second, *The Hill and the Valley*, set in Wales. Full of the organising ambitions of farmers or landlords, these texts portray the type of industry and effort regarded as necessary for the improvement of society. Moreover, the ambitious, territorially improving eye of Martineau shows itself as adept at discussing the agri-economical attributes of the Orient as those of Britain, extending the usefulness of political economy, while gratifying and in some senses revering the benefits of empire. Indeed, in stories such as *Demerara* (set on a plantation in British Guiana), *Cinnamon and Pearls* (based in Ceylon), or *Homes Abroad* (Van Diemen's Land), much the same sort of experiences are relayed as in her British-based texts: planters or farmers of one sort or another draining and improving the soil, for their own benefit, but for the benefit of imperial society also. She is not above critizising certain aspects of colonialism, such as slavery; however, it is possible to read Martineau's broadly positive representations of colonial life as having directly contributed to the success of the series. Quite simply, Martineau conveyed the notion of empire, as well as the benefits of political economy, exceptionally well.

Not all reviewers of the day were as supportive of the project as she would have liked; the *Quarterly Review* in 1833, for example, was especially harsh: 'Miss Martineau has, we are most willing to acknowledge, talents which might make her a useful and an agreeable writer. But the best advice we can give her is, to burn all the little books she has as yet written, with one or two exceptions.'[13] Fortunately for Martineau the advice went unheeded, and the series brought success and independence, despite the adverse publicity. That said, the volumes can certainly make for tedious reading, as the author espouses her theories with a deadly seriousness, and in the didactic manner of much, particularly early, nineteenth century writing.[14] Indeed, it was not until *Letters* that Martineau seemed to properly connect with Ireland, when readers declared an interest in something more than tidy advice on economics, enmeshed within a fictionalized form. By 1852 they wanted to see proposals being applied meaningfully, it would seem, and *Letters* would gratify this desire in fresh and dramatic ways.

THE CULTURE OF TRAVEL

So, what exactly was it that brought Harriet Martineau, accompanied by her niece Susan, back to Ireland in 1852? At a very basic level her second trip to the country was the result of a commission from the *Daily News* for a series of articles on Ireland. The economic and political implications of the Famine (1845–52) aroused considerable interest, and there was widespread curiosity as to how the country was to manage with necessary reforms. But travel itself, that aspect of Martineau's personal and professional life which accounted for a good deal, was an additional factor. Four travelogues, including *Letters* and a confusingly entitled poetics of travel – *How to Observe: Morals and Manners* – suggest that the travel narrative form was one to which she was certainly drawn. Her two American travel narratives were published within a year (1837–8), both of them very polished productions, both of them generally well received. Indeed, there is evidence in the American tours of a level of engagement that could only come from considerable sympathy for travel and the travel narrative form: the Mississippi, Niagara, the South, slavery, prisons – all are discussed, and at considerable length, in her three-volume *Retrospect of Western Travel*.[15] Moreover, when it comes to the results of Martineau's Middle Eastern trip, *Eastern Life, Present and Past* (1848), the same sense of excess and amplification, and the same degree of ambition, is evident: desert travel, visits to a hareem, a Nile journey.

   Although travel writing suggested much more than a form that could encapsulate the many stranded interests that Martineau had developed during the course of her long career, it had other attractions. It was expressive of an individual voice in a way that many other forms of writing were not, and it captured something of the adventuring spirit which many women felt increasingly able to articulate. As Alison Blunt has suggested, travel itself 'seems independent, individualistic, and active, unlike the mass, essentially passive consumption associated with tourism'.[16] Martineau was certainly independent and, despite the order and routine she attempted to impress upon her life, a good deal more impetuous than we might think. With regard to both her American and Irish trips, there is a good deal of organization and preparation evident from her published texts. Yet the story of how she travelled to the Middle East gives a radically different impression of this most independent narrator. Originally on a family visit to Liverpool, Martineau embarked, almost on a whim, on a journey of considerable difficulty, with friends whom she had simply bumped into over the course of a vacation. For a figure who suffered generally from poor health, and who always carried an ear trumpet because of her deafness, such a decision says much for her determination and spirit: 'In the autumn of 1846, I left home for, as I supposed, a few weeks, to visit some of my family and friends. At Liverpool I was invited by my friends, Mr. and Mrs. Richard V. Yates, to accompany them in their proposed travels in the East.'[17] And off she went, for eight months, to record the highlights and complexities of the Middle East.

Martineau's writing constitutes part of a development that saw travel literature move away from the somewhat stuffy, formula-bound disclosures of the eighteenth century, towards the grander narratives of the nineteenth. The cultural pilgrimages to continental Europe continued well into the 1800s, of course, but an appetite for more exotic locations allowed the form – hybrid and fluid at the best of times – to make ever more interesting alliances. The critic Mary Louise Pratt suggests that the travel narrative was reinvented at the beginning of the nineteenth century, and became associated with renewed possibility and potential.[18] No doubt scientific discovery, the development of empire, and the proselytizing mania of Christendom also contributed, but an evidently impressive volume of material was produced from the early to the mid-nineteenth century which suggested a different set of criteria, and a sometimes different set of objectives.

Travel was opening up, it seemed, and publishers and businessmen alike were keen to join in on the rush. John Murray's 'Handbooks' were launched in 1836, Baedeker's 'Guides' first printed in 1839, and the famous Cook's excursions introduced in 1841. However, unlike many eighteenth century tourers who looked for self-improvement and excitement amidst the cultural excess of continental Europe,[19] many nineteenth century travellers revelled in the sociological potential of travel, and in particular, how 'weaker' or less industrially developed countries might be 'improved'. Clearly inspired by the sort of ethnological and anthropological work increasingly conducted from 1830 onwards,[20] such travellers wrote within an expanding methodological climate, mindful of the benefits of a cross-disciplinary approach, and of the subsequent effect on market growth.

An additional element in the midst of all this activity was the increasing visibility of women, as travellers and writers both. The significance of Martineau's *Letters* deepens if viewed in the context of a growing body of women's travel writing, which had begun in the late eighteenth century, and which had achieved considerable acclaim by the middle of the nineteenth. Texts such as Mary Wollstonecraft's *Letters Written During a Short Residence in Sweden, Norway and Denmark* (1796), Maria Williams's *A Tour in Switzerland* (1798), and Anne Plumptre's *Narrative of a Three Years' Residence in France* (1810), not only contributed significantly to the form's development, but helped to establish women's presence in the field. Indeed, by the middle of the nineteenth century the number of female-authored travel texts were so numerous that Lady Eastlake, writing in 1845 for the *Quarterly Review,* had no less than twelve to assess in the course of a single review. Travels to Egypt, New South Wales, Texas, Mexico and Madras, Eastlake's spatially diverse texts embodied the geographical, but also literary ambitions of many well-connected and educated women. In fact, the reviewer's gender-specific assessment praised these texts for the spirit of independence she saw as necessary for successful travel, but also because they were so much better written than men's: 'Who, for instance, has not turned from the slap-dash scrawl of your male correspondent', she asked, 'with excuses at the beginning and haste at the end, and too often nothing between but sweeping generalities – to the well-filled sheets of your female friend, with plenty of time bestowed and no paper wasted, and overflowing with those close and lively details which show . . . that observing eyes have been at work?'[21]

Although a complex set of reasons may be offered for the proliferation of nineteenth century, female-authored travel literature, the critic Shirley Foster attributes a political rather than generic motivation to this growth: 'The concept of escape is of particular significance here. To a greater or less extent, the women voyagers saw their journeying as a release, an opportunity to experience solipsistic enjoyment and to enrich themselves spiritually and mentally.'[22] Whether Ireland afforded such women as visited her in the course of the nineteenth century the sort of intellectual gratification that destinations further afield could provide is difficult to say. But certainly the increasing interest in Ireland as a suitable destination, from which a wealth of political and social reportage could be easily extrapolated, became firmly established in the minds of several British travellers. Henrietta Chatterton's *Rambles in the South of Ireland* (1839), Emily Taylor's *The Irish Tourist* (1843), and Henrietta Pendleton's *Gleanings from the Islands and Coast of Ireland* (1856), to name just a few, displayed a keen interest in the country's political difficulties as much as its scenic attractions, thereby testifying to the extent to which travel was also linked with personal, intellectual development. Not all of these writers produced texts of scintillating political commentary by any means, but their developing interest in the country signalled a phase in which complex images of Ireland became more available, and women travellers more visible.

From her tour of Ireland in 1852, Harriet Martineau produced a series of impressions about the general welfare of its inhabitants, plus a compendia of resolutions and recommendations for their future improvement that sits comfortably within this framework. In many respects Martineau was no different from other travellers who regarded the country as a convenient, off-shore location in which economic and political dissatisfactions abounded. However, Martineau was also making a contribution towards the broader development of travel literature, and to associative disciplines such as anthropology and geography, disciplines which could weld an empire together. Indeed, it is interesting to note how this interest in travel developed at precisely the moment of European overseas expansion, of how the traveller was invested with a level of importance at such a politically expedient moment. This is not to suggest that every missionary, anthropologist or minerals expert who happened to publish their travelling experiences regarded their efforts in quite this vein. However, there is little doubting that travellers who displayed consistently high levels of anthropological and ethnological data did much to sustain empire politics. Harriet Martineau's *Letters* is geared more towards an appreciation of Ireland's economy and infrastructure, on how best to get the country moving after the Famine, than on specifically graphic accounts of the native Irish or their landscape. Nevertheless, much of her text is taken up with advising – presumably future British governments – on how best to deal with issues of religious, educational and cultural importance. And it is against this backdrop that *Letters* should also be set.

MARTINEAU'S TRAVELS

The *Daily News*, first edited by Charles Dickens, took a liberal line on most issues, and in the early 1850s was especially interested in receiving an informed and up to the minute report on Ireland. If the 1840s had been a decade of increasing misery for Ireland, so too had it been a period of increasing interest in its potential. Reports and memoranda, schemes and provisions of one sort or another, competed with the impressions of various travellers who visited the country and carried details of the Famine away with them, as from a war zone. In response to the growing journalistic interest in Ireland, Martineau was contacted by the then editor of the *Daily News*, Frederick Knight Hunt, in April 1852, and asked if she would be interested in occasional leader-writing. After what Martineau, in her *Autobiography*, describes as a 'frank and copious' correspondence, a face-to-face meeting, sometime in the summer of 1852, took place:

> He came to us at Portobello; and for two half days he poured out so rich a stream of conversation that my niece could not stand the excitement. She went out upon the shore, to recover her mind's breath, and came in to enjoy more. It was indeed an unequal treat; and when we parted, I felt that a bright new career was indeed opened to me. He had before desired that I should write him letters from Ireland; and he now bespoke three per week during our travels there.[23]

Later, in a letter to Frances Ogden, Martineau expressed similar excitement. 'Everything prospers', she declared, 'We are to have a charming home at Dublin, – with capital (ci-devant) quakers, – old correspondents of mine, and hearty friends, – with the very best connections for my objects. I don't mean to tell any of the mouldy old Unitarians there of my visit.'[24] Ireland had always interested Harriet Martineau, had appeared in countless articles and letters, was the subject of two trips, and was the place where she planned her successful *Political Economy* series. In other words, although there has been relatively little made of her relationship to the country, or how constant an issue it was for her during her long publishing career, Ireland was a topic and a place to which she felt drawn. That said, her feelings about the country were undoubtedly mixed, and one can only guess that Ireland's intractable economic and political fortunes frustrated her enormously. In the first volume of her *Autobiography* she simply related her Dublin experiences in the light of her plans for the publication of the *Political Economy* series. Given that she spent approximately four months in the capital, such silence is particularly disappointing. Martineau's Dublin recollections, such as they are, constitute little other than a recital of planned or executed correspondence to London publishers. There is no detailing of her information-gathering episodes for the *Ireland: A Tale* volume, nor anything of the social contacts she made, or of how she felt about the place or its inhabitants.

Perhaps it is for these reasons that Martineau's visits to, and subsequent publications on, Ireland are remarkably under-researched.

Her *Ireland: A Tale* has been republished, and described in the introductory essay that accompanies it, as a 'remarkable novel'.[25] But *Letters* has not been so fortunate. Given the politically sensitive period in which *Letters* was written, but also the impressive stature of the figure whose work they are, one wonders why this is the case. Is it that *Letters* is less interesting, or less impressive when set against her other work, say on the Crimea? Perhaps it is because there is some confusion concerning the form of the *Letters* themselves, their part-journalistic, part-travelogue presentation leaving readers unsure about their status, and how they should be read. *Letters*, it must be remembered, was originally viewed as a set of journalistic pieces and nothing more. It was not envisaged as an instalment towards a larger project, but simply regarded as a series of newspaper items. Readers, in other words, would have viewed them as part of a continuing engagement with Ireland, as constituting part of a larger discussion about the country and its various difficulties. But unlike the serialisation of texts that was being conducted elsewhere, there would have been little thought of *Letters* taking on a more permanent form. It was only when, as Martineau tells us in the Preface, they were so well received that it was thought suitable to publish them as a complete volume: 'These Letters were communicated to the "Daily News" during my journey in Ireland last autumn. A reprint of them, as a volume, has been asked for, and I now obey the call'.

Whatever else we might say of the text's relationship to journalism or, indeed, of the less than stable definitions associated with the travel narrative form, *Letters* appears as a coherent and relatively seamless piece. It can be read as a series of distinct journalistic pieces that concentrate on particular political or social issues, such as landlordism, emigration or workhouses, but because it also conveys movement and progression, and sets various localities in contrast, or in relation, to one another, *Letters* appears like a conventional travel narrative. Moreover, throughout the text Martineau describes herself as a traveller, discusses her journey in terms of scale and hardship, and stresses the importance of particular locations and venues. In other words, the text has many of the attributes of the travel narrative form, despite its origin as a series of reasonably discrete pieces. The journey, she tells us in the Preface, is more than 1,200 miles long: from Derry to Belfast, and then onto Dublin, across the Irish midlands to Galway, to Achill Island, Connemara, Killarney and Valentia. Subjects touched upon include the manufactures of the north of Ireland, agricultural improvements generally, railways, and the loss of the Irish woods. Indeed, Martineau is what many travellers to Ireland rarely are: adaptable and curious, but also intellectually astute, and an able, if often provocative, commentator on the variety of topics she combatively discusses. Tenant right, Irish landlords, the 'rival' Churches, the role of women and emigration; all are tackled by Martineau in a lively and thoughtful manner. We may not always be impressed by her efforts at balanced and objective reporting, but her more difficult moments are offset by elements of surprising honesty and intelligence.

Letters is an intriguing narrative of post-Famine Ireland, and a significant contribution to the literature of nineteenth century Ireland generally. Moreover, the text works effectively as a single volume, bringing together diverse issues in a relatively composed and coherent manner. It conveys a sense of all that is best about travel literature – opinionated, transient, and impressionistic – while at the same time offering a picture of the country that is frustrating, even occasionally unpalatable to read. In her *Autobiography* Martineau says of *Letters* that their production 'was a pure pleasure, whether they were penned in a quiet chamber at a friend's house, or amidst a host of tourists, and to the sound of the harp, in a *salon* at Killarney'.[26]

Pleasure is not necessarily the sense that predominates when reading the text, however, and not just because the narrator occasionally challenges the reader's patience, but because there is displayed an attitude towards Ireland that sees the country less in terms of its human complexity, than as a laboratory which requires only sociological analysis, and frequently cold and unfeeling sociological analysis at that. Having said that, the idea that Ireland could be improved on the basis of radical economic theory was an opinion that could be easily discounted, even by Martineau herself. Only the following year, whilst writing a review essay for the *Westminster Review*, she stated:

> The world is weary of the subject of Ireland; and, above all the rest, the English reading world is weary of it. The mere name brings up images of men in long coats and women in long cloaks; of mud cabins and potatoes; the conacre, the middleman, and the priest; the faction fight, and the funeral howl. The sadness of the subject has of late years increased the weariness. People who could read with enjoyment Abdallatif's descriptions of famine, or Defoe's of plague, turn away from narratives of similar woes in Ireland, because they are too real and practical to be an intellectual exercise or pastime – to serve as knowledge or excitement. Something ought to be done for Ireland; and, to readers by the fireside, it is too bewildering to say what.[27]

Weariness of Ireland, of its pitiful politics and dissatisfactions but, more importantly, of the 'realities' of Irish life, is clearly articulated here. Plague or famine are all very well, but only as remote sources of enjoyment or instruction, particularly if associated with exotic locations. However, when those concerns are rendered real and, more problematically, given the kind of visibility that the Irish Famine received, then they become far too painful to consider.

WRITING IRELAND

In many of the critical readings of Martineau's work praise is usually paid to the author's championing of certain issues: abolitionism, women's right to work, the improving qualities of education, the position of the poor. Gaby Weiner, in the Virago republication of her *Autobiography*, describes Martineau's position as 'a response to several powerful calls on her intellect; her outrage at any social prejudice or injustice'.[28] Martineau pledged her resources in the fight against all sorts of iniquities, it is clear, and she gladly took on those whom she regarded as exploiting their privileges and power. Women, in particular, she believed to be considerably less involved about issues concerning their lives than men. For example, in *Society in America* she wrote passionately about slavery, but she also reserved a chapter of her book to the role of women, particularly their political status within society:

> Governments in the United States have power to tax women who hold property; to divorce them from their husbands; to fine, imprison, and execute them for certain offences. Whence do these governments derive their powers? They are not 'just' as they are not derived from the consent of the women thus governed.[29]

And in text after text, the same sentiments are articulated, with Martineau's sense of outrage at seemingly preposterous legislation and institutions forcefully argued.

In *Letters* Martineau reveals a similarly concerned persona, affronted by the destitute nature of many of the country's inhabitants, at the high levels of ophthalmia recorded amongst Famine survivors, at the pitiful working conditions and wages endured by the peasantry. Letter IX, entitled 'The Women', opens by simply stating that it is 'the industry of the women which is in great part sustaining the country'. She discusses the traditional areas of occupation for women, but goes on to claim that women dominate 'the flax-fields . . . potato-

fields . . . harvest-fields . . . bog [and] . . . warehouses'. Although she
appears encouraged by their participation in a diverse economy, she
nevertheless fears for their economic futures. Martineau's feminism
welcomes advances for women in Ireland, as in America, but her
economic background questions the exploitative nature of the new
system of Irish female employment. As she points out, when men
struck for wages, 'their work was given to girls, at 8*d.* per day',
retarding the economic progress of both sexes. Martineau argues,
therefore, for a raising of standards and wages, and states that
advancement for Ireland must come through the 'due reward' of
masculine and feminine labour, on an equal basis.

Throughout her text Martineau makes equally balanced assess-
ments, revealing a capacity for objectivity and fairness. She speaks
movingly about the plight of tenants, for example, who are forced to
accept that improvements to their homes might mean significantly
increased rents, and certainly no compensation for work undertaken.
Similarly, there is a balanced critique of the Established Church,
whose tithe-gathering powers she finds divisive and unjustifiable. One
particularly notable observation, in Letter XVI, concerns the different
types of settler to Ireland, and how they are perceived by the native
inhabitants in the aftermath of the Famine. Martineau speculates that
settlers who come to the country to improve the land, hire local
labour, and generally contribute to the local economy, are to be
welcomed and congratulated. However, she points to a different type
of resettlement which the native Irish, and implicitly she herself, finds
less attractive. It appears, she remarks,

> that the good feeling towards settlers does not always extend to those
> who make the rearing of stock their object. They buy up or lease land
> for a sum or rent nearly nominal, when, as in the case of Lord Sligo's
> lands, the depreciation in value is excessive. They graze their cattle for
> almost nothing, employing next to no labour, and make vast profits.
> There is nothing really unfair in this. They give what the land, in a
> season of adversity, will bring, and they use it in a way most profitable
> to themselves. Nobody has a right to complain of this as dishonest. But
> we cannot wonder if the suffering neighbours are quick to feel the
> difference between this method of settling and that of men who come
> to till the ground and employ labour. Men see cattle growing fat
> among the enclosures where their neighbour's [sic] homes used to be.
> Their neighbours are gone – over the sea or into the grave – for want
> of work or food, and one herd of cattle succeeds another, to be sent
> away to England, and fill English pockets with wealth, while the Irish
> peasant remains as poor as ever.

However, although Martineau displays concern for the oppressed at certain moments in the text, she also reveals a surprising degree of insensitivity, something remarked upon by critics of her other works. Indeed, in many of her writings, commentators have noted the complex nature of Martineau's responses, and indicated that while she aligns herself with progressive institutions and movements one moment, she is capable of sounding not only tiresomely judgemental, but even conservative, the next. For example, Valerie Sanders argues that Martineau occupies a series of sometimes incompatible positions in her texts. Sanders's enquiry, which covers much of Martineau's output, suggests a figure of considerable originality, an 'influential, if always controversial, literary figure', whose reputation for radical and free thinking was not always consistent: 'Her outspokenness on some issues makes her sound surprisingly modern, while her reticence, or conventionality, on others roots her firmly among the more conservative Victorian teachers. Just when she seems to be endorsing the most radical ideas, she drops back into line with the most traditional.'[30]

Not surprisingly, *Letters* displays the same sense of duality, particularly at those moments where a sympathy for the disadvantaged clashes with her deep-seated desire to see the benefits of modernization enacted. At several moments in the text, in other words, particularly unsettling images arise. In Letter XVII for example, Martineau describes the departure of an emigrant family near the town of Castlebar. It is a peculiar passage, which attests to the trauma of parting, while denying the validity of the emotion displayed, and the economic circumstances which encouraged it:

> [W]e were startled – to say the truth, our blood ran cold – at the loud cry of a young girl who ran across the road, with a petticoat over her head, which did not conceal the tears on her convulsed face . . . The last embraces were terrible to see; but worse were the kissings and the claspings of the hands during the long minutes that remained after the woman and children had taken their seats . . . we became aware . . . of the full dignity of that civilization which induces control over the expression of the emotions. All the while that this lamentation was giving a headache to all who looked on, there could not but be a feeling that these people, thus giving vent to their instincts, were as children, and would command themselves better when they were wiser.

Martineau's ambivalance over this incident is both typical and alarming. Within a single paragraph, she acknowledges simultaneously the despair of the moment – 'all eyes were fixed on the neighbours

who were going away forever' – yet attempts to minimise it: 'The
woman's face was soon like other people's, and the children were
eating oatcake very composedly.' As an individual, Martineau
responds to the emotion; as an improving economist, who sees in
emigration a means of modernizing the country, she displays
impatience with these wilfully childish people who cling to outmoded
associations and practices.

Certain themes recur in *Letters* which demonstrate deeply held
political, religious and economic concerns. In her progress throughout
the country, for example, she returns again and again to questions of
land ownership, the position of women, the role of priests in Irish life,
and to the figure of Daniel O'Connell (who died in 1847), the leader
of the Irish Emancipation movement. What her treatment of each of
these diverse topics display in common is a forthright criticism of the
backwardness of much of Irish life, a great deal of which she
attributes to the Catholic clergy. Yet there is one issue to which
Martineau consistently turns: the belief that the future prosperity of
the country lies in large-scale emigration by the Irish, and a resettlement of the country by thrifty English farmers and industrialists.
This notion of the resettlement of Ireland in the 1850s may seem a
rather odd response to the narrative of despair and destitution the
Famine so readily engendered. However this most intriguing element
of post-Famine discourse is what *Letters* specifically explores. The
notion of emigration as a solution to Irish problems had been aired
long before the Famine, but the publication of the 1851 census
appeared to clarify the issue to the satisfaction of many. Famine-
related mortality and emigration had seen the Irish population decline
significantly from 1841; yet until the census was published no one
was quite sure how far the figures had dropped, or whether pre-
sumptions regarding regional variations in decline would be borne
out. The publication of the census, revealing a decrease from 1841 to
1851 of 1,659,330 persons, put an end to speculation. It gave specific
details about male to female ratios, but it was the precise population
figures, region by region, and town by town, that had the greatest
impact. These figures would excite interest in the country in ways that
only five years earlier were unimaginable.[31]

Reading the census, then, could be a fairly complex, though
interpretively rich moment. On the one hand, it could be read as a
narrative of political and economic misfortune, with widespread
disease, malnutrition and death marking its climax; but it could also
be interpreted in terms of anticipatory capital and resettlement – a

narrative position quickly adopted in the 1850s and 1860s. Not surprisingly, in the ten years following the publication of the census figures many hybrid narratives, in which promotional rhetoric was conflated with the travel narrative form, systematically endorsed the notion of Irish resettlement potential. In addition to Martineau's *Letters*, texts such as Henry Ashworth's *The Saxon in Ireland; or, the Rambles of an Englishman in Search of a Settlement in the West of Ireland* (1851), William Bulloch Webster's *Ireland Considered as a Field for Investment or Residence* (1852), Thomas Miller's *The Agricultural and Social State of Ireland* (1858), and Henry Coulter's *The West of Ireland: Its Existing Condition and Prospects* (1862), all represented Ireland as a more attractive resettlement option than many of Britain's other colonies. A reviewer of Henry Ashworth's text, writing for *Fraser's Magazine*, concluded that 'English capital, instead of being transported to New Zealand, Canada, or Port Phillip, would find a much more profitable investment on the western coast of Ireland, which, in addition to all the local attractions he ascribes to it, possesses the very important advantages of being within twenty-four hours of London'.[32] And Martineau's *Letters*, in its frequent exhortations of Irish resettlement as the panacea for Ireland's woes, demonstrates precisely the same opinions. In fact her view of emigration, particularly in Letter XXVII, links Irish political and religious dissatisfaction, emigration, and the census firmly together:

> The late census shows the population of Ireland to be one-third less than under ordinarily favourable circumstances it would be. Those who have gone away are Catholics – of the class that sustains the priesthood; and the children that will be born to those emigrants in their new country would have been the support of the Romish church at home. Of those who are to fill up the gaps in the population, some will be Protestants from England and Ireland; more will be educated Catholics out of the National Schools; and others will be the children of the Catholics now and hereafter educated at the Queen's Colleges, in disregard of the discouragement from head-quarters.

The census gives encouragement, it is clear, because it anticipates a future population of amenable citizens, a new Irish shorn of the malevolence of Catholic doctrine and Catholic politics.

Although the census is important to Martineau, it functions as part of a wider discourse on Ireland, which links progress with scientific advancement generally.[33] The development of railways, canals, and bridges, or the work of the Belfast Social Inquiry Society – linked to the Statistical Section of the British Association for the Advancement of Science – establish a model of scientific improvement for Ireland as the necessary way forward. The Chemico-Agricultural Society of Ulster, as well as the work of figures such as Alexander Drummond or John Frederick Hodges, are not just admirable institutions or individuals, but signs of improvement on a largely bleak and wasted landscape. They exercise a particular fascination for Martineau because they are indicative of tangible scientific improvement, but also because they stress the direction she feels the country must take if it is to improve. Indeed, as early as Letter II, Martineau rhapsodizes about the benefits of one particular branch of scientific improvement: the agricultural science demonstrated at the Templemoyle agricultural school in County Londonderry. Everything about this school, from the elevated site on which it stands, to the principles of discipline it instils in its pupils, is a marvel to her. From the Edenic description of its location, Martineau invests the institution itself with a striking benevolence:

> The situation of the establishment is beautiful. The house stands near to the top of a steep hill, looking down upon a wooded glen, and abroad over the rich levels stretching to the Lough, and over the Lough to the mountains of Donegal and the grand Coleraine rocks. The path to the front door rises through garden, nursery-ground, and orchard; and behind the house and offices the land still rises till it overlooks the whole adjacent country.

From this centre of civilization, Martineau envisages what she calls 'the missionaries' – young men trained at the school – issuing forth to civilize a barbarous terrain in the interests of economic improvement.

Although her primary concern in this letter is with agricultural improvement, Martineau also emphasizes the contrast between modern English farming methods, which guarantee prosperity, and outmoded Irish ones, which are specifically associated with decay and decline. Thus politics and economics are conflated to stress the necessity for greater intervention on the part of the government to forcibly improve Ireland:

> The wretched potatoes, black, withering, and offensive, seemed to have poisoned and annihilated every growth within their boundaries; but in every enclosed pasture the weeds had their revenge. This is a proud country for the ragwort. In every pasture, as far as we could see, it

grew knee-high, presenting that golden harvest which may please the eye of an infant, but which saddens the heart of a well-wisher to Ireland.

The importance attributed by Martineau to marigolds, ragwort and weeds, the embodiment of Irish agricultural ineptitude, is typical. She deplores what she sees as the Irish refusal to improve property, but frequently ascribes it to an inherent tendency in the Irish rather than a lack of agricultural investment or estate management.

The point about the Templemoyle seminary is that it functions for Martineau as a symbol of what Ireland might be, were English and Scots scientific agriculturalists to take the country in hand. Indeed, Martineau sees science as the solution to all of Ireland's difficulties, and tirelessly promotes the benefits, as she sees them, of rational, scientific progress. In this regard she represents Ireland, and Ireland's relationship to Britain, in a typical manner. Ireland can occasionally appear picturesque, bountiful and fertile, but rarely as a convincing instance of modernity. Rather, she is trapped in an undignified, premodern narrative of programmatic decay, a disgrace to both herself and Britain. Degenerated, if beautiful, Ireland encourages Martineau to see the assistance that the country desperately requires as a blessing, and the visitation of famine a pitiful but necessary cleansing act. It is for this reason that Martineau and many of her contemporaries, such as Ashworth, Webster and Miller, investigate the agricultural worth of the country in the 1850s, and with particular relish after the publication of the census figures.

The picture of obstructive counter-modernism that Ireland presents, then, is handled by Martineau – for all her apparent distaste – in an opportunistic mode. The general terms of her critique focus on the poor husbandry of the Irish, their illogical and childish attachment to Church and land, and their ignorance of basic economic principles. A discernible difference appears between the north-east and the more westerly and south-westerly parts of the country. Belfast and Antrim, and especially the London Companies' estates, appear as relatively competent arenas where agri-economical success is, if not flourishing, at least in better shape. However, the closer she gets to Galway, Mayo and Clare, the shriller her criticism and the deeper her despondency. The north of the country does not escape criticism entirely, being noted for its paucity of woodland, but when this is set against the horrors of the West, especially enclaves such as the Claddagh, it is positively idyllic. Barefooted children, vistas of bogland, priestly interventions in everyday affairs: the west of Ireland is less an area of calculable social interaction than a nebulous collection of names and images. Indeed, the enthusiasm she feels for the science and practice of agriculture at Templemoyle gives way to a specifically developed depression on the bogs of the west and south-west of the country. And yet it is precisely the disregard for basic principles that Martineau despairingly describes which allows her to anticipate a future based on a reorganization of the country along British lines. If Ireland is poorly utilized, then the answer is clearly the importation of individuals who can more successfully manage the land; if the people are disgracefully misled by their priests, then National Schools and the Queen's Colleges will educate them out of such ignorance, and away from their influence.[34]

While there is something distasteful about the belief in Irish barbarism and British civility that can be found in so many British-authored texts from the mid-nineteenth century, Martineau consistently viewed herself, and Ireland, in just such terms. She sailed to the city of Derry, when Belfast or Larne would have been more convenient, because Derry was where she could get a proper sense of the work of the London Companies. In Letter I, for example, she explicitly states that the purpose behind her decision was to see 'some of the most prosperous parts of the country, in order to carry elsewhere the hope that the use of similar means may produce a similar prosperity'. The Fishmongers' Company, she is happy to relate, is doing some excellent work: reclaiming land, replanting trees, building schools and churches. In Letter II, having travelled just five miles from Derry in the direction of Limavady, she notes with some satisfaction the sharp difference between the Grocers' estates and their native Irish neighbours'. On an estate 'which lies between the lands of two of the companies' she finds 'cottages whose thatch is sinking in or dropping off and . . . puddles of green slime', whose inhabitants live next to 'green ponds'.[35] The influence of the Companies, 'great though it be, is not all-powerful in improving the cultivation of the land in their neighbourhood'.

Although Martineau's assessment portrays the work of the Companies as less than complete, the impression of preferable systems of management and economy is prevalent. As suggested above, the work of the Templemoyle agricultural school is seen as a beacon, an institution devoted to rigorous agricultural methods based on the most modern economic principles. Its one major failing is that many of its young men emigrate after graduating from the college, so that rather than improve the lands around them, they take their expertise away from the place which requires it most. Still, the impression is that these institutions, like the London Companies, offer the best that Ireland can get. English and Scottish influences, it is clear, offer a lifeline to Ireland; through estate management, education, and investment. And all along the route from Derry to Belfast, Martineau consistently evokes this vision. In Letter III, for example, we are told of abundant fowls, high-yielding milking cows, and salmon-fisheries on the River Bann. The Clothworkers' estates near Coleraine come in for some criticism, but as the narrator winds her way towards Belfast the most outstanding impression is of improvement and industry.

The circumstances of Martineau's arrival in Belfast, in Letter IV, is curiously convenient. The city is covered in fog, we are told, 'which hung over the district as we entered it [and which] was so dense as to allow nothing to be seen beyond the road'. Like Derry and Dublin, this is a city of industry and of evaluations of future prosperity, rather than individual contact, and Martineau refuses to take us much further than within sight of the city limits. And like Derry and Dublin, Belfast remains strikingly obscured, an indication of her preference for rural economy above all else. Indeed, even the Belfast to Dublin road, never the most remarkable of routes, offers considerably greater comfort than might have been expected: 'Some really good wheat-crops are seen here and there,' remarks a satisfied Martineau. Wheat-crops, turnips, oats and potatoes – these are the items to which Martineau's observing eye is consistently turned. Moreover, when her attention moves from the relative prosperity of Leinster, Queen's County in particular, towards the west of the country, this appetite for landscape appreciation will prove a deadly gift. Travelling by train through Kildare, we are told that there exists 'the best crops that have come under our notice thus far in Ireland'. Good signs, the reader might think. But the spectre of the West – famine-stricken, destitute in terms of manufactures and industry, politically unstable, and synonymous with evictions and emigrations – lies ahead.

'If we should encounter a wilder barbarism in remote places, it will, at least, not be jumbled together with an advanced civilization,' writes Martineau on 31 August 1852. Letter XI, simply entitled 'Galway', signals a new phase in the Martineau itinerary. Where she resided when she stepped from the train at Eyre Square is not known. How she dealt with porters, where she dined, whom she met, what personal effects she had to stock up on, or found wanting within the cobbled streets of the town, is not known either. What we do know is that part of the journey by train from Dublin was uncomfortable (acute bends which apparently shook the carriages precariously), while part of the rest of it was dull (the bog of Allen, the section of railway between Lord Clancarty's residence at Ballinasloe and Galway city). Furthermore, we know, or are quickly informed, that here, in direct contrast to much of what has preceded it, lies mayhem and uncertainty. Around County Londonderry there was the work of the London Companies, and in the vicinity of Lisburn and the outskirts of Belfast stood the scutching-mills and the flax mills of serious and sure-minded men.

However, in Galway city, in the Claddagh and, by reputation, on the Aran Islands, lies a different story. In fact, one gets the impression that here, finally, Martineau has found what she has been really looking for. On putting into port at Derry she mentioned that it was her purpose to compare, not just record, the various impressions of Ireland. Those parts of the north of the country under the sway of external influences, that show some signs of improvement and profitability, elicit approval. In the west of the country, however, even in a place such as Galway with its recently arrived railway and newly built Queen's College, there is only disdain and despair. Galway is less a place or region, suggests Martineau, than 'a spectacle never to be forgotten by an Englishman'. And as for the poorhouses and work-houses of Kilrush, the religious fanaticism of Achill, the emaciated and ophthalmic victims of Ennistymon, these are worse and worse; although rarely, the reader will notice, does Martineau actually write of the hardships themselves. Whenever a sense of desperation arises, Martineau's keen sense of editorial propriety (or ideological commitment to a different agenda?) quickly intervenes. Near Coleraine, for example, she tells us that there is no need to 'describe the mournful spectacle of the people'. Having crossed the district of Erris, she declared, 'Of the horrors of the famine we shall say nothing here.' Outside Castlebar, she insists, 'there is no need to describe again the condition of the land and the people'. And after the briefest of discussions on the problems of subletting, she concludes, 'it is the old story, which we may spare ourselves the pain of telling again'.

But the question raised is this: just who exactly is being spared the pain, and why? Is Martineau concerned for the reader's feelings to such an extent that she would disclose certain aspects of her trip, while repressing others? Certainly a sensitive narrator, unwilling to pornographize human misery, is only too welcome, particularly in the nineteenth century when a catastrophe could be seized upon to effect a territorial advantage. But there is something unsettling about these discursive ellipses, about a narrator who so clearly wishes to talk about some things, like the benefits of emigration, but who so determinedly avoids others. A series of formally provocative reasons may lie behind the absence of *Letters* from the Martineau canon, but perhaps a simpler reason lies in her presentation of Ireland: ridiculing and criticizing the country in some matters, while ignoring or excising others in the interests of ideological purity. Is this the real reason for the 'loss' of *Letters*, for the fact that they remain surprisingly obscure since their first appearance? Granted, a great deal of material from the Famine period has remained similarly displaced. But when we consider how difficult it might have been to square Martineau's *Letters* with the broader reputation she had for many liberal agendas, the notion of political selectivity becomes especially pronounced.

Harriet Martineau is forced to concede the unnecessary harshness of several aspects of contemporary Irish life during the course of her 1852 trip, yet she finds much of the country's intractability to be associated, in her own mind at least, with a lack of knowledge and with an unwillingness to adapt to different agricultural and social methods. Solve these difficulties, she seems to suggest, and the result will be greater economic success and, ultimately, greater political stability. The country has seemingly withstood the epistemological advances of Britain for long enough; it is now time to put the place in order, to bring about a state of relative prosperity, to break down the country's subordinate, yet unknowable presence. Fortunately, Martineau has overlooked one thing: that the strategy of social engineering she has in mind might not mesh so easily with the complexities of Ireland. As she sails into the city of Derry to confront these problems, in early August 1852, this most complex of narrators is on course for a challenge.

1. Walker's Pillar, walls of Londonderry.

Harriet Martineau's Preface

THESE LETTERS were communicated to the 'Daily News' during my journey in Ireland this last autumn.[1] A reprint of them, as a volume, has been asked for, and I now obey the call. My readers will take them for what they are – a rapid account of impressions received and thoughts excited from day to day, in the course of a journey of above 1200 miles. I have thought it best not to alter them, either in form or matter. There would be no use in attempting to give anything of the character of a closet-book to letters written sometimes in a coffee-room, sometimes in the crowded single parlour of a country inn, – now to the sound of the harp, and now to the clatter of knives and forks, and scarcely ever within reach of books; therefore have I left untouched what I wrote, even to the notices of passing incidents as if they were still present, and references to a future already fulfilled.

The issue of the Letters in this form enables me to render one acknowledgment which I was rather uneasy not to be able to make at the time – an acknowledgment of my obligations to the members of the Dublin Statistical Society[2] and of the Belfast Social Inquiry Society,[3] whose tracts, before interesting to me by my own fireside, were of high value in my journey, by directing my observation and inquiries. They not only taught me much, but put me in the way to learn more. When I had the honour of meeting Professor Hancock in Dublin,[4] and told him how freely I was using his ideas in my interpretation of Irish affairs, he made me heartily welcome to all such materials as might be found in his tracts, saying that all that any of us want is that true views should spread, for the benefit of Ireland. He can afford to be thus generous; and I, for my part, must request my readers to ascribe to him, and the other economists of those societies, whatever they may think valuable in my treatment of economical questions in this volume; the rest is the result of my own observation, inquiry, and reflection, on the way.

H. M.
THE KNOLL, AMBLESIDE,
December 20th, 1852.

Lough Foyle and its Environs

August 10, 1852

TRAVELLERS usually enter Ireland by Dublin; and Dublin being a good deal like other large cities, and having the varied population of a capital, there is so little that is distinctive at the first glance, that the stranger exclaims, 'I thought I was in Ireland; but where are the Paddies?' The Paddies, and the true signs of the times in Ireland, may be better seen by dropping into the island at almost any other point of the coast. For some reasons, it may be well to begin by steaming into Lough Foyle,[1] and landing at the famous old Derry,[2] whose prefix of 'London' seems rather an impertinence when one is fairly among the Paddies. It is true that, by entering Ireland from this point, the traveller's attention is first given to districts of country which have for centuries been managed by Englishmen, and largely peopled by Scotch, – it is true that the lands of the great London corporations cannot be taken as specimens of Irish tillage and management;[3] but it may be well to see, in the first instance, what the Irish peasantry can be and can do in a region where the peculiarities of land proprietorship in Ireland are suspended or extinguished. It may be well to see first some of the most prosperous parts of the country, in order to carry elsewhere the hope that the use of similar means may produce a similar prosperity. There are quite enough of the Catholic peasantry dwelling on the lands of the London Companies to give the stranger a good study of the Paddies, and moreover to show what the relations of the 'mere Irish'[4] may be with the residents of English and Scotch descent.[5]

After entering Lough Foyle at Portrush,[6] we were struck by the extent of cultivation on both shores. Fields, green or tinged with the yellow of the harvest month, divided by hedgerows into portions somewhat too small for good economy, stretched over the rising grounds which swell upwards from the Lough. Here and there are labyrinths of salmon-nets, marking the fisheries of the Companies.[7] Then follows an odd spectacle – a low embankment and railway, apparently through the water, near the south-east shore, enclosing an ugly expanse of mud or shallow water. There was a company established in London a good many years ago for the purpose of reclaiming large extents of land from the bed of Lough Foyle; and this is the point which the operations of that company have reached, – or, as we fear we must say, where they have for the present stopped. The undertaking cannot be called a failure. By the terms made with the Fishmongers' Company, that corporation was to have 500 acres of the reclaimed land; and of this 250 acres have been cropped for five years, and have proved fertile to the last degree. This bit of experience has proved useful. Looking towards the Lough from any high ground for miles inland, one sees level tracts of a peculiar yellow or brownish soil. These are the '*slob* lands,' retrieved from the shallow waters.[8] Antiquarians and naturalists are of opinion that this method of procedure is simply a continuation of what has been done for many ages, by natural or artificial means. The heaps or mounds of gravel, earth, and stones which are found scattered over the bog districts which are stripped of peat are called 'derries;' and here, once upon a time, flourished clumps of oaks, rearing their heads over the forests of firs which filled up the intermediate spaces.[9] Below the roots of the bog firs, now dug out for sparkling fuel in the rich man's house, and for torches or candles in the poor man's cabin, are evidences that the waters once covered all the low grounds, and that the habitable portions of the whole district were only the rising grounds and 'derries,' which were so many islands and promontories stretching out into a world of waters. Thus the changes going on are not new, though proceeding more rapidly continually. The reclamation is not only from the Lough. The bog is incessantly lessening. Two thousand acres have been brought under tillage on the estates of one of the London Companies.[10] There is plenty of lime in the district, and the Lough furnishes any amount of sea shells for the carriage. As the peat is cleared off, the subsoil is fertilized by these means, and presently repays cultivation. To the farmers whose lands lie along rivers and railways it must answer well to import coal, and spare for more profitable works the labour hitherto spent on cutting and drying peat; but the people who live in the mountains, away from means of transport, will doubtless burn peat, and nothing else, till the bogs are wholly exhausted, – a period which seems already within sight.

After passing the salmon-nets we came upon a fine tract of woodland, on the north-west shore of the Lough, where it stretches down from the ridge of the low hills to the very seaweeds which the tide washes up. Some good houses peep out from among the trees. It was not till we had travelled some distance inland that we learned to appreciate that tract of woodland. The woods have shrunk and disappeared over whole districts where formerly they were cherished for the sake of the large exportation of staves, and use of timber which took place under the old timber duties. When the demand for staves died off, and even the Companies found that their own carpenters could put down floors for them as cheaply by buying foreign timber as by employing labour in felling and seasoning their own trees, there was, for a time, a somewhat reckless consumption of wood. But now the process of planting is going on vigorously; and the last ten years have made a visible change. In the moist lands the alder flourishes, attaining a size which we never before saw. Larch and fir abound, and great pains are taken with oak plantations. Huge stacks of bark for the tanners may be seen here and there; and the wood is readily sold as it is felled.

The changes in the productions and exports are worth notice. Formerly there was much linen manufacture here; but that is over: Belfast seems to have absorbed it. A good deal of flax is grown, and sold to Belfast; but the clack of the loom is scarcely heard.[11] Again, there was a great exportation of pigs and pork prior to 1846;[12] but the potato-rot has almost put an end to pig-keeping. Scarcely any cured pork is sent out. Live cattle are an article of increasing export, – the fat to Liverpool, and the lean to various parts for fattening. Almost all the oats and other grain raised are now exported, the people finding it answer to sell their oats, and eat Indian meal, which they import from America. One consequence of this is a marked improvement in their health.[13] The disgusting diseases which attended upon an almost exclusive oaten diet have disappeared; and certainly a more healthy-looking population than that about Newtown-Limavady we do not remember to have seen. There is a large export of butter, eggs, and fowls. On the whole, the change is visible enough from the old manufacturing to the modern agricultural population; and it is very interesting to the observation of an English visitor.

From the site of the new Catholic chapel on the estates of the Fishmongers' Company a wide view is obtained,[14] extending from the high lands of Donegal on the other shore of the Lough to the Coleraine mountains. Within this space the divisions of the soil indicate pretty accurately the classes of its inhabitants. After the Rebellion,[15] the victors drove the Catholics into the mountains, and the alluvial lands – all that was fertile and valuable – were taken possession of by the English and Scotch Presbyterians.[16] The arrangement was so marked and decisive that the mountaineers are called 'Irish' to this day. For a long time past the 'Irish' have been creeping down into the low grounds. At first, the Protestants emigrated in a much greater proportion than the Catholics;[17] and a Protestant farmer often left a Catholic substitute in his farm. Now, the Catholics are beginning to emigrate in much greater numbers; but, as the Protestants go on emigrating also, so that the total population is in course of reduction, there is more and more room left in the low country for the mountaineers, who find themselves able to come down, and hold their ground among the thriving Presbyterians. We find here little or nothing of the feuds which divide the two classes in too many places. We find, on the Fishmongers' property, schools where children of all faiths sit side by side on their benches, as their respective pastors do in their committee-room.[18] The priest, the clergyman, and the Presbyterian minister act together, on the National system,[19] in perfect harmony. Some zealous young priests awhile ago insisted that the Catholic children should read the Douay version of the Scriptures.[20] The clergyman and agent wisely consented, stipulating only that it should be the Douay version, without note or comment. It was presently found inconvenient to use it; the priests declared that really the difference to the children was so small as not to compensate for the inconvenience, and they themselves proposed to return to the use of the accustomed books. No Ribbon Society[21] exists among the Catholics in this neighbourhood; and nothing seems to be needed in the way of precaution but a little watchfulness against infection brought by navvies and other strangers, and a careful impartiality between Catholics and Protestants in matters of business, and moderation in spirit and language on political matters, on the part of official men and magistrates. We find a Company building a handsome Catholic chapel, and their agent presenting its painted window;[22] we find the gentry testifying that, while the Protestants are certainly the more industrious people, the Catholics are more honest and the women more chaste, – facts which are attributed to the practice of confession by those who are best aware of the evils belonging to that practice. On the whole, Catholic servants are preferred as far as the mere domestic work is concerned; that is, the female servants are Catholics. But it is not denied that the very safest – those who are living, and have lived for thirty years, on good terms with all their neighbours – do feel safer for having Protestant men-servants. There is enough of distrust – not of individual neighbours, but of the tyranny of secret organization – to make even the securest prefer for men-servants persons who are out of the reach of such organization.

West of Ulster – Weeds – London Companies – Templemoyle Agricultural School

August 11, 1852

B Y THE TIME we had left Londonderry two miles behind us, we thought we had seen more weeds in a quarter of an hour than in any whole day of our lives before. In every little field of oats – thin, scattered, stunted oats – there were long rows and wide parterres of wild marigold; a pretty flower enough, but out of place in a corn-field. As for the turnips, they were as modest as the violet, hiding themselves under the shadow of bolder growths of weeds. The wretched potatoes, black, withering, and offensive, seemed to have poisoned and annihilated every growth within their boundaries; but in every enclosed pasture the weeds had their revenge.[1] This is a proud country for the ragwort. In every pasture, as far as we could see, it grew knee-high, presenting that golden harvest which may please the eye of an infant, but which saddens the heart of a well-wisher to Ireland. The stranger is assured, as to the marigold, that it is not a sign of the worst state of the land; that, when the land is getting exhausted, the marigold comes first, and after it the poppy. He is told, as to the ragwort, that it is a sign of the land being good, – that bad land will not grow it: no great consolation, where it usurps every other growth. It takes up all the potash in the soil, one is told; and on it goes, taking up the potash, for anything that anybody seems to care. In one case alone we saw pains taken about it: from a corner of a field two men had removed a heavy cart-load which they were going to add to a manure-heap.

At a distance of five miles from Derry[2] there is a settlement which looks, from a little way off, neat and prosperous.[3] That is the beginning of the Grocers' estates. A few miles further, there is an enclosure which challenges observation at once. It contains a

30

plantation, chiefly of fir and larch, drained in a style which makes one ask whom it belongs to. It is the beginning of the Fishmongers' property. These London Companies remember that Westminster Abbey and Westminster Hall were built with oak from this county; and they are disposed to enable a future generation to build immortal edifices of oak from this district.[4] The outlying fir plantations are only a token of the interest taken by the Companies in restoring the woods of Ulster. For some miles forward the marigold scarcely appears, only peeping out humbly, low down in the corn; and the ragwort is nearly confined to the fences, – till, once more, both burst upon us again in full glory, in the neighbourhood of cottages whose thatch is sinking in or dropping off, and of puddles covered with green slime. We are now on an estate which lies between the lands of two of the Companies. What we have said of it is enough. What we saw shows that the influence of the Companies, great though it be, is not all-powerful in improving the cultivation of the land in their neighbourhood. The people who live under that rotten thatch, and beside those green ponds, dwell in sight of the slated cottages and the heaps of draining-tiles of the Fishmongers. The agent of the Fishmongers hopes to live to see every cottage on their estates slated;[5] and then, as now, we suppose, men will be botching their thatch on that wretched inter-mediate land, just as if there was no slate-quarry within an easy walk.

Seeing these things, certain anecdotes about Irish tillage recurred to our minds. We remembered having heard of the delighted surprise of a farmer who had scribbled or shovelled his field four inches deep, and thought he had dug it, at being shown that a rich loamy soil lay six inches deeper, – a mine of wealth which he had never opened. We remembered having heard of the reviving spirits of some despairing peasants when shown how easily they might raise cabbages in the place of their perishing potatoes. We remembered how some who had agreed to try turnips, and had duly sown their seed, actually cried when their instructor began thinning the rows, and said he was robbing them; and how they got no turnips bigger than radishes. Remembering and seeing these things, we inquired about the state and prospects of agricultural instruction, and particularly about the Templemoyle School.[6] The Templemoyle School was within reach, and we went to see it. We wish that everybody who cares for Ireland would do the same.

This Agricultural Training School was instituted in 1826 by the North-West of Ireland Agricultural Society. The land belongs to the Grocers' Company; and that and other companies, and a few of the neighbouring gentry, supported the school till it could maintain itself. It is now self-supporting; but great good would arise from its being more generally noticed – more abundantly visited – and its merits being more generously acknowledged. A strong interest about it was excited in England by Mr. Thackeray's report of it in his 'Irish Sketchbook;' and there have been more recent notices of it in reviews of that book and elsewhere; but it appears to us to deserve a more steady interest and observation than it has met with.[7] One asks what Lord Clarendon[8] was about, that he never honoured Templemoyle with the slightest notice, while in every other way promoting the great cause of agricultural instruction in Ireland.[9] He never came, nor sent, nor was known to make the slightest inquiry about the institution, during the whole course of his government, while exerting himself in the most excellent manner to send out instructors from the National Board and through private efforts.[10] Perhaps he and others thus paid their compliment to the great companies of Ulster, leaving it to be supposed that whatever was under the care of the corporations must necessarily flourish. But there is no kind of effort which is not stimulated by sympathy – no cause which is not the stronger for appreciation; and it might be a benefit to the whole country if its due place of honour were given to Templemoyle. Public attention seems to be almost entirely absorbed by the plan of sending out instructors from the National Board. That plan is good, and the service rendered has been very great; but the Board farms are of a much smaller extent than that of Templemoyle, which comprehends seventy-two acres; and the Templemoyle course of training must be the more enlarged of the two, in proportion to the superiority of its field of experiment. The institution has sent out men who have written valuable agricultural books. It has sent out surveyors and civil engineers of merit, masters of agricultural schools, an editor of an agricultural newspaper, and land-stewards and agents, besides all its farmers and instructors in agriculture. The 'Quarterly Review' has complained of this as a practical failure, insisting that all the pupils shall be agricultural instructors, and nothing else, except by some rare accident.[11] But, whatever may be thought of this, we have here a proof of the extent and depth of the education given, – an education which enables the pupils to be not mere common farmers, but scientific managers of the land.[12]

By inquiry, we found the state of the case to be this, in regard to the missionary view of the institution. There are beds for seventy pupils; and the place was overflowing before the famine reduced the means of the whole farming class. The number now is fifty-eight.

Since the occupation of a large part of the missionary field by Lord Clarendon's instructors,[13] there has been an increased tendency in the Templemoyle students to emigrate. No one can wonder at this, for they must feel themselves better qualified to succeed as emigrants than most of their neighbours who go out; and they do not like the prospect – so common for the last few years – of sinking at home. Now, therefore, during the present rush of emigration, about one-third of the pupils go with the stream. Natural as this is, it is a pity. The institution is not intended for the training of emigrants; but we own we do not see how it is to be helped, while every class of the population yields up a large proportion of its numbers to the colonies or to the United States. Of the remaining two-thirds, about half are believed to go home to their fathers' farms, or to settle on one of their own, or to follow other occupations, while the rest become, under one name or another, agricultural missionaries. In 1850 there were three hundred and two who were cultivating their own or their parents' farms. To us it appears that these young men are missionaries of a secondary order. To us it appears that the scientific cultivation of three hundred farms throughout the length and breadth of Ireland must be nearly as efficacious in the improvement of agriculture as any amount of instruction that could be given by lectures and itinerant practice, by the same number of men. We must remember how the influence of a resident improver spreads through his neighbourhood, and how it is deepened and expanded by the circumstance of residence. If, therefore, taking the number of students at sixty-three on the average, and the course at three years (though it is sometimes four, and even five), and allowing one-third of those who leave each year to emigrate, we have, as the result of the Templemoyle training, seven in a year who go forth through the country as agricultural missionaries, and seven more to settle down as scientific farmers, or managers of the land in one way or another. If this is not approved, or if vexation is felt at a small sprinkling of shopkeepers and clerks coming out of the institution, those who recommend the pupils must take more care to ensure the devotion of their candidates to agricultural pursuits. The pay, too, is very low – only £10 a year; and it may easily happen that a place is occasionally given as a charity, or to some hopeless youth who has never succeeded elsewhere. But the very small amount of misconduct – the extreme rarity of expulsion – proves that there cannot be much of this kind of abuse.

The situation of the establishment is beautiful. The house stands near to the top of a steep hill, looking down upon a wooded glen, and abroad over the rich levels stretching to the Lough, and over the Lough to the mountains of Donegal and the grand Coleraine rocks. The path to the front door rises through garden, nursery-ground, and orchard; and behind the house and offices the land still rises till it overlooks the whole adjacent country.[14] The soil and aspect are unfavourable. To the young men it is certainly the pursuit of farming under difficulties; but this is better for them than success coming too easily. The price given for the land was 10s. the statute acre, and the value is now at least doubled. Besides feeding the whole establishment, the produce brings in a yearly increasing profit. We have said how low is the payment by the pupils. Yet, within ten years, there have been additions of new dormitories, an infirmary, washing-rooms, a museum of models of farming implements, an improved cow-house, and an excellent house for sheep, the introduction of which, with all modern improvements in the management of them, is an important new feature in the education given. The land is divided into nine portions, five of which are regularly tilled on the five-shift rotation, and the other on the four-shift. Every part of the work is, sooner or later, done by the hands of each pupil, the only help hired being for the drudgery, which would be mere waste of time when once learned. From the first attempt to plough a furrow or set a fence, to the highest skill in judging of stock at fairs and markets, the pupils are exercised in the whole of their art. The art being pursued during one half of the day, the other half is given to the science. The mathematical master is superintending the studies in school and class-rooms, while the agricultural master is in the fields and yards with the other half of the pupils. The cows and pigs are fine, and the sheep a source of both pride and profit. Lectures on agricultural chemistry are given, of course; and some members of the establishment visit the great agricultural shows in all parts of the kingdom, to keep up with the world in the knowledge and use of all discoveries and implements.

There seems to be nothing wanting, as far as the visitor can see, but the presence of a matron, or the occasional visits of ladies, to see to the opening and cleaning of windows, and some domestic niceties; and we emphatically declare the encouragement of a wider notice and appreciation of this highly important institution a matter of national concern. It would be renovated and cheered for ever if Prince Albert, with his interest in agricultural improvement, would pay it a visit. And why not? In some one of her healthful and pleasant cruises, the Queen will surely, sooner or later, visit the famous old Derry, to whose stout heroic loyalty once upon a time she owes her crown.[15]

May she come soon! and then Prince Albert, and perhaps the Queen herself, will remember that Templemoyle is only six miles from Derry, and will go over and see the crops, and the maps, and the museum, and the joyful students, and will leave certain prosperity behind them.[16]

The Derry and Coleraine Railway – Produce and Traffic of the District – Beautiful Scenery – What can Public Works do for Ireland?

August 13, 1852

THE IMPRESSION which every day's observation strengthens in the traveller's mind is, that till the agriculture of Ireland is improved, little benefit can arise from the large grants which have been, and still are, made for public works.[1] If public works which are designed to open up markets for produce should stimulate the people to the improvement of production, it will be a capital thing; but, till some evidence of this appears, there is something melancholy in the spectacle of a great apparatus which does not seem to be the result of any natural demand.[2] We saw yesterday nearly the whole line of the intended railway from Coleraine to Derry. If we had looked no further than the line, it would have been an imposing and beautiful spectacle; but we saw other things which sadly marred the beauty of it.[3]

Much of the benefit of this railway will depend on whether the Bann river can be made navigable from Lough Neagh to the ocean.[4] Lough Neagh supplies a vast body of water to the beautiful river Bann; and its shores ought to supply a great amount of produce. With railways from Belfast and Carrickfergus meeting at Antrim,[5] and running round to where the Bann issues from the Lough, large districts will be put into communication with the sea at the north, if only the difficulty of the bar at the mouth of the Bann can be got over.[6] Money is granted for building two piers. Some wise men assure us that they will be effectual; while other wise men consider the opening of the navigation to be a hopeless matter. A small harbour has been made secure for little vessels at Portrush; and those who despair of the mouth of the Bann, wish that something more extended and effectual had been done at Portrush. Whoever may be right, and whoever wrong about this, there is to be a railway from Coleraine to Londonderry: and, as there is one in progress between Londonderry and Enniskillen, the circuit will, by the help of existing railways, be almost complete.[7]

This Coleraine railway was originated, with sanguine expectations, by a company, a few years ago. Not only was the traffic expected to be great, but a grand scheme of reclaiming 20,000 acres of land from Lough Foyle was connected with it. These 20,000 acres, at a rent of £3 per acre, were to yield a revenue of £60,000, on the security of which money to any extent might be raised. Already however there has been a Government grant of £70,000, and the proprietors are believed to have spent £200,000 of their own, while there is, of course, no prospect of money coming in at present, however well the project may answer hereafter. A great sweep was made out over the surface of Lough Foyle to comprehend the 20,000 acres. Then, as it was not supposed that the railway could be strong enough to meet the tides, it was carried nearer inshore, and an embankment was carried over the original line for as far as it went. The railway works proceeded, the embankment has stopped, and it is understood, though not officially declared, that it will not be resumed. If so, the main source of anticipated profit is cut off, and the shareholders' gains must depend, not on the sale or letting of the reclaimed land, but on the railway traffic. This must be vexatious enough to the shareholders, and especially if what is said be true, that the railway is, after all, strong enough to have borne the stress of the outer line of waters.[8]

Before it has well left the Lough, the railway will receive the flax of the country-people for Coleraine. The people are cutting the flax at this time, and some are steeping it, as the traveller's nose informs him, from point to point on his road.[9] As for the growing flax, a novice might be excused for carrying away the news that the flax has a yellow flower, and is now in bloom, so abundantly is the wild marigold intermixed with the crop. In other fields the lads and lasses are pulling the flax, – some few skilfully, the greater number un-skilfully, – and making their handfuls into sheaves. Others are laying them in the turbid water, and keeping the bundles down with stones; while some, again, are taking the plant out of the ditches, and spreading it to dry. The traveller is told that various new methods of preparing flax have been tried, and that the old ways are found to be the best. Time will show whether they are right in throwing away the seed altogether, and in spreading their processes over a period of time which embraces many risks. If they are right, then the new railway will carry plenty of flax to Coleraine.

It has been hoped that it would carry plenty of potatoes, as well as cattle, butter, eggs, and fowls, to Derry for exportation. The fowls are indeed abundant, – pecking about on the mud-floors of the cottages, under the shelter of the peat-heap, which is handy to the fire. The cows are, for the most part, in good plight, either led about by a child, or tethered in a pasture, as even a single sheep may here and there be seen to be. We heard of one cow, properly considered a great marvel, which yielded 17$\frac{1}{2}$ lbs. of butter per week – that is, from 37 to 40 quarts of milk daily – for a considerable time. It is true, she was exhausted, and had to be killed, after this feat; but there seems to be little doubt that the cows in this region do flourish, and afford a profit. Hence appears the wisdom of some of the Companies in gradually abolishing the small pursuit of weaving, which used to go on in whole rows of cottages by the roadside, where no such wretched cabins are now to be seen. The Companies have paid for the emigration of the inhabitants; have removed their cabins, and put good gardens in the place of them;[10] and the flax which was woven here is now all sent to Coleraine.

And the potatoes – what of them? Alas! there is a dismal story to tell. Where the stench of the steeping flax intermits, now comes that of the rotting potatoes. At the point where the new railroad, coming from the Lough, passes under the bold headland of the Coleraine rocks – a noble headland, 1300 feet high – there is a plain, stretching out to the margin of the waves. It fills up the wide space between Lough Foyle, the Coleraine rocks, and the sea. We were told, rather to our surprise, that it is the largest plain in Ireland. This is the plain to which we owe the Drummond light. Lieutenant Drummond, engaged in the trigonometrical survey of Ireland, and desiring to obtain for the base of his triangle the vast space from this plain to the Scotch islands, and knowing that the Paps of Jura are visible in clear weather from the crest of the rocks, was stimulated to devise the most brilliant light that could be had, to shine from the Scotch to the Irish heights.[11] Hence the invention of the Drummond light, – a benefit which, whether practically great or not, is almost forgotten in comparison with the more heart-moving services which that gallant man[12] afterwards rendered to Ireland at the cost of his life.[13] This plain consists of a soil which is, throughout, fit to be a valuable manure. It is called sand, but it is wholly composed of comminuted shells. It is in great request by some agriculturalists, who understand their business; and potatoes, grown in breadths which are deeply trenched, extend almost to the margin of the tide. The potato-rot had hardly been known before in this neighbourhood. In 1846, and ever since, specimens of failure were very rare. But this year the visitation has come. There was scarcely a green patch to be seen yesterday as we passed over this plain. We need not describe the mournful spectacle of the people, here and there, forking up the roots to see if any could be saved, and elsewhere leaving the whole growth to its fate. They can hardly be blamed for having planted potatoes, so many years of impunity having appeared to warrant the venture; but, as to other parts of Ireland, it certainly appears as if men had had as broad a hint as could be well given to leave off staking so much on a crop which, from some unknown cause, seems to require a suspension of its cultivation, till either soil or root shall have become renovated by the intermission.

Before the railway disappears behind the rocks, it will have received, from the inland roads, oats, a little barley, and less wheat. Then, for a space of some miles, it can hardly receive any products but fish. The beauty of the region is so extreme that the stranger thinks little of anything else. Below the noble crowning precipices stretches a steep green slope which melts into the white sand of the beach. In spring this slope is one gigantic primrose-bank, wherever the woods allow the blossoms to be seen. Then succeed blue-bells, and the roses of which attar of roses is made.[14] There is now a perfect wilderness of bushes and trails, clustered with hips, which show what the blossoming must have been. The few houses have fuchsias growing higher than the eaves; and the tall hedges are starred over with the blossoms of the blue periwinkle. These are the sights which the railway traveller will see, – every garden free from blight, and something very like an eternal spring reigning under the shelter of these crags. The myrtle flourishes here, as in the south of Devonshire; and there is little but the roar of the Atlantic to mark the presence of winter. Far away on the one hand stretch the headlands of Donegal, on the other the ranges of the Giant's Causeway; while, as we have said, Scotland is visible in clear weather. In every chasm of the cliffs is a feathery waterfall, whose spray is taken up and scattered in the sunlight by every passing breeze. Further on come archways through the limestone, and tunnels running into the black rocks. At Coleraine the produce of the salmon-fishery on the Bann will, of course, be received, and more rural produce from the interior.

But how easy would it be to double or to treble that produce! The Clothworkers' estates lie near Coleraine,[15] and really they seem scarcely better than their neighbour's. The absurd gate-posts, like little round tents – the rusty iron, or broken wooden gates – the fences which fence out nothing, but nourish thistles, ragwort, and all seeds that can fly abroad for mischief – the over-ripe oats, shedding their grain for want of cutting, while the hay is still making – the barley so cut as to shake it all manner of ways – the stinking potato-fields – the men coming home from the weekly market tipsy and shouting, – the cabins with windows that will not open, and doors that apparently will not shut, – these are mischiefs for which nobody in particular may be exactly responsible, but which make us ask of how much use railways and harbours and reclamation of land can be, so long as people cannot bring out its wealth from the soil which is actually under their feet and hands. If, as some people hope, the railways will improve the tillage, it will be, as we said before, a capital thing. Let us hope and watch for it.[16]

The Linen Manufacture – Flax growing and Dressing

August 17, 1852

THE LINEN manufacture is the one only manufacture which has ever fairly taken root in Ireland. Having come in when the Revocation of the Edict of Nantes sent a crowd of ingenious foreigners into our islands,[1] and having now attained such perfection that, if only the patterns were as good as the fabric, the damasks of Belfast would cover all the royal dinner-tables in Europe, this manufacture may be regarded as the one great unmixed good in the industrial aspect of Ireland.[2] If the population employed in it were not originally, and are not yet, the Celtic, so much as the descendants of the Scotch, there seems to be every inclination to extend it among the inhabitants of other parts of Ireland; and the services of the Celtic cultivators being required to furnish the flax, the benefits of the manufacture are as thoroughly Irish as could be desired. When Lord Clarendon obtained a grant of £1000 a year for the Flax Improvement Society of Ireland,[3] it was under the engagement that the money should not be spent in Ulster, but wholly in promoting the growth of flax in the western and southern parts of the island. It was supposed that Ulster could take care of itself, every farmer who chose to grow flax being near the great market of Belfast, and sure of selling all that he could possibly raise, if the quality were good. It is estimated that no less flax is wanted than the produce of 500,000 acres to supply the demand of the manufacturer, while not more than 60,000 acres are growing flax in any one year. This means that an inferior flax is supplied to the United Kingdom from abroad, while there seems to be no reason why Ireland should not yield all that is wanted, except some very few of the finest sorts from Belgium. So much for the demand.

As the flax imported from Russia and other countries is, for the most part, inferior to the Irish, it appears that the natural advantages for flax-growing in Ireland must be all-sufficient.[4] Is it a remunerative crop to the grower? The present eagerness about flax-growing in England shows that this question is in the way of being completely answered: and the reports of English flax-growers seem all to agree that, under proper management, it is about as lucrative a business – that of flax-growing – as any man can now follow – short of gold-digging. We hear of a profit of £10, of £18, of £25, per acre, and even a good deal more, while assured that flax is not an exhaustive crop. Now, if this be true, or the half of it, what a prospect is opened for Ireland! She is the special grower of a product of this extraordinary value; and, with all the advantages of that special qualification, she may expand – she is even solicited to expand – her cultivation of flax to eightfold what it is now, to meet the manufacturing demand of today, – without anticipating the increase which is sure to take place.[5] It seems as if a resource like this might fill up an abyss of distress, – as if a harvest like this might reconcile the cultivators to a surrender (temporary or permanent) of the treacherous potato. With these facts (or, at least, authorized statements) in view, we have observed the flax-grounds all the way from Londonderry to Belfast; or rather to within a few miles of Belfast, for the fog which hung over the district as we entered it was so dense as to allow nothing to be seen beyond the road, for some little distance round the city.

Flax appears to us to stand third, as to extent of cultivation, among the crops we have seen; but we are not certain that turnips may not come before it. There can be no doubt of oats coming first, and potatoes next. The oat-crop is as good this year as it can be under such imperfect care as the Irish farmer bestows. The potatoes are little better than a putrid mass of waste. As for the flax, the climate and soil must be suitable, or Irish flax would not bear the name it does. The first requisite as to the management is that the ground should be well drained and subsoiled. The roots of the flax go down two feet, and they must have air and a loosened soil: this they certainly have not, as a matter of course, or in any systematic way. Flax should never follow roots immediately; and it should be grown only once in eight or ten years, we are told by the experienced; but there are some farmers who grow it after potatoes, and much oftener than once in eight years. The soil should be pulverized and cleared of weeds, and levelled till it is like a lady's parterre; but no soil in Ireland, as far as we have yet seen, is so treated: and, not satisfied with leaving the native weeds in all their rankness, the farmers are tempted by the low price of Russian flax-seed to buy it in preference to home-saved seed, offered even under the highest sanctions, though the Riga seed contains invariably a very large proportion of weeds. The crops should be weeded when about two inches high, and, as careful foreigners tell us, once or twice afterwards; but here the flax crops are, at this moment, as gay with a dozen varieties of weeds as the oats and the pasture-fields. The lower part of the stalk is thus choked up and discoloured and weakened for want of air and sunshine, besides the soil being exhausted by the weeds, and the steeping and dressing injured by their intrusion. And no less a sum than £300,000 a year is spent in the purchase of foreign seed, while the farmers of Ulster lose the whole of their own seed. At the end of the first ten years of the existence of the Royal Flax Society, it was computed that the waste, from the throwing away of the seed, amounted in that time to £2,000,000.[6] The farmers say that the fibre would be spoiled if the plant were allowed to ripen its seed; that, if pulled at the proper time for the fibre, the gathering of the seed would cost more than it would be worth for the feeding of cattle. The answers to these objections are of a practical sort. The seed is advanced enough to ripen of itself, and to produce excellent crops, if the plant is allowed to grow, not too long, but till the stalk is two-thirds yellow; and if the grower will sell his crop to the preparers, instead of preparing it himself, they will take care of the seed. These are facts abundantly proved by experience. It is also proved that one-fifth of the ground will grow seed to sow the whole; and that if the grower will not try the more economical plan of saving all the seed, it would answer better to him to let one-fifth of his fibre grow too woody than to buy weeds from Riga. There must be bad management somewhere when Ireland grows flax and loses the seed, while England is growing flax for the sake of the seed.[7]

Next comes the pulling. The ground being too often uneven, the roots do not come up 'square;' and, the farmer's family of all ages turning out to the work, some of it is ill done, the roots not coming up 'close,' and the stalks of different lengths being laid together. The steeping is done in pools or ditches. If the water be soft and favourable, well and good. If there be not enough of one kind of water, the produce of the same rood of ground may present as many different values as there are pools or ditches used. The process depends on so many accidents that it is all a chance whether the steeping will take six days or six weeks. Then comes the spreading, with all the liabilities of letting the flax lie too long, or not long enough; and then the same risk, all belonging to uncertainty of weather, about its standing in the stook or shock. When the beetling[8] and dressing are done, and the flax is brought to market, the farmer finds that he gets 6s. where the patentees of Schenck's system get 9s., though no farmer sells his best crop to Schenck's patentees.[9]

Some of this waste, vexation, and loss arise from bad farming, evidently enough; but much also proceeds from the want of division of employments. The time was when, in England, the farmer's family prepared, spun, and wove their own wool and flax, and wore their own homespun; and it would be merely a continuation of this old practice – merely an ignoring of the manufacturing system – if the Ulster farmers grew and prepared their flax for family wear. But they claim precedence in flax-growing; they claim to supply the manufacturers of Belfast who are to weave table-cloths for all royal dinner-tables; and if they are to do this, they must study and obey the requirements of the manufacturing system. They must learn to see that it cannot but answer best to them to devote their care to the improvement of their crop, and to sell it to establishments where the steeping and other preparation is done on scientific principles, and with the certainty which science alone can give.

There are about eighteen establishments under Schenck's patent in Ireland. The one we saw is in the neighbourhood of Belfast. The others are scattered over every part of Ireland where flax is grown; but the effect they have produced is as yet scarcely perceptible – so wedded are the cultivators to their old methods.[10] When the Government grant was obtained by Lord Clarendon for growing flax in the west and south, people asked what was the use of it while the cultivators could have no market for their crops. The answer was that there must be a clubbing together to set up scutching-mills,[11] which are reckoned to save 16s. 8d. per acre over hand-scutching. In distressed districts however hand-scutching was encouraged, for the sake of the increased employment of labour. As might have been expected, it was found impossible to continue the business on so false a principle. The privileged encroached on their privilege. The best workers turned out only 6lbs. per day, and some no more than 2lbs. Where the patent process is fairly set up, a market is provided; the remuneration becomes a regular trading matter; and, if the system could be extended to embrace the privileges offered by the times, a very considerable portion of Ireland's poverty might be abolished. At present, as we have said, scarcely any impression is made on the flax-growers of Ireland.

Under Schenck's patent, – of American origin, and established nearly four years in the neighbourhood of Belfast, – the steeping is done in vats, by means of steam-pipes, and with water of the best quality.[12] The process occupies from one day to four or five; but it can never fail of complete success. The same certainty attends all the processes.[13] It was at once found that £170 worth of labour saved £1200 worth of seed. That which is ripe enough is sown: the rest is sold for cattle-food. The first year nobody would sell the proprietors any flax; and now they can obtain it only within a range of eight or ten miles round Belfast, and they are sure of not obtaining the best. It is only when the farmer is doubtful of his crop that he offers it for sale. The second year the proprietors obtained a good deal, paying for it by the acre. Now they obtain more still, and buy it by the ton, which suits them better than having to watch the cropping of the produce they have bought. But the quality is so variable, – often from mere unskilfulness on the part of the grower, – that they long for the time when they shall be able to make their own requisitions as to the quality of the article in which they deal.

The question is – a question of unspeakable importance – will that time come before it is too late to secure this natural branch of industry to Ireland? There are some who fear and believe that other countries will be too quick for her, and that she will miss this much of her possible salvation. Look at the facts again, and say if this be likely. Ireland pays away £300,000 a year for seed which she merely wastes at home. She grows flax (on the whole very badly) on only 60,000 acres; whereas there is a demand, addressed peculiarly to her, for the produce of 500,000 acres. This is no new-fangled product, but exactly that which has been her own for centuries. At the same moment with the demand arises a new and sound method of avoiding the risks and losses of the old unskilled method of treatment. Under all this incitement, she has no opponents, but the offer of every possible assistance.

What follows? That if she misses her advantage, the world will say she deserves no pity. It does not follow that the world will be right in saying so. Some who look deeper may feel that she is more to be pitied than ever; for there must be some dreadful mischief at work to paralyse action in so plain a case. If such a painful spectacle should be seen as the flax cultivation passing from Ireland to some other soil, it will be owing to the same causes, whatever they may be, which deprave Irish agriculture generally to a lower point than can be seen in almost every other country in Europe. What those causes are, we shall better understand when we have looked beyond the province of Ulster.

Agricultural Improvement in Ulster

August 18, 1852

WHILE ALL Ulster is noisy with outcries and controversies on the subject of tenant-right[1] – while some of the elections are a public scandal, and political quarrels run high – there is a society modestly at work which, if properly supported, might do more for the benefit of the population than all the politicians in the province, with all their din. Professor Hodges,[2] who fills the agricultural chair in the Queen's College at Belfast, is the main support of the Chemico-Agricultural Society of Ulster.[3] He is the society's chemist, he lectures, and he superintends the preparation of its journal.[4]

We have given some account of how the tillage of the province appears to a stranger. We must have conveyed some impression of the crying need of knowledge, of consultation among landowners and farmers, of union to obtain information about the latest improvements, and so on. Bearing this in mind, and remembering also that this society is universally praised where it is noticed at all, – that it sits apart altogether from political quarrels, and is allowed on all hands to be much needed and a pure benefit, what may be supposed to be the degree of support it receives?

Last year's report informs us that the annual subscriptions amounted to £182. 5s. 6d. Well may English newspapers and Irish advocates describe such means as 'ridiculously small.' Dr. Hodges' 'Lessons on Chemistry in its application to Agriculture' is used as a text-book in all the rural schools of the National Board; he carries on an extensive correspondence with associations, British and foreign; and the Journals of this society are known to have given a great impulse to agriculture in Ireland.[5] One of the most zealous members is Mr. Andrews, the first Irish pupil of Mr. Smith of Deanston, and the man who subsoiled the first bit of Irish ground in 1833. Yet 'some of the larger landed proprietors have not renewed their subscriptions;' the amount received for advertisements last year was three guineas, and, as we have said, the subscriptions amounted to only £182. 5s. 6d., though sixty-five new members had joined.

What does this mean? English men of business would say at once that the Ulster people do not wish for agricultural improvement. And why do they not wish for it? Because, as the residents tell a stranger, it would do them no good. And why? How should a better method of tillage do them no good? To this there are many answers.

We hear most about old habits. It is an old habit of the Irish – even in Ulster, where they say they are half Scotch – to like division of lands, and not to like division of labour. The most zealous improvers can get nothing done thoroughly well that they do not effect with their own hands. Mr. Andrews himself cannot get his corn so stacked as that the ears do not hang out from the eaves to the base. Every labourer wants to be doing everything, – if possible on his own account; and he stands, in comparison with the Lincolnshire labourer, like the old nail-maker described by Adam Smith, who forged every separate nail, in comparison with the nail-cutter of the present day, who can supply more in a few hours than our whole nation formerly could in many months.[6] The great Companies have steadily set their faces against a subdivision of farms which should bring back the old evil of every tenant being a Jack-of-all-trades on a deteriorating patch of ground; but it needs to be on the spot to learn what difficulty they have in carrying out their own steady determination. The agent finds that where the tenant and his sons cannot divide the land, they secretly divide the produce; it is only by a painful interference with family arrangements, that, in certain cases, a virtual subdivision of farms can be prevented. Tenants who would do this have not attained to any desire for improvement in the science and practice of agriculture. These are the men who ask what chemistry can possibly have to do with their business; and who hold, with regard to the land, that 'whatever is is best.'

Such men would however be displaced in a trice by better farmers, if there were not obstacles to men becoming better farmers. The obstacles are, that, in the present state of the law, the tenant has no lease, or none that he can depend on; he has often no capital, being stripped of it by the process of entering upon his farm; and his political have been, till recently, no less striking than his legal discouragements. The difficulty of obtaining valid leases from the owners of encumbered estates[7] in Ireland has been fatal to the good cultivation of land. In Scotland the law gives the priority to a farming lease over every other claim whatever; and Lothian farmers would as soon think of squatting as of sitting down on any farm without the security of a long lease, – of nineteen years at the shortest. They will have nothing to do with leases of lives, because their operations proceed on a basis of calculation and foresight; and they bar accidents, as far as men of business can. When they are sure of their nineteen, or thirty-one, or more years, up rises their tall chimney; their steam-engine begins to pant, their subsoil to come up, their stagnant waters to run off, their money to disappear in the soil, and their hopes to stretch forward over a score or two of years, and embrace a compensating average of seasons. Their land becomes a perfect food manufactory; a perfect treat to the eye of the veriest old square-toes,[8] who fidgets at the sight of a weed, and cannot sleep for the thought of a hole in a fence. If the landlord thinks it right to guard against the exhaustion of the land during the last years of the lease, this is managed by simply prescribing the course of cultivation during those years. But the ordinary case is, that the relation answers too well to both parties to allow either to wish to part, and in that case it is the tenant's interest to keep up the quality of the land throughout the period. Very different is the case of the Irish tenant. During all the long period that estates have been growing more encumbered, it has cost him more and more to ascertain the validity of a lease, till he gives the matter up. The law has given the preference to every claimant over him; so that, after all his pains, the mortgagee might at any moment step in between him and his landlord, and claim his farm. And then, up to 1832, a sort of honour was paid to tenants for lives above tenants for terms of years, the first being admitted to the franchise, and the other class being excluded from it. All this is now rectified: but the prejudice in favour of the chance tenure remains for awhile. In 1832 the franchise was extended to leaseholders for terms of years; and in 1850 the better principle was introduced of proceeding on the value of the holding, instead of regarding the form of contract between landlord and tenant.[9] But the notion of the superior dignity of a tenancy for lives is not worn out yet; and thus, even where leases exist, the least secure kind are preferred to those which admit of steady calculation and foresight. Agricultural science and art are not likely to be very ardently pursued amidst such a state of affairs. A tenant is not very likely to lock up his capital in buildings, and sow it in the soil, when he cannot reckon on remaining long enough to recover it.

But he seldom has capital. A Scotch landowner takes care to ascertain that the candidate for his farm has the means to do it justice. The Irish candidate may perhaps present himself with a handful of money, when he applies for the land; but the outgoing tenant is sure to strip him of it by claims for improvements. In Ireland it is the tenant who builds the dwelling and everything else: the landlord lets the bare land. The outgoing tenant is under the strongest temptations to lay on his charges well. We are all apt to over-estimate our own doings and our own possessions – very honestly. Every old lady who has house property chafes at any mention of deterioration, and estimates her property higher, instead of lower, every year. Much more may the outgoing tenant overrate the value of what he has done and spent on the farm which he mourns over leaving; and the intense competition for farms removes all check upon him. Rather than miss the farm, candidates will vie with each other in paying his price; and the successful competitor enters, spending his capital upon his predecessor's so-called improvements, so as to have no means left for instituting any of his own. And he cannot borrow capital for the conducting of his business, as the Scotch farmer and every other man of business may. In the hope that some remedy for this hardship will soon be provided, we may content ourselves with saying now, that the law surrounds the Irish tenant with such difficulties, that he not only loses commercial credit by proposing to conduct his business with borrowed capital, but it may cost as much pains, expense, and uncertainty, to offer or obtain security for a loan of £50, as to ascertain the title of a large estate. How would a Scotch farmer, or a Manchester manufacturer, or a London merchant, get on with his business, if he were thus precluded from raising the means for carrying on his operations?

And who can wonder at the depressed condition of agriculture under laws, customs, and habits of mind like these? Where is good tillage to come from, and what is to be its reward, under so thankless a system? It seems very creditable, considering all this, that sixty-five new members should have joined the Chemico-Agricultural Society last year. It affords good promise of what the desire for improvement may become in the days of safe leases and command of farming capital. And these days may not be far off. The Attorney-General for Ireland has declared his intention of proposing a reform analogous to that of the Scotch law of eighty years ago, – a reform by which the power of secure leasing shall be largely extended, and by which a lease shall have priority over an encumbrance, instead of the reverse.[10] Then the world may have an opportunity of seeing whether there are natural causes which prevent the agriculture of Ireland from being as good as that of the Lothians. At present the fields in many parts of Ulster are but too like the crofts of the highlands and islands of Scotland.

Ireland Dying of too much doctoring – the 'Tenant Right' question

August 20, 1852

THERE IS something very striking, and not a little pathetic (to a stranger, at least), in the complaints of the suffering Irish that they are neglected, – that a little more law would save them, if they could only get it, but that the Imperial Parliament will not make laws for Ireland; while, all the time, the observer sees that the woes of Ireland arise, to a very great extent, from overmuch law. In the days of the Repeal agitation every repealer had visions of getting a law for this, that, or the other object, never doubting that, in the first place, he should get the desired law from the Irish parliament, and that, in the next, the law would do all he wanted.[1] It never entered his head that he was pining under too many specifics already; and that his welfare would be found, if at all, in committing himself to general laws, through a release from those which were impoverishing his life in all directions. He was like the hypochondriac, who thinks he wants more physic, and again more; whereas what he needs is to 'throw physic to the dogs,' and commit himself to the fresh air, cold water, and cheerful sunshine, which are shed abroad for all. It is not always easy, or even possible, to draw a sharp line of distinction between general laws of society, and those which are special; and, again, between the special laws which are rendered still necessary by former states of society, and those which may be considered done with, and therefore ready to be abolished. But there is one thing quite certain, and that is, that no new special law should be made without well-ascertained occasion – without occasion so decided as to command the assent of nearly the whole of the thinking and informed portion of society. If this be admitted, what ought to be done about this great question of Tenant Right in Ireland?

Few of us can forget that when O'Connell[2] found the repeal movement getting past his management, he allowed the people to anticipate whatever blessed consequences they chose from the acquisition of repeal; he always said, in a general way, that when they had got repeal they could get anything else they liked.[3] What they most wanted was 'fixity of tenure;' so they asked him whether repeal would give them fixity of tenure, and he said it would. There is no doubt that the popular meaning of the phrase was that every man who held a bit of land should hold it for ever – himself and his posterity after him – on the payment of a certain rent, when the seasons allowed him to pay. Before Lord Devon's Commission,[4] the 'almost universal topic of complaint' was the 'want of tenure,' as the witnesses expressed their trouble. O'Connell has long been in his grave; the Repeal agitation has died away;[5] Lord Devon's Commission is now only occasionally quoted; but we find Ulster ringing with cries about tenure, and, among other cries, we find one for 'fixity of tenure,' which the poorer cultivators believe to be uttered by their best friends. Let no one hastily suppose that fixity of tenure and security of tenure mean the same thing. As the stranger sees the matter, security of tenure must be obtained by doing away with a good deal of law; but fixity of tenure would require new law, and a terrible deal of it.

There are some who desire that the proceeds of all the lands should be lodged in the hands of some central administration; and that, after all public obligations are discharged, the rest of the fund should be distributed among those who tilled the ground. We need not do more than state this opinion in passing. Another plan, more extensively talked about, is that of converting the Irish agriculturalist into a peasant–proprietor, by transferring to him the ownership of the land, subject to a fixed rent. There are various ideas about providing for the security of the rent; but the main point of the whole measure is to be, that the transference of the land shall be made as difficult as possible. There may be little use in pointing out to those who would propose such a scheme as this that it is simply a confiscation of property. They must either have got over such a scruple, or have some plan to propose about compelling the owners to sell their land to some who would submit to hold nominal property on such terms. It may be more to the purpose to remind these advocates of fixity of tenure, that the great evil to be dealt with is the badness of the tillage; and that, by universal agreement, this unproductiveness is above everything owing to the difficulty in the transfer of land, which obstructs agricultural improvement. Once make the peasant–proprietor irremovable – once place him beyond the reach of stimulus to learn, and improve and bestir himself, and what a perspective of misery stretches before him and all who can be affected by him! What a tribe of children and grand-children is swarming on the bit of ground intended to support a single couple or family! How, as means diminish, the land becomes impoverished, till the whole concern goes to ruin altogether! The Flemish or Saxon peasant-proprietor is the *bona fide* owner of the land he lives on. He has not only fixity of tenure with a certain rent for ever, but the soil is his very own, as the children say; and it requires all the complacency and affection which attend the absolute possession of property in land to enable the patient drudging Fleming, with his neatness and his accuracy, and his long-established passion for independence, to rear his family first, and then so to dispose of them as to preserve his little estate entire. We need spend no space in showing what are, in comparison, the chances of the Irish peasant.

Next comes the scheme of which so much has been heard in Parliament and out of it – the scheme of a formation, under legal sanction, of a tribunal, appointed by landlord and tenants, with the resource of an umpire, for arranging the terms of the letting of land, and especially for determining the value of the improvements made, and to be left by the tenant. The short answer given by the landlord party is, that they do not wish it; they do not choose to admit any interference between themselves and their tenants. If the case of the landlords were perfectly simple, nothing could be more conclusive than their reply. If they came into the market, like sellers in general, to sell the use of their land to some one who wanted to buy that use, no third party would be wanted here, any more than in any other transaction of sale and purchase. But, in such a case, the question of tenant right – any question of tenure – could hardly have arisen at all. There is a complication and embarrassment, which has occasioned the proposition of a third party to the business; but it does not follow that the remedy will be found in legalizing a third party at all. While everybody seems bent on adding to the complication – on heaping more law on the mass which is already squeezing its vital juices out of the ground – it strikes a stranger that an Irishman here and there is probably right in proposing to undo some of this complication, to take off some of this incubus of law.

The poor Irish say that the landowners made the laws to suit their own purposes. This is very true; that is, that early law-makers in all countries were landowners, and, as a matter of course, and without meaning any particular harm, they made the laws to suit themselves. The poor Irishman now wants his turn: he wants the chance to make some laws to suit himself and his class. But that would be neither wise nor good. Better set about abolishing such as are hurtful of the landlords' laws. One of the most hurtful is that by which the existing owner of the land is prohibited from entering into leasing obligations which shall bind his successor. We have said enough before about the contrast between the Scotch method of leasing and the Irish practice of yearly tenancy. Free the Irish owner from his inability to grant leases for long terms; free him from his inability to charge his estate with farm-buildings and improvements, to be paid for by the extension of the rent over a sufficient term of years; free him from the inability to pledge his estate for a due compensation for the tenants' improvements; release the landowner from these trammels, and he will be in a condition to make a bargain with a tenant for their mutual advantage. The landowner is surely sufficiently punished for his ancestors' selfishness in law-making, – punished by his own restrictions before his posterity; punished in being unable to meet his tenants like a free man; punished in seeing his land deteriorate from one five years to another. It will not mend matters to punish him further (if it could be done) by subjecting him forcibly to the orders of a tribunal who should hardly leave him even the nominal owner, certainly not the master, of his own estate.[6]

There is no question of the fact that the practice of tenant-right in Ulster has been a good thing, – good for the cultivation of the soil. If the tenant could not obtain the security of a lease, he has obtained the next best thing he could get – the custom, sanctioned by the landlords and their agents, that his improvements, from the dwelling-house he built to the last manure he put into the ground, should be paid for by his successor.[7] In the confidence of this repayment he has tilled his land better than tenants in other parts of Ireland have done. But when changes arise – when the tenant's improvements become depreciated in value (like a merchant's stock under a commercial crisis), and he calls upon his landlord to lower his rent because the rent was calculated in proportion to the former value of his tenant-right, then comes the quarrel, as all Ulster has felt for two years past. Some landlords have reduced their rents, and largely; others have declined, never having been aware, they say, that the custom of tenant-right could lower rent. There is no way of settling the dispute through the dispassionate intervention of law; for the law has restricted the owner from making tenant right contracts with his tenants otherwise than tacitly. The consequences of this loose method of transacting business so important, and of turning into a sort of clandestine arrangement the terms on which depends the small amount of agricultural superiority which prevails in Ulster, are that landlord and tenant are now at strife on the most fatal subject about which men can quarrel in Ireland; and multitudes who know no better are crying out for all manner of new laws to coerce the landlord, while he would be but too happy to do what is best for both parties, if only he were disencumbered of that heavy armour of law, under which he cannot stir hand or foot, to help himself or anybody else. When men are allowed to manage their existing property by the use of their present wits, it is sure to be well managed; as long as they are compelled to treat it according to the wits of former centuries, the whole affair must be a sad jumble. Let the Scotch rule be admitted in Ireland – the rule that the first object is to secure the productiveness of the soil – and we shall see a common ground provided, on which owners and tenants can traffic. We shall see long leases, landlords' improvements in loving company with those of the tenant, rich fields, full barns, and rising plantations, with no smoke of the assassin's blunderbuss curling among the trees.

How Ireland is to get back its woods

August 23, 1852

WE HAVE the pleasure of seeing trees once more – real woods; and not merely such young plantations as the Companies have made in Ulster. Till we were passing through woodland again, enjoying the cool light as it came tempered through a screen of beechen foliage, we were not fully aware of the barrenness of the country we had traversed. From the time we had left the Coleraine rocks, we had scarcely seen a clump of well-grown trees. On the high lands of the coast near the Giant's Causeway, no one would look for woods; but, turning inland from those heights, for miles and miles over hill and dale there was nothing to be seen but the brown, green, or yellow surface of heath, root-crops, and harvest-fields. Some of the slopes about the noble Fairhead show young plantations of larch; and the romantic valleys in which lie Cushenden and Cushendall have some well-wooded nooks and recesses. After that the dearth of trees is really sad, even as far as Lord Roden's property, near Dundalk.[1] If one asks why, the answer is that trees will not grow in Ireland. Nobody can believe this who gives a moment's thought to the subject. Trees grow very well wherever resident proprietors like to live under the shelter of woods, and wherever estates are kept in the hands of proprietors. Trees grew very well when there was a good trade in timber and staves.[2] Trees grew very well when miles of forest were destroyed to dislodge outlaws. Trees must certainly have grown very well before the growth of the bogs; for the base of a bog is an almost continuous layer of forest trees. Lord Roden's trees grow very well, and Lord Downe's, and the Duke of Leinster's.[3] Ireland was certainly once covered, to a considerable extent, with forests; and we hope that there will be planting enough in time to come to prove that trees will grow in Ireland, much as they do in other green islands.

From the time that the Carlingford mountains come into view, on the journey from Belfast to Dublin, the scene becomes gay and smiling for an extent of many miles. Some really good wheat-crops are seen here and there. The pastures are as slovenly as possible; but there are fields of well-weeded turnips occasionally, and even two or three of unspoiled potatoes. We remarked here, and also further south, that where the potatoes were worst the poppies flourished most. In some cases, where the potato-stalks had almost vanished in black decay, poppies and other weeds seemed to usurp the whole field. We are far from drawing a hasty conclusion that exhaustion of the soil, such as is marked by the presence of poppies, is the cause of the potato-rot; for we know that the best tillage has failed to avert the evil; but it is worth notice that we have repeatedly seen a field of potatoes yet green and promising, between well-kept fences, and free from weeds, parted only by that fence from a decayed expanse where cattle were going in and out over the hedge, where slimy water stood in the ditch, and the poppy, the marigold, and long purples made the ground as gay as a carpet.

On approaching Dundalk, Lord Roden's woods present a fine background to the yellow oat and wheat fields: and the opening of avenues from the road to church, or house, or river, is a refreshment to the eye after the coast-road of Antrim and the bleachfields south of Belfast. Yet more smiling was a subsequent day's journey which led us through the great plain of Kildare. The heavy wheat-crops and rich oat-fields made us feel that we were rapidly going southwards; and on the further side of Athy the belts of woodland, extending for miles, reminded us amusingly of the assurance we had so lately received, that wood would not grow in Ireland. We asked how the large oaks, the rows of elms, the spreading ash and beech, came to be there; and we were told that Lord Downe's woods were carefully kept up round his mansion (as we saw by driving through the park), and that the Duke of Leinster is a good landlord.

No doubt he is a good landlord; and no doubt a good landlord has some power over the growth of wood on his estates. But there are facts open to the knowledge of all, which show that the landlords are not responsible for the decay of wood in Ireland – nor the tenants either. It is easy to say that men are lazy; that Irishmen are particularly lazy; that people will not look forward; that the sale of wood stripped the land, and that nobody remembered to plant in proportion to the felling; that, as wood became too scarce for fuel, men took to peat; and that there is so much peat, that men don't care about wood; that they are so accustomed to see Ireland bare, that they would not know their own country if they saw it wooded. These things may be facts,

2. Londonderry.

3. The Coleraine salmon leap, Co. Londonderry.

4. The town and bay of Dundalk, Co. Louth.

5. A street in Galway.

6. Galway.

7. A pattern in Connemara.

8. Clifden, Connemara.

9. The Eagle Mountain, Killeries.

but they are not reasons. We are still unsatisfied as to the why of the case. We know that it is a positive pleasure to the landowner to plant; and to the tenant too, in a minor degree. We know that it is quite a peculiar enjoyment to those who are concerned with land to put in seedlings and saplings, and shelter them, and foster them, and admire their growth at six years old, and begin to enjoy the profits of thinning after that time, and reckon complacently the incomings from year to year, and the permanent value added to the estate by means so cheap and easy and pleasant as planting. If, as Sir Robert Kane[4] tells us, during all the consumption of wood, while there was still any to fell no one planted, there must have been a reason for it.[5] When we consider what would have been the difference in the resources of Ireland now if it had been a well-wooded instead of a bare country, it appears that the reason must be a very strange and a very stringent one.

Why tenants-at-will, or on a lease of lives, should not incur the trouble and expense of planting, is obvious enough. By the law, as we have seen before, the improvements go with the land, and the tenant has no claim for compensation. According to the common law, the tenant cannot fell trees, because he is entitled only to their fruit and shade, and the landlord cannot fell them, but by express agreement, because the tenant is entitled to their fruit and shade. Even the power which the tenant once had, of felling what wood he wanted for repairs, was taken away by a statute passed in the Irish Parliament a few years before the Union.[6] The certainty of the total disappearance of woods under a system like this was so clear, that an act was passed in 1766, by which the property of the trees planted was vested in the tenant who planted them; but then, this tenant must have a lease of lives renewable for ever, or for above twelve years unexpired.[7] The much larger class of tenants, with short leases or none at all, were left where they were. Another act gave further scope about felling to the smaller class of tenants, without affecting the larger. By this latter act, passed in 1784, the tenant who had more than fourteen years of his lease before him might dispose of his own trees as he chose, if he had registered them by affidavit within twelve months of planting them.[8] Considering the trouble and expense of this registering, and the small number of tenants included under the permission, it is not very wonderful that after seventy years from the passage of that act, Ireland is still the bare country it is.[9]

And how does the law work with regard to the favoured class of tenants? There is a story on record which opens a curious scene to us. A tenant on a long lease in a northern county planted extensively, and

registered his trees, in compliance with the law. He believed them to
be his own, and loved them accordingly. He sheltered them, fostered
them, and gloried in them; and they grew for a long course of years.
He paid rent for the ground they grew on – and he did not grudge it,
for he believed he was growing a good property for his children. The
time came for a renewal of his lease. There was no difficulty about
that: both parties were willing to continue their relation, and the
terms were readily agreed upon. But then it came out that the trees
could not be made the property of the tenant for a future term. The
only lease which the law allowed the landlord to give was one by
which the tenant was subjected to severe penalties for cutting a switch
off any one of the trees he had planted, and for whose standing-room
he had paid rent all these years. Either trees must go with the land,
and become the landlord's property, or the landlord must, by an act
of liberality, purchase the trees; or the tenant must fell them before
the expiration of his lease – that is, in a few weeks. The landlord was
grieved. It was not convenient to him to buy the trees, as an act of
generosity. He could not legally give them to the tenant, for that
would be alienating so much of the value of the estate. The tenant
could not believe this. He could not credit that such could be the state
of the law; and he naturally supposed that the landlord wanted to
make the trees his own by delay. The man waited till the last day that
he could call the trees his own; then he called in everybody from far
and near to help him; and the woods were felled and removed before
night, amidst the curses of the peasantry on the landlord's name.
They knew nothing about the law: they saw an active improver
desperately cutting down his own beloved woods, to prevent their
becoming his landlord's property; and it would not have been easy to
convince them that the landlord had no desire to possess them. In the
Appendix to the Report of Lord Devon's Commission, there is a
narrative very like this, except that it ended more happily.[10] The tenant
was a well-informed man, who knew that his landlord was not to
blame; and it does not appear that he cut down his trees. But when
asked whether it is likely that he should plant any more, 'No,' he says, 'I
may grow furze, or heath, or brambles, but I won't grow timber.'

It is sad to see Ireland thus stripped of her ancient resources. It is
like seeing the disappearance of the furniture of a sinking house. Not
only is there present poverty, but an exhaustion of future comforts.
Difficulty and embarrassment may be got through, but the recovery
from barrenness is so hard! The woods of Ireland have to be re-
created; and how, if it is nobody's interest to plant, and there is

difficulty and expense at the very outset? The suggestions made by those who know best are, that if there be registration, it should be made to secure a property of such duration to its proper owner for a longer term than the current lease; and that the law should give the property in woods to the occupier, as the supposed planter, in the absence of any declaration or arrangement to the contrary. Thus it would become the interest of the tenant to plant, as it is usually the interest of the proprietor that he should. If the proprietor has any objections or special wishes about the matter, he can arrange his terms in giving his lease. If the island is ever to be re-clothed, and to begin to accumulate a new capital of forest timber, it must be by some such alteration in the law as this; for nothing can be done while the parties interested are kept in a position of common and relative incapacity which would be ludicrous if it were not far too sad for a joke.

Leinster – Irish Industry – Religious Feuds

August 26, 1852

BISHOP BERKELEY would hardly hold to his notion of the constitution of the Irish people, as regards their repugnance to work, if he could now come back, and give a fair study to Irish industry at home and abroad. He set it down as a fact, that in Ireland 'industry is most against the natural grain of the people,' and theorized to his own satisfaction on their being 'partly Spanish and partly Tartars,' and indolent, in virtue of both descents.[1] If he could revisit his earthly haunts, he would find, in his American province, for instance, Irishmen working as well as men need do, and growing as rich as men need be; and at home he would probably find men, women, and children much like what they are elsewhere, working well when they enjoy pay and hope, and dawdling over their business when hungry and discouraged.[2] 'Why and how,' has been repeatedly said to us since we entered the country, – 'why and how should our labourers work well while they are so ill paid? Let the truth be plainly stated, that our people are underpaid, or it may be ever so long yet before we learn that it answers best to the employer to give good wages.' We are willing to state plainly the little we have as yet seen and learned about the quality of popular labour.

Three things are very striking to us under this head – the heartiness of the labour where men are well paid, – the languor of the labour where people are ill paid, and the toil that people will undergo, under the stimulus of hope, even where the gains are very small. We have seen Irishmen working, with every muscle and every faculty, in an establishment where the work *must* be well done, where every man is paid according to his merits, and where the wages are from 8s. to 50s. per week. We have seen men and women lounging, staring about them, and moving slowly (when they moved at all) over outdoor work, the pay for which was 1s. a day for the ablest men, and 6d. for

60

the inferior men and the women. We have seen women bending over their embroidery, as they do all day long, and from week to week, plying their needles without respite, in the hope of making more than the ordinary 6*d*. a-day. We have learned that in the neighbourhood of Dublin women will walk five Irish miles for fruit, and walk all the rest of the day to bring it back and sell it, and be well pleased if they get 1*s*. a day – satisfied if they get 6*d*. There seems to be no room for a theory of constitutional indolence here.

And so we thought from as much as we could see in passing of the harvest-work in the plain of Kildare, and in a portion of Queen's County, last week. What we saw that day certainly surprised and gratified us, after what we had heard of the superiority of tillage, and of the quality of labour, in Ulster. We saw the best crops that have come under our notice thus far in Ireland, with the exception of two or three favoured spots; and the reapers and binders seemed hearty about their business. They were, to be sure, a strange-looking set of mortals, as we passed company after company of them in the yellow sunset light; the women hung round with rags that it was a marvel to see and a mystery to understand; and the men, some gaunt, some stunted, some with flaming red beards, some with shaggy black locks; all bare-legged and all ragged. But they had been working well, and the cabins they were returning to (such of them as were residents) are, according to all sound testimony, a very great improvement upon the dwellings of the labourers of forty years ago; cleaner without and within, more light and airy, and decent in every way.

So much improvement having taken place from natural causes, in spite of singular troubles and difficulties, there would be every hope of an accelerated progression if natural causes could work freely. It was as lately as 1845 that the Report of the Land Occupation Commission declared the condition of the labouring population to be stationary or worse, while that of the farming class had improved.[3] Through the horrors of famine, and the perils of the emigration of thousands of the employing class, the condition of the labourer has improved and is improving. But now, just when good men's hopes are rising, occurs a difficulty, sorrow, and danger which there is no seeing the end of. A new fierceness is infused into the religious strifes of the country. There is no use in now entering upon any discussion about how this fresh exasperation arose. There is no use now in inquiring whose fault it is. 'It must needs be that offences come; but alas! for those by whom they come.' It might be inevitable that new and more deadly struggles between the two churches, and among all churches, should occur; but, for our part, we had rather have cut off our right hand, and have been smitten dumb, than have written or spoken – as premier, priest, parson, or whatsoever else – a single sentence that could tend to exasperate the religious hatred which is now making Ireland a disgrace to the Christian name.

We have been wondering how much is known in England of the subject which is exciting the deepest interest here – the rapid course of conversion to Protestantism in the West. We are told that a population of 13,000 has been added to the Protestant church (the evangelical section of it) quite recently, on the west coast. We may have more to say about this when we have been there; and till then, we will say no more of it. Our present business with this question is as it affects the employment and condition of the labourer – the distribution and recompense of labour.

The last report of the Society for Protecting the Rights of Conscience lies before us.[4] It contains letters which bear so late a date as the middle of last June. The Archbishop of Dublin[5] is its president, and its office-bearers are persons whose testimony would be regarded with respect by the whole of society. The object of the association is to extend support (which means nothing more than bare maintenance) to poor Protestant converts, who have become the objects of priestly vindictiveness. A good deal of money has been raised, but it is speedily exhausted, and more is urgently requested. The Archbishop himself would excuse us and anybody for looking upon this business with some suspicion at first. He is a political economist, as well as a church dignitary; and he would commend, rather than censure, any reluctance to espouse a scheme by which a charity fund is applied to a creation of employments in favour of professors of a particular faith. He is no doubt aware that in cases of religious quarrel there are always ignorant and selfish persons who suppose there is something to be got by a new theological profession, and who try to get it. Perhaps he may know of certain parents of families who have applied to the clergyman to inquire what they shall get if they come to church with their seven, or their five, or their ten children. He knows enough of this aspect of the question not to disapprove of an inquirer's looking closely into the matter, before giving his sympathy to this kind of movement. He may also be aware that it takes some time for English people to become able to believe what the conduct of a Catholic priest in Ireland may be. It was in a somewhat antagonistic mood of mind that we took up this little report: but before we had done with it, we saw that there is really no choice for political economists, or anybody else, as to what shall be done. If the people are to be anything but mere slaves of the priests, and if, being free, their lives are to be saved, they must be employed and fed by their fellow-members of the Church. It is a sad and a mischievous necessity; but a necessity it appears to be. There seems to be no doubt that the converts spoken of in this report are *bona fide* converts, and that they have made, and are making, very severe sacrifices for the sake of their new faith. There is not the least appearance of anything of the nature of a bribe having been offered in any case; on the contrary, the funds are insufficient to afford the merest rescue from starvation to numbers who would at once be provided for and favoured if they would go back under the yoke of the priest. In one district, no one of 800 converts has ever obtained one single day's work from any Catholic farmer or landowner; and the only alternative is work afforded by the society or the workhouse. While the converts were receiving 6*d*. a-day at farm-work and frieze-making, their Catholic neighbours were earning from 10*d*. to 1*s*. 6*d*. In another district Protestant fishermen were not allowed to enter Catholic boats. Even when the owner would have employed a mixed crew, the priest prohibited it, and was obeyed. The priest went further, and told a Catholic owner of a boat that he would incur the curse of every priest for ever if he did not dismiss two of his best men, Catholics, because they had worked for a Protestant employer; and the men were dismissed accordingly, though engaged for the season. In such cases there is nothing to be done, apparently, but to buy boats and nets, and employ the outcasts. This has been done at one place on the coast, where the priest finds means to send a waverer to America, and where, while the priest has taken 30*s*. from a woman for blessing her sick cows, the converts are content with 6*d*. a-day, and release from the tyranny of the priest. One wishes however that the bodily release could go along with the spiritual. We read, in this report, a case wherein the priest was not content with persuading the landowner to turn out a family from their cottage if one boy continued to go to church, but condescended to lacerate the boy's face with his nails, and to lash him with his whip, threatening him with a worse whipping if he entered the church again. In cases like these, there seems no choice but to invent employments, and tamper with the natural course of industry and its rewards.

When we go into some of those parts we shall endeavour to learn what are the state and prospects of industry amidst these perturbing forces. Meantime, we are of opinion that there is little to choose between the Catholic and the Protestant temper – taking society all round. No priests in the country can be more ferocious in their language than, for instance, a host of the shopmen of Dublin – Protestants from Ulster. These young men came from the north, often sadly ignorant – scarcely knowing how to read and write. The shops in the Irish towns open late, and close very early – at 6 or 7 o'clock. Too many of these young men spend their evenings in idleness, probably at the public-house; or, if reading, knowing of nothing better than a newspaper, as newspapers are in Ireland. These are the valiant host whom their disgusted employers sometimes hear talking greedily of 'wading knee-deep in Catholic blood,' and so forth. The placards in Dublin streets, with their tall type of vituperation, are painful to the eyes of a stranger. It is a stranger's business to read them; but it is an embarassment to stand to do so. It is a pain to overhear the talk of poor men about the coercion they are subject to – whatever amusement their native wit may infuse into the topic. 'By Jasus,' said one poor man to another, the other day, 'I don't know where to look to for meself. The priest says if I don't vote agin for his mimber, he'll keep me out of heaven; and me landlord says if I do, he'll turn me out of me cabin on earth. What I'll do, I don't know.' 'Thry the say,' suggested his comrade. According to the report above referred to, the priest and the land- (or water-) lord are to be found there too.

The Women

August 27, 1852

CONSIDERING that women's labour is universally underpaid, in comparison with that of men, there is something very impressive to the traveller in Ireland in the conviction which grows upon him, from stage to stage, that it is the industry of the women which is in great part sustaining the country. Though, in one view, there is moral beauty in the case, the symptom is a bad one. First, the men's wages are reduced to the lowest point; and then, capital turns to a lower-paid class, to the exclusion of the men, wherever the women can be employed in their stead. We should be sorry to draw any hasty conclusions on a matter of so much importance; but, recalling what we have seen since we landed, we cannot but declare that we have observed women not only diligently at work on their own branches of industry, but sharing the labours of the men in almost every employment that we happen to have witnessed. As an economical symptom, the employment of the least in the place of the most able-bodied is one of the peculiarities which marks the anomalous condition of Ireland. The famine time was, to be sure, an exception to all rules; but the same tendency was witnessed before, and is witnessed still. At that time, one of the London Companies sent directions to their agent to expend money to a certain amount, and on no account to allow anybody on their estates to starve. The agent determined to have a great piece of 'slob' land dug, – employing for this purpose one boy out of every family of a certain number, with a staff of aged men for overseers, to superintend and measure the work. Spades, from a moderate to a very small size, were ordered; and a mighty provision of wheaten cakes was carried down to the place every day at noon. The boys were earnest and eager and conscientious about their engagement. They were paid by the piece, and they worked well. Some little fellows, who were so small that they had to be lifted up to take their wages, earned 5s. a week. They grew fat upon their wheaten food, and their families were able to live on their earnings; and if the Company did not gain, they did not lose. But it must have been a piteous sight to see households supported by their children and grannies, instead of by the strong arm of him who stood between. The women were at work at the same time. The women of Ireland so learned to work then that it will be very long indeed before they get a holiday, or find their natural place as housewives.

We do not say recover their place as housewives; for there is abundance of evidence that they have not sunk from that position, but rather risen from a lower one than they now fill. Some years ago, the great authority on Irish peasant life was Mrs. Leadbeater, whose 'Cottage Dialogues' was the most popular of Irish books till O'Connell's power rose to its height.[1] In the suspicion and hatred which he excited towards the landlords, and the aristocracy generally, works like Mrs. Leadbeater's, which proceed on the supposition of a sort of feudal relation between the aristocracy and the peasantry, went out of favour, and have been little heard of since.[2] Elderly people have them on their shelves however, and we know, through them, what was the life of the Irish peasant woman in the early part of the century. We know how, too often, the family lived in a mud hovel, without a chimney, all grovelling on the same straw at night, and perhaps with the pig among them; and at meals tearing their food with their fingers, and so forth. We know how the women were in the field or the bog, while the children were tumbling about in the manure at home. Those who have been to Stradbally, Queen's County, where Mrs. Leadbeater lived, are aware of the amelioration in cottage life produced by the efforts of her daughter-in-law, by the introduction of domestic industry in the place of field labour. The younger Mrs. Leadbeater taught fancy knitting to a bedridden woman and her daughters, many years ago, for their support. The example spread. Women came in from the reaping and binding, – girls stayed at home from haymaking, and setting and digging potatoes. They kept their clothes dry, their manners womanly, and their cabins somewhat more decent. The quality of the work grew finer and finer, till now we see issuing from the cabins of Stradbally the famed 'Spider Mitts,' 'Impalpable Mitts,' 'Cobweb Mitts,' or whatever else English and American ladies like to call them. Upwards of two hundred women and girls are employed in this knitting; and people who knew Stradbally thirty years ago are so struck with the improvement in the appearance of the place, that they declare that the lowest order of cabins appears to them to be actually swept away.

Stradbally is only one of many such places. In every house of the gentry one now sees sofas, chairs, screens, and fancy tables spread with covers of crochet-work – all done by the hands of peasant women. In the south and west, where the famine was sorest, terrible distress was caused, we are told, by the sudden abolition of the domestic manufacturers on which a former generation was largely dependent. The people used to spin and weave linen, flannel, and frieze, which were carried to market, as were the knitted stockings of Connaught. In the famine, the looms and spinning-wheels disappeared, with all other cabin property. It is very well that, when this had once happened, the same manufacturers should not be restored, because they are of a kind surely destined to destruction before the manufacturing system. The knitting goes on; and it may long go on, so superior as knitted stockings are to woven ones in point of wear. And a variety of fine works are going on, in wild western districts, where the workwomen who produce such beautiful things never saw a shrub more than four feet high. In the south-west, lace of a really fine quality is made in cabins where formerly hard-handed women did the dirtiest work about the potato-patch and piggery. Of the 'hand-sewing,' some mention has been made before. We are assured at Belfast – and it only confirmed what we heard in Scotland – that no less than 400,000 women and girls are employed, chiefly by the Glasgow merchants, in 'hand-sewing' in the Irish cabins. Their wages are low, individually; but it is a striking fact that these women and girls earn from £80,000 to £90,000 per week. It is a regular branch of industry, requiring the labour of many men at Glasgow and Belfast, to stamp the patterns on the muslin for the women to work, and, again, to bleach it when it comes in 'green' (that is, dirty – so dirty!) from the hands of the needlewomen. They earn but 6*d.* a-day, poor things! in a general way, though at rare times – such as the Exhibition season – their pay amounts to 1*s.*; but it must be considered that their wear and tear of clothes is less than formerly, and that there must, one would think, be better order preserved at home.

So much for proper 'women's work.' But we observe women working almost everywhere. In the flax-fields there are more women than men pulling and steeping. In the potato-fields it is often the women who are saving the remnant of the crop. In the harvest-fields there are as many women as men reaping and binding. In the bog, it is the women who, at half wages, set up, and turn, and help to stack the peat, – not only for household use, but for sale, and in the service of the Irish Peat Company. In Belfast, the warehouses we saw were more than half peopled with women, engaged about the linens and muslins. And at the flax-works, near the city, not only were women employed in the spreading and drying, but in the rolling, roughing, and finishing, which had always till now been done by men. The men had struck for wages; and their work was given to girls, at 8*d.* per day.

Amidst facts like these, which accumulate as we go, one cannot but speculate on what is to be the end; or whether the men are to turn nurses and cooks, and to abide beside the hearth, while the women are earning the family bread. Perhaps the most consolatory way of viewing the case is that which we are quite willing to adopt, – that, practically, the condition of women, and therefore of their households, is rising. If there is something painful in seeing so undue a share of the burdens of life thrown upon the weaker sex; and if we cannot but remember that such a distribution of labour is an adopted symptom of barbarism; still, if the cabins *are* more decent, and the women more womanlike, it seems as if the process of change must be, on the whole, an advance. As to the way out of such a state of things, it seems as if it must be by that path to so many other benefits – agricultural improvement. The need of masculine labour, and the due reward of it, must both arise out of an improved cultivation of the soil; and it is not easy to see how they can arise in any other way.

While thinking and speaking of cabin life, it occurs to us to notice the remarkable appearance of health among the very lowest of the peasantry whom we have yet encountered. What we may see in the West we cannot anticipate; but we are assured that the same fact will strike us there, – that there also we shall see grown people and children grovelling in filth, with a manure-heap on the threshold, a stagnant pool before the door, and rotten thatch dropping on the stale straw on which they sleep, and they nevertheless stout, clear-eyed, and ruddy. From this we except, of course, particular situations and circumstances in which ophthalmia and fever arise, such as crowded dens in towns, and over-peopled workhouses.[3] What this mischief amounts to may be partly judged of by the number of one-eyed people, and persons marked with the small-pox, who may be seen at assemblages like Donnybrook Fair; where we observed more than can easily be seen at once, anywhere out of Egypt. But these people are not usually peasants, living in country cabins. As to the cause of the apparent health, it is said to be nothing else than the antiseptic properties of the peat. We know how charred and powdered peat is valued as a deodorizing agent. Plenty of this crumbled peat lies in and about every cabin, on the mud or flint-paved floor, on the threshold, in the pool, and dropped about on the manure. If this is the real reason of the undeserved healthiness of the ordinary Irish cabin, it is as well that the English should know it, for the sake of many thousands of poor fever patients who might be made the better for the 3,000,000 of acres of bog which might be emptied out, greatly to the advantage of Ireland.

Railway from Dublin to Galway – Bog of Allen

August 29, 1852

T HE RAILWAY from Dublin to Galway carries the traveller completely across Ireland – from the Irish Channel to the Atlantic – in six hours. The speed is not great – a little short of twenty-one miles an hour; but the punctuality is remarkable. The Dublin and Galway Railroad is not a very easy one to travel on in regard to steadiness. For the third of the line nearest to Dublin there are many curves, and pretty severe ones, so that the shaking of the carriages is disagreeable. For the rest of the way the road cuts straight through bog, with very narrow intervals of more solid ground; and a little jumping is not therefore to be wondered at, or found fault with. The marvel would have been, a quarter of a century ago, that the weight of a railway train should ever be carried across the bog at all.

The road traverses the great limestone basin which occupies the centre of Ireland; and there is scarcely any variation of level all the way. The engineer's difficulties were wholly with the consistency of the soil, and not at all with any hills and dales. One pleasant consequence of this is that the traveller sees for miles on either hand, and is not blinded and stunned by being whirled through cuttings. To us it appears as if there was scarcely a mile of cutting the whole way. Some who know the road may ask what is the good of this, considering what it is that is to be seen. But when one's object is to study the face of a country, nothing comes amiss, – neither Salisbury Plain nor the Bog of Allen. We (two of us) determined to use our opportunity of passing through a dead level of nearly 125 miles, to see everything on both sides the road, – and a diligent look-out we kept.

First, about the potatoes. We can safely say that we did not see one healthy ridge of them between Dublin and Galway; and we believe there is not one. It appeared indeed as if, in despair, the people had left the potatoes to their fate without a struggle. In the greater

number of cases the field was so gay with poppies and other weeds as
to leave only a black shadow of the potato-plant in the midst; and,
quite universally, the ridges were so choked with grass and weeds that
no care could possibly have been taken of the crop at any time this
season. The oats were as weedy as many that we have before described;
and some of the pastures as overgrown with thistles and ragwort; but
they did not present the same evidences of reckless despair as the
numerous potato-fields. Some of the pastures were so fine, of so pure a
grass and so brilliant a verdure, that there would have been unmingled
pleasure in looking on them but for the drawback that the hay is not
yet carried. There it stands in cocks, in these last days of August, to
catch the rains which are coming up with this west wind from the
Atlantic: and a sad pity it seems. We do not expect to see much more
such grass; and we can scarcely see finer anywhere. The limestone
bottoms favour pasturage so much, that we hope the day may come
when, in all the intervals of the great central bog, there may be a most
advantageous stock farming carried on. In those days the hay will, we
suspect, be saved six weeks earlier; though it should in fairness be
said that we are told that English critics have no idea what allowance
it is necessary to make for the caprices of the Irish climate.

As we proceeded, we looked with a regretful interest on the trees,
where we saw them grouped in any beauty – as they were, if we are
rightly informed, nearly the last we shall see for some time to come.
Among the wild scenery of the west coast we shall see quite another
kind of beauty. The College at Maynooth appears to be surrounded
by gardens and thriving plantations; and some old trees hang about
the neighbouring ruins of the ancient castle of the Fitzgeralds of
Leinster,[1] and clothe the entrance to the estate of the Duke of Leinster.
There are large plantations again on the estates of Lord Clancarty, at
Ballinasloe, though there we have entered on the bog country, which
extends all the way to Galway.[2] A more desolate tract of country than
that which stretches forward from the boundary of Lord Clancarty's
liberal improvements, we are hardly likely ever to see.[3] It makes the
imagination ache, like the eye. What it must be may be in some
measure conceived, if we remember that Ireland contains very nearly
3,000,000 of acres of bog: that six-sevenths of this amount lie
between lines drawn from Wicklow Head to Galway, and from
Howth Hill to Sligo; and that, within that space, the greater proportion
of bog lies west of the Shannon. When Cromwell transplanted all
disaffected families from other parts to Connaught, and when
Connaught became the proverbial alternative of hell, the great bog

was no doubt the uppermost image in men's minds.[4] The disgraces of Connaught certainly recur with strong force to the traveller's mind when he traverses that bog for the first time.[5]

The depth is at the deepest part forty-two feet: at the shallowest, where it is worked, about six feet. The deep and wide drains are satisfactory to look upon; and so are the blue smokes where heaps of peat are burning with an intermixture of clay, – working the process of reclamation; and so, perhaps, are the dismal patches of thin and feeble oats, where, wholly surrounded by black bog, the reaper and his children, bare-legged and half clad, suspend their work to see the train go by. The vast 'clamps' (stacks) of peat, the acres upon acres covered with little heaps of the drying 'bricks' of turf, the brown and black terraces, just sprinkled with new heather and weeds, may be dreary; but they are not dismal; for they tell of industry, and some harvest of comfort, however small. But there are other sights, – groups of ruins, as at Athenry – staring fragments of old castles, and churches, and monasteries; and worse than these, a very large number of unroofed cottages. For miles together, in some places, there is scarcely a token of human presence but the useless gables and the empty doorways and window-spaces of pairs or rows of deserted cottages. There is something so painful – so even exasperating in this sight, that one wishes that a little more time and labour could be spared to level the walls, as well as take off the roof, when tenants are either ejected, or go away of their own accord.[6] Yet, while substantial stone walls are thus staring in the traveller's face, what cabins – actual dwellings of families – are here and there distinguishable in the midst of the bog! styles of mud, bulging and tottering, grass-grown, half-swamped with bog-water, and the soil around all poached with the tread of bare feet. In comparison with such places, the stony lands near Galway (a vivid green ground, strewn with grey stones) look wholesome, and almost cheerful, but for the wrecks of habitations. From the time that we enter upon the district of the red petticoats – the red flannel and frieze, which form a part of the dress of most of the Galway people – things look better than in the brown and black region of the bog.

Yet we were accustomed, a year ago, to hear the Bog of Allen called the Irish California. This was in our minds as we passed through it yesterday; and we had not forgotten it when we were in Antrim; and we went down into Kildare on purpose to see about it. The interest excited a year ago by the news of Messrs. Reece and Owen's patent, and by the promise that peat should be converted into divers useful substances by a process yielding enormous profits, was not only natural, but thoroughly justifiable. If it were really probable that the substance which occupies nearly 3,000,000 of acres of the surface of Ireland could be turned into wealth, the fact would be of such incalculable importance to the whole people – and to our whole empire – that no degree of earnestness could be ridiculous or misplaced. Men of business distrusted the statement of probable profits; and men of science were aware that difficulties, many and great, usually occur in reducing scientific prospects to commercial facts, under a delegated agency; but none were willing to discourage a trial, or to prophesy failure in the pursuit of so great a good. As far [as] we can make the matter out, the results thus far have not been very encouraging; but still, so great is the stake, the scientific and practical seem to agree to treat the enterprise gently and cheerfully, in hope of better days.[7]

This is a matter about which the public can form some judgement for themselves, without taking the trouble that we have taken, of going to the works of the Irish Peat Company, four miles from Athy.[8] The first annual meeting of the company took place in London at the end of July; the report was printed in the London papers the next day, and it has been copied all over the country. Each reader of that report can judge for himself as to whether, if the Bog of Allen had been the mine of wealth supposed by the patentees, this company's report would have been what we see it is. If the wealth be there, it will come forth through the retorts, pipes, and hydraulic presses at the works. There is no opposition, we believe, no enmity to meet, no antagonism whatever but that of Nature; and therefore the thing, if feasible, will be done.

On inquiry about this matter at Belfast, we found that the experiments tried at Antrim had come to nothing. The thing was completely over there; and we were informed that the only place where any works were going on was at the establishment near Athy. In Dublin we could not find that any interest was felt, or that any products had ever been seen. We therefore went down into Kildare to see for ourselves. We found the bog lands of the company, consisting of 500 acres, lying close to the railway, the managers of which have acted in a most liberal spirit to the company – as the report informs us – even constructing a siding at their own expense. There was the furnace, with the gases blazing within; and there was the hydraulic press, full of paraffine in its woollen cloth; and there were barrels, with more or less of tar, and spirit, and oils. The distillation was

going on; and three or four men were about the place. We were told
by the agent, afterwards, that fifteen people are employed on the
works, besides those engaged in digging the peat: but three men had
been so burned the day before, as to need removal to the Kildare
Infirmary; and the foreman had that morning burned his hand. We,
no doubt, saw the place at an unfavourable time; and the works have
never fully recovered their spirit since a fire which took place in
February last, by which £300 worth of peat was burnt. The agent
told us of intended new buildings, new furnaces, etc.; and we see by
the report that the shareholders (who are not the public at large, but
a few gentlemen interested in the enterprise) are called upon for a
payment of £2 per share, in addition to the £4 already received.
When these new buildings are up, and the furnaces at work, we shall
be better able to judge of the prospects of Ireland with regard to her
bogs. At present there has been an expenditure of above £12,000,
without (as we understand the report) any profit to the company. The
agent speaks of 'difficulties;' and such certainly beset all new
undertakings. He declares that all the original chemical statements
have been verified, and all promises fulfilled. If so, success must soon
stifle all cavil. Meantime, the observation is natural, that there are no
sales made except in London. If the products are of the value and
immediate use alleged, it seems strange that they should not find a
market nearer home. On the whole, while every one appears to wish,
sincerely and earnestly, that the bogs of Ireland may be turned to a
richer and more speedy account than by the old method of toilsome
and gradual reclamation, the hope of such an issue of the new
experiment seems to weaken with time. If the wealth is so very great,
it is strangely slow in coming in; and, while no one will say that peat
is not convertible into candles, naphtha, oils, ammonia, and gases,
there is more and more hesitation in saying that the conversion will
ever be worth while. The consolation under this doubt is, that the
experiment, if sound, cannot fail soon to vindicate itself.

Galway

August 31, 1852

WHATEVER we may find that is strange in the wild parts of Ireland, we shall hardly find anything stranger than this town of Galway. If we should encounter a wilder barbarism in remote places, it will, at least, not be jumbled together with an advanced civilization. See here what has struck us already.

We approached the place through a series of limestone bottoms which ought to afford the finest pasturage. Nothing can be fresher, sweeter, or more delicate than the grass that grows there, though there is no great weight of it. The people destroy these slopes and levels as pasture, breaking it up to grow potatoes, of which they lose this year 80 per cent. As, owing to natural advantages, nothing can altogether stop the grazing, butter of the finest quality is sold in Galway (none being exported) at 1s. a lb. throughout the year; the pound consisting of 28 oz. Yet there is no manure whatever saved or made from any kind of stock or land-growth. The people will have seaweed, and no other manure whatever. Now, see what a story belongs to this seaweed. It is the red weed, which is thrown up in vast quantities, in every bay and on every promontory, from the north coast of Mayo to the extreme south-west of Ireland. After all is taken for manure that the people will use, two-thirds are left to rot and be lost. A professor of chemistry[1] examined this weed, and saw reason to be confident that, if properly burned, it might be made an article of profitable production. He is certain that the extinguished kelp fires might be profitably relighted all along the coasts, not for the sake of the soda, which was the product formerly sought by kelp-burning, but which can now be had more cheaply from common salt, but for the sake of the iodine and potash salts, which this particular weed yields in abundance, when burned in a certain manner. He went over to the island of Arran, and there arranged his plans. He purchased seven stacks of the weed, at £1 per stack, and he promised £3 more for the burning. This burning would take one man three weeks, or three men one week. One need not say that this pay is much higher than could be obtained by selling the weed for manure, even if there had not been abundance for both purposes. All was agreed upon; and the professor paid half the money into the hands of the priest, in the presence of the men, promising the remainder when the work should be finished. In the morning, as he was proceeding to the spot with the rake he had brought over for the men's use, they met him, and, under various pretences, threw up their bargain.[2]

There is a fish abounding in these bays, and near the land (for the Claddagh fishermen will not go far to sea) called the basking shark.[3] To what extent it abounds may be judged by the fact that eighty were taken last season, under all disadvantages. Each fish yields six barrels of oil; and the liver of a single fish fills one of the Claddagh boats. The oil is almost inestimable as a commercial resource, if its value was understood; but the people do not understand or believe it; and they sell it all, as train-oil, to a purchaser from Dublin, who comes and buys it up.[4] This oil burns with a light as brilliant as sperm; and the professor of chemistry here vouches that its value for medicinal purposes is nearly or quite equal to that of cod-liver oil. Yet, there is no inducing the Claddagh men to use any harpoon in pursuing the basking shark, but the antique one, which allows many more fish to escape than it secures. We were, the other day, in a boat with a man who last season struck seven fish which escaped, and which he might have secured with a proper harpoon: and he sticks by the old one yet. To appreciate the mournfulness and vexatiousness of this perverseness, one must walk through Claddagh, looking into the houses as one goes.[5]

It is a spectacle never to be forgotten by an Englishman. Claddagh is a suburb of Galway – a village of fisherman's cabins.[6] The cottages are in rows; and there are therefore streets or alleys, where grass springs between the stones, or moss tufts them, and where a stunted elder-bush, or other tree, affords a strange little patch of verdure in the dreary place. The rest of the verdure is on the roofs. Nettles, docks, and grass grow to the height of two feet, and the thistle and ragwort shed their seeds into the thatch. Where the thatch has tumbled in, the holes are covered with matting, kept down by large stones, which make new holes in the rotten mass. The once white walls are mossy and mouldy. The sordidness is indescribable. But infinitely worse is the inside. Some have no windows at all. Voices were heard from the interior of one where there was no window, and where the door was shut. In several, men were mending their nets by the light from the door; in one we saw, through the darkness, a woman on her knees on the mud floor, netting, at a net which was suspended from the roof; and again we saw, kneeling at a bench, a mother and daughter, whose faces haunt us. The mother's eyes were bleared, and her hair starting like a patient's in Bedlam. Elsewhere we saw a litter of pigs wallowing in the mud close by the head of the bed. Many mothers in the street, and even in the fish-market, were performing that operation on their daughter's heads or on their own persons, which is apt [to] turn English stomachs in Naples or Lisbon. But enough. This mere fragment of description will show something of how the Claddagh people live, while the basking shark abounds on the coast, and dozens of Claddagh boats are laid up in the harbour. On inquiring whom this village belonged to, we were informed that it has lately been purchased by a Mr. Grattan, and that he is hoping to induce the people to use a modern harpoon which he is sending them. But, till this is achieved, what is to be done about those cabins? How can any man endure to call them his?

There is a clergyman on the island of Arran who has set up a trawling-boat, with a crew of two men, said to be Scotch. The success of this little fishery is what might be expected on such a coast, and what might attend any other well-served trawling-boats. It is necessary to be cautious in receiving details in this part of the world; but the profits of that fishery are said to have been, in the past season, from £12 to £16 per week. The Claddagh men attacked the boat, and threatened, in all seriousness, the life of the clergyman. He applied to Government for protection, and a steamer has been sent in consequence. Some Claddagh men were asked, in our presence, the other day, whether it would not be better for them to try for a share in so profitable a fishery; and why they did not club together to get trawling boats, and prosper like the clergyman. They replied that they had their own boats in the harbour; that they were poor men; that they did not want any new ways; that they had always been used to their own boats; and so forth. The answer to all proffers of advantage to the people here is, that they don't want any improvements.[7]

'Here is the barbarism,' you will say; 'but where is the civilization?' You have had news of the railroad. Here is a new canal – a massive and admirable work, to all appearance, opening the great lakes to the bay. A short canal connects Lough Mask with Lough Corrib; and this new line, very short also, with some improvement of the navigation of the river Corrib, and some deepening of parts of the lake, establishes an admirable waterway for the conveyance of produce from the interior. Of the interior and its produce we may say more when we have seen them. As to the aspect of Galway, the place seems to have been furnished with a vast apparatus for various social action, for which there is no scope. Here is the railroad, with, as yet, very little traffic. Here is this canal, with, as yet, no trade. Here is a nobly situated port, with, at present, no article of export. Here is a great hotel, built apparently in some prophetic anticipation of custom in future years. Here is the very handsome Queen's College, with its staff of twenty professors, and its forty-two scholarships, while its halls echo to the tread of seventy-five students.[8] The number on the books is about one hundred and twenty; and the attendance is seventy-five. The grey marble edifice stands up strangely amidst bare plots of ground and desolate fields, heaped up or strewed over with stones, and inlets of water, which glitter in the sun on every side. The sea runs in wherever it can find an opening; and there is the river Corrib, and the canal; and a cut through the rocks for the water-power which turns the great wheel at Franklin's marble-cutting establishment. The amount of water-power would make a great manufacturing centre of the place at once, if Galway were in America; here it seems to add to the desolation of the scene. Well, there is, besides, the new workhouse, also of grey stone; and the model schools under the National Board – the most hopeful feature, perhaps, of the singular scene. Across one arm of the bay there are woods; and, when your boat approaches the beach there, you see gay gardens, productive orchards, rows of stacked corn and hay; and, across another inlet, more stacks, another orchard, verdant pastures, a pretty farm-house, some splendid stock; and you believe you have found one piece of sound prosperity on the shores of Galway Bay. You find that the tenant of the farm is the agent of the whole estate, under whose management it has reached this prosperity; but he is going away. His stock is to be sold off; the pastures he has retrieved to their natural use will be broken up into potato-grounds. He is the Professor of Agriculture in the college.[9] He has only five pupils there, but his example on this farm might have done more than his instructions in the college. Why is he leaving his farm? Because the noble owner of the property which has been so much benefited by his science and skill died of cholera last year, and the widow will not (possibly cannot) grant the tenant a lease which will justify his remaining on his farm.

So much for the agriculture. We have seen how it is with the fisheries and the seaweed. There are marble quarries at hand, – the fine black marble of Galway, and the green marbles of Connemara, so well known by name, but which so little use is made. With all these resources, and many more, Galway has no trade; and people who desire improvement look for it from the place being made an American packet station. For passengers, and mails, and latest news by the electric telegraph, it may serve; but surely not for goods traffic: the trans-shipment for the passage of the Irish Channel must be a fatal objection.[10] However this may be, we would fain see the Galway people using now their great advantages, while awaiting what the future may bring. The difficulty seems to lie in the absence of a middle class of society. The people are, in this, like the buildings. There are imposing edifices – hotel, college, schools – and there are the thatched cottages of the old town, and the Claddagh cabins. If, after looking round for middle-class abodes, you think you have discovered a row or group, you find they are convents, and you are shown the cross upon the roof. In the same way, you find two kinds of aristocracy in the place – the proud old families, either rolling in their gay carriages through the narrow old streets (and past, among other houses, the weedy grey mansion of the Warden of Galway), or secluding themselves within their own gates, because they are too poverty-stricken to come abroad; and the implanted society of the college professors and their families, and other officials. Between these and the poor you find scarcely anybody – the poor, of whom not one in forty can read, and whose ignorance is of a worse kind than an absence of all notion of books. There are a few shops, languid and old-fashioned; and there must be industrial people of sufficient intelligence to carry on the business of life: but there is no substantial, abounding middle class, from whom the rise of a place of such capabilities might be confidently expected.

Of the religion of the region we will say little till we know more. Taking all the Irish colleges together, there was a decided increase of Catholic students after the Synod of Thurles.[11] This is a cheering fact. In the Galway College and Model Schools the proportion of Catholics and Protestants accords very fairly with that of society generally. The Vice-president of the College is a Catholic;[12] but he has lost caste among his own order, who are vehemently opposed to the institution; he has been absent for six months past – gone to Rome, to represent the mistakes that the Pope has been led into about these colleges. We shall see whether any good results from his voluntary mission.[13] Meantime, we have seen something. We yesterday turned, after leaving the college and schools, into the parish chapel, – a dim, large, sordid-looking building, with a shadow of an old woman on the steps, selling rosaries; and four blind, crippled, and decrepit persons within; two telling their beads on their knees, and two asking charity. All this we should have expected; and the dressed altar, and the confessionals. But there was more, which we could not have anticipated. Panelled in the wall, there was a barbarous image of Christ, for the most part hung with cobwebs, but with one leg and foot black and shining – no doubt with the kisses of worshippers; and worse – there was another panelled image, a bas-relief, of God the Father, as a hideous, bearded, mitred old man; and God the Son, as a lamb with a human face, equally hideous. We turned away, and, when in the open street again, felt as if we had passed, with one step, from the recesses of a pagan temple into the vestibule of our own home.

Connemara

September 3, 1852

THERE ARE few things in the world more delightful than a drive at sunset, in a bright autumn evening, among the mountains and lakes of Connemara. A friend of ours describes the air of his favourite place by saying it is like breathing champagne. The air here, on such an evening, is like breathing cream. It has the best qualities of the sea and land breeze at once. Then there are the grand bare mountains, the Bennobeola, or Twelve Pins, with caprices of sunlight playing about their solemn heads, and shining into their dark purple depths; and below are waters untraceable and incalculable. We are here at the ends of the earth, to all appearance; for the land is as a fringe, with the waters running in everywhere between its streaks. There are salt waters and fresh: bays, lakes, rivers; dashing torrents; mirror-like pools; a salmon-leap here; an inlet for shellfish there; and, receding behind, Ballinahinch Lough, with its little island, just big enough to hold the old castle, now a ruin, where tradition says that 'Dick Martin' used to imprison people who were guilty of cruelty to animals.[1] Then comes a basin of turf – a filled-up lake, as any one may see, with the last little pool in the middle fast turning into bog. Close at hand are broken banks, gaudy with heath and bog flowers in vast variety; and beyond spreads the bronzed moorland, with foreign-looking goats, black and white, browsing in a group; and sea-gulls dipping, as if they took it for the sea. Along the road are brown-faced girls and boys, all healthy-looking, and many handsome; and women finishing their reaping and binding for the day, – their madder-red petticoats and blue cloaks throwing a wonderful charm of colour into the scene. And next, we cannot but observe that cottages are whitewashed as we approach Clifden. This was noticable in the neighbourhood of the mansion lately called the Martins' Castle; and pleasant it was to see neat white cottages up on the hill-sides, each with its 'stooks' of oats before it. In proportion to the sweetness of such an evening drive is the strangeness of entering the public drawing-room at the inn, where there are ladies and clergymen, all intensely occupied with the condition of the people. There are Bibles open and shut. There is talk of a Protestant lecture this evening; of Protestant prayers in the morning, preparatory to an examination of the children in the principles of Protestantism. Ladies are busy with crochet-work, or with their accounts of crochet-work sold, or in teaching poor women crochet. The ladies relate that they have thus far sent out teachers to instruct the poor women in cabins in crochet-work, with the simple object of earning their bread: but that now, as these pupils have been almost all Catholics, they shall alter their plan, and give this instruction only in connection with sound Protestant principles. They tell how wonderfully the ministry of Mr. —— has been blessed, from his plan of speaking plainly; that he has plainly told the people, 'If you attend to what the priests tell you, you will go to perdition; if you learn of me, you will be saved;' and this plan, they say, has 'certainly been wonderfully blessed;' 'the people are coming over by hundreds, and the answers given by the children are really astonishing.' This is one statement, earnest and sincere, whatever else it may be.

Another is, that the people were terribly neglected by the priests, and that the novelty of being sought, caressed, and flattered, stimulates their ambition, while it excites their affections; that the native shrewdness is called forth, and that it is true that the answers of the children are wonderful – that, in fact, their aptitude at theological controversy is something truly frightful to witness; that their new religion will probably turn out a very transitory matter; that, in regard to this very crochet-work, on which their bread depends, the women do one or two pieces admirably, and then grow careless, preferring to do two collars that shall bring a shilling each, to doing one which shall bring in six; that their characteristic versatility and slovenliness will presently extend to their religion; and that, when the first excitements of praise, gain, notice, and gratified affections are over, it is probable that nearly all the converts will fall back under the old-established power of their priests. They will go back, as Gavan Duffy said, to the old Holy Well.[2]

There is a third account given to the inquirer. It begins like the last, with the declaration that the people were deserted in their need by the priests, who really refused the offices to the dying on which salvation is supposed to depend, when all hope of pay was gone. It is said that the people have fairly found out that the priest's attendance depends on his pay, and that he desires to keep them ignorant: that the grand benefit of the present movement is that it teaches the people something, and rouses the priests to better behaviour, and the people to require it: that the practice of the clergy on both sides teaching that their antagonists are carrying their hearers to hell tends to make the people reject both doctrines; and that in fact a total infidelity, such as now prevails largely among the educated, in this region of strife, will probably prevail ere long no less extensively among the poor and ignorant.

Here you have the various local opinions, as they have reached us, on a subject which is occupying more attention here at present than any other. From the temper in which it is discussed by the most zealous, it is far from being agreeable to the stranger. And it must not be forgotten that we have at present heard only the proselytising side. At Dublin we found in the National Schools that two or three hundred teachers, from all parts of Ireland, can live and learn together, Catholics and Protestants, at the very age of theological passion – from seventeen upwards – without a word of strife for years together, while earnest in their work as any of the apostles of the west. Here, in the west, we find it taken for granted, or as proved, that the two faiths are opposite as heaven and hell, and that their professors can make no terms whatever with each other. It is perhaps fair to remark that, in the Dublin case, the Church, strictly so called, – that is, the laity in conjuncion with the clergy, – are engaged in the work of education. Here, in the west, it appears to us that the enterprise is mainly engrossed by clergymen and ladies. If so, the difference in temper and spirit is easily accounted for. Of this we shall know more as we proceed.

Before we left Galway, we saw increasing reason to believe that the fearful apparent wretchedness of the people is no necessary indication of poverty. The five pigs wallowing near the bed's head is an instance. At the present value of pigs here – a value greatly enhanced by the potato-disease – these five must be worth many pounds. Elsewhere, we have seen a very fine cow, or perhaps two, belonging to a hovel so wretched that you would suppose the people had no prospect of another meal. The pawnbrokers' shops at Galway reveal a great deal. We find that the people have no idea of selling any of their possessions when they want money, – of traffic, in fact. They beg, they pawn, they resort to every possible device before they think of selling a pig, or anything else that they have; and the collections of rags – Irish rags – at the Galway pawnbrokers' are a singular sight. They would melt the heart of any stranger, unless he should learn that the owners of some of the tatters had pigs or cows or other stock at home, to the value of many pounds. The peasants do not like to be supposed to have any property; they do not like paying rent, on this account; and they prefer paying it, if they must, in some sort of barter. All this is a painful evidence of what sort of treatment they must have been subject to, some time or other; and it makes their present case so difficult to deal with, that one is not surprised to find their most spirited and humane and patient friends despairing of ever teaching them to live cleanly and respectably. But the case may, it seems to us, be fairly regarded as now a hopeful one. We may be somewhat misled by the charms of what we have seen of Connemara; but we are certainly in better spirits about 'the poor Irish' than we have ever before been since we entered the country. We should never have conceived beforehand that Connemara would be the place where we should feel cheered: but so it is.

In the first place, the healthful appearance of the people is something quite remarkable. Men, women, and children are plump, brown, clear-eyed, comfortable-looking in face and limb. We are told that about one-fifth of the population on and around the Martin and D'Arcy estates (now bearing those names no longer) died during the famine.[3] A good many – nobody seems to know how many – but certainly no great multitude – have since emigrated. Those who remain used to think they could live on nothing but potatoes. In one mansion that we have visited, the servants thought all was over when they were restricted in regard to potatoes, and supplied with Indian meal and other things. Last year, when the potatoes were good, and they were told they might return to them, they begged for a portion of meal also. Six years ago, a girl on the estate said, 'O ma'am, I hope the Lord will take me to himself before I have to eat turnips.' She was soon glad enough to get turnip-tops, poor thing! And yesterday, an intelligent lad, who was our guide to Clifden Castle, took pains repeatedly to explain to us what turnips were, with a zeal and pride which showed that the growth was new here, and highly esteemed. According to his testimony the ragged people here get meat sometimes, and a good deal of meal. Is not this good, as far as it goes?

The castle at Clifden, a part of the late D'Arcy property, is inhabited by a gentleman who is said in the neighbourhood to have done much good by 'teaching the people better ways.'[4] They were his turnips that were, with his other crops, shown us with so much pride. And very well they looked. The quantity of land that goes with the mansion is, we were told, 250 acres, which feeds 'an illigant stock,' and leaves a good deal for sale, and of course employs many people.[5] It was a ragged boy who said, in answer to our remark on the whitewashed cottages which shine all around on the hill-sides, that you may always know that the people are well-doing within when you see whitewash on the outside. We saw some fair plots of oats and turnips before these places; and girls feeding calves, and here and there a vast hydrangea flowering near the door. From the inlet below, fish come up all the year around. The men bring in large turbot, which sell for 1s. 4d. or 1s. 6d. each; and the boys wade at low tide for shellfish. The salmon-fisheries, belonging to the Martin estate, employ not less than fifty persons on the average of the year. The tin for the cases is imported from Cornwall, and the cases are made on the spot. Flags are imported, and used for floorings (better than mud!) and also for the grinding and polishing of the marbles of the district. These importations take place at the little wharf erected by the late Mr. D'Arcy, whose unfinished monument (begun before the famine, and left stunted) deserves to be completed by grateful admirers, and to stand for future generations to be proud of, on its commanding summit, visible far over sea and land.[6] What the present exports are it is not easy to make out, without closer inquiry than we have yet had time for; but it is easy to see what they might, and probably will, be. The agent of the Law Life Insurance Company's property (late the Martins'), is gradually reclaiming extents of bog, which will yield a great amount of produce.[7] The success thus far affords a sure promise of this. Some small openings have been made in the centre of a valley, which reveal not only the green marble of which the celebrated chimney-piece at the Martins' is made, but that there are mountains of it; and the same elsewhere with the black. The red sea-weed, mentioned before, abounds in all the bays. The sea, lakes, and rivers yield a vast wealth of produce: so might the surface of the ground: so does its interior. It is true the hill-sides are deformed by the staring gables of deserted dwellings; it is true that gardens of the castle are damp and weedy, and the noble fig-tree trailing from the wall; it is true that the D'Arcy monument is unfinished, and the town of his creation more dependent for subsistence, just now, on the influx of tourists, than a steady trade; it is true that the timid have a genuine side of the question as well as the hopeful. But it is also true that the two great estates have come into new hands, by which they may obtain that improvement which was before impossible; and that the people are fed and in health; and that their district is full of natural wealth; and that strangers know it; and it is true beyond controversy that the condition and temper of the peasantry are improved. At this agreeable conclusion we stop for to-day.

The People and the Clergy

September 5, 1852

THE MOST experienced travellers find one piece of experience ever fresh and striking – their inability to anticipate, through any amount of previous reading and inquiry, what they shall see and what they shall think in a new country. After wide travelling, extended over many years, we are now feeling this as freshly as in our first journey; and we need not be ashamed to own it, as the same acknowledgement is made by some persons who were likely to know a good deal more beforehand about the Irish than ourselves – the English settlers in Connemara. Some of them declare that, while in no one respect disappointed, they find the Irish people with whom they have to do, and their circumstances, different from what they expected. After a long course of reading and thought on Ireland and its main interests, there were two things, among others, about which we felt ourselves pretty well assured – that in the wild West we should find the peasantry poor, to the point of hunger; and that we should be in some sympathy with the Catholics – priests and people – under the injury of the establishment, over their heads, of the religion of the minority, and under the suffering of the contumely with which they are treated by the insolent Protestantism of the country. Do not be alarmed. Do not suppose that we are any nearer than formerly to sympathy with insolence – Protestant or Catholic – or to approbation of the establishment of the religion of the minority over the heads of the majority. We will presently explain what we mean.

Since we wrote last we have seen multitudes of the peasantry and town labourers; nearly all, in fact, that there are to see; for they are a people who do not stay much within-doors at this season (to which, indeed, there is little temptation), and we have not seen one unhealthy-looking person. Our attention has been particularly directed to this since we entered upon what are especially called the famine districts. We have passed through the districts of the English settlers; we have skirted the lonely Kylemore Lough, and crossed the moorlands at its head; we have travelled the length of the wild Killeries (where it was scarcely possible to believe ourselves within the bounds of our own empire), and traversed the dreary tract which lies between the Erive and Westport; we have left Connemara behind us, and penetrated some way into Mayo, and we have as yet seen only the same stout, brown, clear-eyed health that we have spoken of in former letters. We are now about to plunge into the very wildest part of the island – beyond Achill to the Mullet, which was depopulated by the famine. If we have a different story to tell after being there, you will soon know it. Meanwhile, I tell you what we have found. From every cluster of hovels by the roadside – from behind a dunghill on which a noble eagle is somehow secured – from over the fences – from all imaginable places – children, lads, lasses, sometimes women, rush forth, with bundles of stockings and socks, with crystals, or bits of marble or of coral, and run beside the car, with their light, easy, bog-trotting pace, for miles, begging, more or less earnestly, or, in some cases, apparently for the sport. They seem to have lost no breath, at whatever distance they may stop; and they do not look as if they had ever known what sickness was. Several are marked with small-pox; and cases of the loss of an eye are frequent in the towns; and we have observed an unusual proportion, we think, of club-feet. But in the faces and forms we see no signs of deficient nourishment, or of the diseases which are generated by bad air and light, damp, and over-crowding.

The testimony of good judges seems to be uniform as to the industry of the labouring classes under fair circumstances, – that is, when they can make money only by industry, and when their labour is fairly paid. If they can beg they will. If they fancy they can find a short cut to wealth, they will try it, eagerly enough; but, settled down under a just employer, out of the track of tourists and of conflicting religionists, they will work as well as anybody. They are also very provident. It is this part of the experience of the English settlers which has surprised them most. The labourer will live upon almost nothing, and lay by all he can save, till he has enough to take him to England, or to America. He does not like to be known to have anything; so he will not let the most honourable and benevolent gentleman take care of his money, or put him in the way of getting interest for it. The long accumulated suspicion of many generations cannot be dispersed at once; and the peasant would rather forego the interest on his money than let anybody know that he has it: so there is no knowing what he does with it, except when he buys a cow or other stock. The unwillingness of the people to traffic – to sell anything that has once been their own – has been already mentioned. They hold fast by any investment they have made, and evidently consider that they are robbed if they have to part with it. At the time of the famine some persons went on their own horses to obtain relief from the board; and one man got it who was found to have been, at the moment, the owner of fifteen cows. These were people who would not have stolen anything under any pressure; but they had a notion that what was once theirs was theirs always, by right. Wherever we have been, and from all sorts of authorities, we have been assured that there is a fine natural sense of justice among the Irish, under whatever strange perversions: and it certainly appears as if, among their most insufferable encroachments and their wildest eccentricities, they had some distorted conception of justice in their minds. In school, and in domestic service, it is found that they rather lack truthfulness; that in regard to honesty, they are about on a par with the English and that, as to other matters, their morality may be sustained at a high point, if their sense of justice be duly respected, and made the point of appeal. This being the case, the shameless and absurd begging, by those who are not in need, is indeed sadly *infra dig*. The other day we were walking on a half-private road, where two lads were raking and smoothing the approach to a pretty residence, by whose owner they were employed and paid. They asked us for money for mending the road, and were refused. A little further on, their spade, of unusual shape, was standing against the wall. We felt the weight of it. 'There, now,' said they, 'you must give us something for using our spade.' 'Give me a halfpenny,' cried a girl. 'What would you do with it if I gave you one?' 'I would buy a book with it.' 'Can you read, then?' 'No.' This one had the grace to run away. Probably their parents, or the habit of a life, may set these children and grown-up young people to run miles after a car; but our impression is, that they like the fun of it: and they certainly look as well fed and merry as the tourists about whom they swarm.

As for the other matter, it becomes a more painful one to hear of, and witness, and think and speak about, the further we go into the wilds. This is no reason for silence, but the contrary. There is no need to explain that we are wholly unconnected with the conflicting religious 'interests' in this country, and that our sole 'interest' is in seeing the people wise, good, and happy. We have hitherto taken for granted that the Catholic religion was a real faith to its professors, animating their hopes, and more or less securing their morals. We have steadily contended for their rights of conscience, and, as they have been conventionally (since they ceased to be legally) oppressed, we have found our sympathies unavoidably siding with them – including the priests with the laity. We are compelled to say that the further we go, and the more we learn, the more completely that sympathy dies away. We little thought ever to have written this; but this is what we have to write. We find, from universal testimony, – and by no means from that of the zealous 'Protestants' we have met, whose word we would not take in this particular matter, – that it is a settled thing in the popular mind that 'the priest is no good where there is no money.' Those who cannot say, of their own knowledge, that it is true that the priests refused the last offices 'essential to salvation' to those who could not pay, admit that everybody acts on the certainty that it is useless to send to the priest unless the fee is ready. Again, the fee must be ready, if by any conceivable means it can be scraped together, and for purposes incessantly recurring. A peasant would never think of using a chair, or other article of furniture, till it has been blessed by the priest, which blessing costs half-a-crown. There is scarcely an incident in life in which the priest, and consequently his fee, is not mixed up; and we are unable to learn what the priest does beyond such paid services as these. He is the policeman of his church; and it does not seem clear what he is besides. We have endeavoured to learn which alternative of two very sad ones we must suppose to be real, – that the priest believes in the necessity of blessing furniture, and of extreme unction, or that he does not. If he does, what are we to think of his money stipulations? If he does not, what kind of a priest is he? In either case, what is the plight of the people – of that multitude whom I now see kneeling, not only on the steps of the chapel opposite, but on the pavement outside the railings, filling up its whole breadth? The Catholic and the Protestant zealots seem to be trying, as for a wager, which can fastest drive the people into an ignorant contempt of all faiths whatever. The struggle for victory is as morally bad for the ignorant witnesses as it is painful to those who are out of the battle. They know very well that Protestant ladies are trying in vain to get their tracts laid about in hotels, where the Catholic or politic owners will not suffer them to lie for an hour. Some have much sadder cause to know what the conflict is. Yesterday, we were issuing from the Killery Pass – feeling more as if we were in Norway than anywhere else, with this true fiord before our eyes – when we perceived (what is never to be seen in Norway) a most wretched-looking hamlet, in a slight hollow, high up on the mountain-side. But for the hovering smoke, we should never have supposed those cabins to be dwellings. We asked what that wretched place was.[1] 'Oh,' replied our Catholic driver, 'the people there are all Jumpers' (Protestants).[2] We inquired further, not seeing the connection between religion and wretchedness. He said, in simple reply to our questions, that the people were Jumpers because they were too poor to help it. That the clergyman (whose pretty house he pointed out) got money from England, and offered work to everybody who would go to his church, and refused it to all who went to mass. The priest had no money, and so the people were obliged to be Jumpers; but they would not be so when they could help themselves. They loved the priest, and wished to go to mass; and when he called and threatened them with what would happen if they did not, they promised to go; but they were obliged to break their promise or starve. Such is the Catholic account of the matter, on the spot. Whether the Protestants would allow it to be correct or not, this report shows what is the popular feeling on the subject of the religious conflict.[3] Then we passed the new church, rising under the hands of people thus driven to the work, and thus 'converted.' Next, we met a band of boys, – clean, intelligent-looking, and well-mannered. They pulled their forelocks, and did *not* beg. We observed on this to the driver, who said that children don't beg on their way to school. All hail to the schools! happen what may outside. The schools are our ground of hope: we were going to say our *only* ground of hope, but we will not say that yet. Nor will we say what the difficulty is of forming an opinion or a wish on the management of ecclesiastical affairs in Ireland, till we see whether more light arises from further travel.

English Settlers in the 'Wilds of the West'

September 7, 1852

THESE WESTERN wilds are the region for English settlers. The further we proceed, the more of them we find; and we must say that, as far as our observation goes, they seem to be heartily welcome. In old days we used to believe (and we find that some residents think so still) that the peasantry, all over Ireland, had a strong distaste to working for wages; and that the one good thing in life, in their estimate, was to have a bit of ground on which they might be independent. We now find indications of a very different feeling wherever Englishmen have settled. Mr. A. is a very fine man, who employs sixty people or more, who would be starving but for him. Mr. B. is a gentleman who has a very fine wife, who has so many people come that they keep much company, and spend a good deal of money. Mr. C. has a very fine place and garden, and it employed plenty of people for a long while to raise it and get it into order. Mr. D. has a very fine mill; and it is a fine thing for the place – it employs so many people. Mr. E. has a very fine farm, and the people are sure of work and wages all the year round. And so on, from one county to another, in the west.

Mr. Robertson, the agent on the Martin estates, now the property of the Law Life Insurance Company, has lived in the country for many years and is much esteemed and trusted by his neighbours. It is he of whom we used to hear that he had no locks and bars on his doors, as there was nobody to be afraid of. He is the lessee of the Martin fisheries, and he employs fifty persons, on the average of the year, on the salmon-fishery near the Martins' Castle. His bog reclamations answer well, and employ much labour. There was some discontent about the 196,000 acres of that property being all transferred to one company; but there was nothing else to be done, as the company had claims exceeding the value of the whole estate. It is not yet divided, to be sold in portions. It has been so laid out that the saleable parts could not be disposed of without throwing away every chance of making anything of the more unproductive. Time will remedy this; and the management of the estate will proceed with a view to a future division and sale. Meanwhile, there is no necessity for a forcible clearance, nor even for the company to enable the people to emigrate. Some have earned the means, and are gone; and more employment is found for those who remain. The other great domain, the D'Arcy estate (about a fourth of the size of the Martins'), is divided, and has been sold in portions, of which two or three are bought by Englishmen. Our guide at Clifden told us that the castle and lands belonging to it are bought by a 'Mr. Eyre, the head banker of London.' Mr. Scully, his agent, now resident at the castle, is gratefully spoken of throughout the neighbourhood, for the pains he takes to improve the people's ways and promote their welfare.

On leaving Clifden for the north, we see, on the first water-power, and at the foot of a little wooded ravine, a large mill, with a dwelling-house beside it. A new settler lives here – with a Scotch name – and he is evidently the great support of the population round him. After ascending the swelling moorland above, we see, far off and away, the lovely coast, with its bays, promontories, valleys, and islands – as sweet a scene as ever basked in autumnal sunlight. The driver points out what he calls the light on yonder hill: this 'light' being a clearing where green fields and stubble shine amidst the surrounding moor. This is Mr. Twining's, of Clegan – too far off for us to visit; but a letter of Mr. Twining's has been published, in which he speaks hopefully of the capability of the district.[1] We turn down to the right, and see a church, a large expanse of drained bog and of advanced cultivation; and a large, eccentric-looking abode. This is Mr. Butler's, a settler of many years' standing.[2] Some way further on, amidst a scene of remarkable beauty, there is a handsome house, with its roof-tree just laid, and workmen busy about it. In the sloping fallow before the door, two men are harrowing. There is a pleasant and cheery look about the place. It is Captain Fletcher's. Then follow immediately half-a-dozen or so of brilliantly clean dwellings, some gardens, really verdant fields, a post-office, a shop, a school-house, up the hill on the left-hand side; and on the right, charmingly seated on its green bank, and with garden sweets about it, the grey stone house of James Ellis, whose name is his sufficient eulogy.[3] This Quaker family lives among an exclusively Catholic peasantry, on terms which it would do the conflicting zealots elsewhere good to witness, – if they could go to hold their tongues and learn, instead of preaching mischief where all is now peace. This Friend, who values his own faith as much as any M'Hale[4] or Dallas,[5] employs a large number of labourers, who are all Catholics; and they find they can all be religious in their own way, without any strife.[6]

Somewhat further on, towards Kylemore Lough, in a solemn seclusion, at the foot of dark mountains, stands the abode of Mr. Eastwood, another English gentleman, who is improving a large estate there.[7] After that, there are no more dwellings for many miles, except the little Kylemore Inn, and some cottages beyond. The moorland is too wild for settlement, and the misty mountains allow too little sunshine to encourage tillage. The singular and glorious Killery follows, with its admirable road, one of the benefits left behind by the lamented Alexander Nimmo.[8] Then comes the Jumper village I told you of, with its new church and pretty parsonage at the extremity of the fiord. Further on, when the Connemara mountains are left behind, and the moor looks as if nobody had ever crossed it before, we come upon the plain, domestic-looking Catholic chapel, and, almost within sight of it, the national school-house of Carrekenedy. That school-house is a pleasant token of English care to light upon in the wilds.

We are now approaching Lord Sligo's property.[9] The road continues most excellent to within five miles of Westport, where Lord Sligo's 'demesne' skirts the town. This young nobleman seems to be much beloved, Protestant as he is, by his Catholic neighbours. In the morning, one may see him handing round the plate in his own church in the park for contributions for Protestant schools, – the police of the neighbourhood being on the floor of the church, and the soldiers in the gallery; and in the evening you may hear from his Catholic neighbours how good he is, – how just and kind to his tenantry and labourers, how generous as a family man, how self-denying under the reduction of fortune caused by the adversity of the country. The reduction of rents and increase of burdens that he has had to bear for his share are no secret, and should be none. There is no disgrace in the fact; and there is honour in the way in which it has been met. From Westport, for some miles on the road to Newport and beyond it, the aspect of things is more dreary than anything that had before met our eyes in Ireland. We need not describe it. Those soaked, and perished, and foul moorlands, relapsed from an imperfect cultivation; those hamlets of unroofed houses, with not about one or two roofs in sight; little bridges, with their centre-stones tumbling out; graveyards overgrown with thistles, while cattle go in and out over the crumbling earthen fence; signs of extensive former habitation, amidst which we may see two or three human beings moving about like chance survivors of some plague, – these features of a lapsed country are understood at a glance; and here we found them. But presently we met a gentleman, riding a fine horse, and looking as if business carried him on so briskly. He touched his hat: we inquired who he was, and found he was another English settler – Captain Houston – who is gratefully spoken of for his excellent and extensive farming; and he is only one of seven or eight settlers who have large farms near Westport.

As soon as we enter the island of Achill we see a large house half built; and superintending the work is the owner, Mr. Pike, a magistrate of the island – better known as the late chairman of the committee of the Birkenhead improvements.[10] This gentleman is one of the party of friends to whom one-half of the island of Achill has lately been sold; the other half being purchased by the Protestant mission in the island.[11] The island – not much smaller than the Isle of Wight – has been for seventy-two years the property of the O'Donnells. By the recent sales in the Incumbered Estates Court of the lands of Sir Richard O'Donnell, this little dominion has come into the hands of English improvers. Mr. Pike employed fifty people last winter. At this season, when they can well take care of themselves by harvest-work, etc., he dismisses them, to be taken on again as soon as they 'feel the pinch,' as they say. He is going to plant very largely. His experience in the planting of the new park at Birkenhead, and the skill of a man whom he has brought over to direct this part of the business, guarantee his success; and in half a century there may be woods clothing the bases of the magnificent hills of Achill, sheltering its valleys, and imparting an air of civilization to the wildest shores that the most romantic traveller could wish to see. We have more to say about Achill hereafter. Our mention of it now is merely in connection with the subject of the settlement of Englishmen in Connaught.

The one thing that everybody – high and low, Protestant and Catholic – says about this is, that Ireland is perishing for want of capital; that there has been too much labour; that the land is very fine, and the sea most productive, – that there is, in short, every conceivable material of human welfare, if only the people had the means of obtaining and using them. We hear, in these western parts, no political murmuring whatever. O'Connell's name has never once been mentioned to us since we landed, except when we were passing his house in Merrion-square, Dublin, and looking at his door-plate:

nor has Repeal been spoken of, except when the subject was introduced by ourselves. The complaint is of want of capital; and the settlers are popular because they bring it.

All the while, Irish capitalists were keeping money invested in public securities to the amount of nearly forty millions, up to the time of the opening of the Incumbered Estates sales. Very few English and Scotch have been purchasers there, in comparison with the Irish. Out of the first five hundred and eighty-seven purchasers, only thirty were English and Scotch. The capitalists of Ireland are not the pauperized tenants and embarrassed landlords; and hence it is that the English settlers are so welcome as they are. But that there are capitalists enough in Ireland to redeem her from her poverty is proved by the equality of the rate of interest received by holders of stock in Ireland and England. (The 1 per cent. more charged on Irish mortgages is owing to the greater irregularity and risk in Ireland, and so is the limit of 6 instead of 5 per cent. in the usury laws.) As long as tens of thousands of Irish capitalists send forty millions of money to England, to receive only 3 $1/4$ per cent. for it, it is clear that the thing wanted in this undeveloped country is not capital, but inducement to employ it as strangers are beginning to do. It is with great pleasure that we find how very large a majority of the purchasers in the Incumbered Estates Court are Irish; and yet it is with great pleasure that we see our countrymen scattered over these western wilds, each a centre of industry and a source of plenty. The Irish purchasers furnish a practical answer to the complaint of want of native capital: and the English and Scotch open up a prospect of national union, political peace, and social regeneration in that part of the United Kingdom which the most sorely needs it.

Achill

September 14, 1852

TWENTY YEARS ago, there were no roads in the Island of Achill. The people were as truly savage as any South Sea Islanders. When we were crossing the mountain – walking along precipices at a great height above the sea, on our way to Keem – we were told by a gentleman who has known the place for a quarter of a century, that we could not have taken that walk twenty years since, for fear of the natives. The island, whose coast measures eighty miles, was then one vast tract of moorland, yielding nothing but grouse and fish. Its boats were the old curraghs, frames of wood covered with tarred canvas, as indeed too many of them are still. Of all the poor inhabitants of the west of Ireland, the very poorest were the people of Achill. They were then to others what the people of South Inniskea now are to them; the people who worship a stone, dressing it in woollen, and praying to it for wrecks![1]

The first road in Achill was made by the Government about twenty years ago; and there are now several: but so few in proportion to the extent of the island, that the traveller is annoyed at the loss of time and the fatigue incurred by the great circuits that have to be made to get from place to place; and there is no making any short cuts, as the whole surface is bog.[2] Before there was any road, there was a coast-guard; and a tower, conspicuous on a mountain, shows where an officer and a few soldiers were stationed in the days of the war, looking over the sea in opposite directions, and keeping watch against invasion. The coast-guard were less 'dull' then than now. Smart affairs with smugglers were of frequent occurrence in the days of high duties, when the deep coves of Achill offered great facilities for introducing a variety of articles from France, Holland, etc. At present there is no smuggling whatever, and the coast-guard find their station horribly dull.

Seventeen years ago the Protestant mission, of which so much good and evil has been said, was established in Achill. Mr. Nangle is now about to leave the station which he has held through this long course of years.[3] He is going to a rather humble living in Sligo county. Our impression is that when he has left his work, and the result of his sojourn can be estimated with impartiality, he will be found to have borne a great deal with courage and patience, and to have done a great deal of good. Whether there have been faults in the doing of his work we have no wish to inquire. Our business is with the results, and they have satisfied us that Mr. Nangle's residence has been a great blessing to Achill. In the early part of his residence there his life was in danger: he was thrice shot at, and once knocked down by a stone, and nearly killed. It is told with laughter now in the drawing-rooms at Achill, that in those days there was only one hat on the island (outside the mission, we suppose); that it was hung on a pole near the Sound, whence it was taken by any person going to the mainland, to be hung up again on his return. Now, there are schools, not only at the mission settlement, but scattered about the island, where boys and girls are taught in both the Irish and English languages. We saw the eager, intelligent, vigilant little boys of Keel – the Catholic Keel – at school, and we saw that there was no dawdling there. The school was dark and poor-looking, but the children were wide awake, and well-mannered, and clean, though, of course, barefoot and ragged. The houses of the settlement occupy two sides of a square; and apart stands, on a third side, the dwelling of Mr. Nangle. There is a little church, and a post-office, and a humble inn; the houses are all whitewashed, and all but one slated. On a hill behind Mr. Nangle's are some unroofed cottages; and close by, a more dreary sight still, the hamlet of Dugort on the cliff, with its filth and apparent misery. We inquired how it could have happened that, in full view of the settlement, this place could, at the end of seventeen years, be what it is? The answer was that the property of the place has till now been Sir Richard O'Donnell's, and that all the mission could do was to educate the children of the Catholic parents living there, hoping for the effects to appear in the next generation – as in Keel and other Catholic places. Now, the mission having bought half the island, the influence of its presence upon the population may be expected to be much greater.[4]

It has already been very great. The skirts of Slievemore, the highest mountain in Achill, which rises behind the settlement, are enlivened with tillage, from a considerable height down to the boggy plain. It is a cheering sight to see the farmhouse from afar off, with its range of handsome stacks, and the sloping fields, some with green crops (so green in contrast with the bog), and others with oats and rye falling under the sickle of the reapers. It is cheering to see the healthy faces of the women, who, a dozen in company, file out of the field by the roadside, each carrying a horse-load of fine oats to the stack. It is cheering to see the boys – ready for a job, but not begging, and looking like civilized beings. The women we meet in the road are knitting. The people in the fields are really working hard. There is life throughout the settlement. That much a stranger can see for himself, without entering into any disputes as to whether things might have been done better. There are contradictions among the residents as to whether the children are or are not improved in morals, in truthfulness, and honesty, by the education at the Mission Schools. One employer says they are, another says they are not; but the last admits that this may be from the influence of the parents, and the habits of many generations overwhelming that of the recent education.

For a long course of years there was a quietness which might almost be called peace in Achill. The mission pursued its work quietly; and the island was blessed with a quiet priest, who diligently minded his own business, of which he had quite enough, and let other people alone. Before the famine there were 6000 people in Achill; and there are now about 4000 – a population sufficient to occupy the clergy, without leaving time for quarrels.[5] But, since the Papal aggression business, the renowned 'John Tuam'[6] has become dissatisfied with the quiet priest, who is understood to have had the utmost difficulty in keeping his situation, and who is virtually superseded by a priest of the temper of 'John Tuam' himself. The last petty sessions show what a state the island is now in, and is likely to be in henceforth. A month ago Dr. M'Hale visited the island, and opened a Catholic chapel not far from the settlement.[7] He left behind him the two priests who are to be tried for assaults on the Scripture Readers belonging to the mission. Without prejudging a matter which stands over for trial,[8] we can state these particulars of the case which are declared and admitted on both sides. The admitted facts are, according to the report of petty sessions, that the two priests collected the people in the village of Keel (Catholic, and the largest place on the island); that they supported each other in instigating the attack by which a Scripture Reader was stoned, knocked down among the turf, and beaten; that one of these priests, foaming at the mouth with passion, called the readers 'damned devils,' and the Protestants 'jumper devils' and 'stirabout jumpers;' that he charged the parents with sending their children to school to lose their souls, to be 'justified by stirabout and redeemed by porridge;' that he bade the people 'scald, scald,[9] and persecute to death' the Protestants of Achill; that he pronounced his curse and the curse of God on any one who should sell them a pint of milk or a stone of potatoes; that he said he had but one life, and he 'would willingly give it to drive out these devils, and see Achill great, glorious, and free, as it was before they came.' An impartial person, arrived from a place where such quarrels are not heard of, happened to be present, and to see the convulsive rage of one of these priests; to see him run after a woman, who escaped by a stratagem from his blows; to hear him say that to think of the settlement made his hair stand on end; to see him endeavour to enter the girls' school, presided over by a modest young woman; and to hear him, when the door was (by order of her superiors) shut against him, shout out against her, in the hearing of the crowd, names too foul for repetition!

In following a road across the bog, towards the north-east of the island, we came upon piles of stones which scarcely left room for the car to pass. On inquiry we found that a nunnery is about to be built there – another broad hint of the religious warfare which may be expected now that Dr. M'Hale's attention is riveted upon Achill. It was by mere accident that we discovered that, of all the population of the Catholic village of Keel, there are no adults who dare go out after nightfall, for fear of the fairies. Dr. M'Hale's emissaries fear nothing so much as the emancipation of the people from fear; and nothing arouses their wrath so quickly as the sight of that book in which the people read, 'For ye have not received the spirit of fear, but of power, and of love, and of a sound mind.' A tract has been published (in not the best spirit) which contains the report of the trial of a Sligo priest, some time ago, for an assault, – the motto of which tract is, 'The servant of the Lord must not strive,' etc. That priest was punished by imprisonment, and his flock and their neighbours regard the sentence as a piece of Protestant persecution, and English oppression of Ireland. On the other hand, the Catholics complain that disreputable converts, and men who will do anything for a maintenance, are sent out by the Protestant zealots to distribute tracts and read the Scriptures; and that they go armed with leaden life-preservers, with which they lay about them, on women and others, on the slightest occasion, or none. Thus is the religion of peace preached in these parts.

Our visit to Keel was on our way to the most romantic and melancholy spot that even romantic and sombre Achill can show; the place which once was Keem – still spoken of in the Irish guide-books as living, and moving, and having a being on earth. Proceeding from Keel, we went through the village of Dooagh – sordid, like the rest – and began to mount by a good hill-road, till we found ourselves at a grand height above the sea, which, seen from hence, had the deep blue of the Mediterranean. The view of the coasts was superb, from the precipices of Achill, where a woman and seven children were blown into the sea, from the mountain path, one stormy night, to the faint, far distant headlands of Connemara. We saw the entrance of the Killeries, and Clew Bay with its islands (like a shoal of seals), and many islands and rocks besides, with here a glittering lighthouse, and there a few scattered boats – mere black specks on the shining sea. Another turn, and a most touching scene was before us. The road – a very good one, in excellent repair – wound down and down to a little cove where the waters, in the shadow of the rocks, were of emerald green, and the narrow beach of the purest sand. On a green slope behind, under the shelter of high mountains which clasped it round, stood the remains of Keem, – a village of roofless stone cottages, now becoming grass-grown, and silent as the death that laid it waste. The people lived chiefly by fishing; but they had some potato-grounds too. When weakened by the famine (which they had somehow struggled through), the cholera came upon them, and carried off a third of their number. The rest went away – some to America, others to wherever they could find food. So the eagles look down from their perch on the ridges above, and see only the places where people once were – smugglers of old, and fishermen since.[10] There is a little potato-patch on the margin of the sand; and one solitary roofed dwelling stands beside it. Some way up the hill-side there is a heap of stones among the heather, and a man or boy may now and then be seen searching and knocking among the stones. This is what is called the amethyst-mine, and some fine amethysts have, we are told, been found there.[11]

The best tillage is towards the south of the island, where oats grow to great perfection, as well as the other crops mentioned before. The freshwater lakes yield trout of a large size; and the sea is alive with fish. Fine lobsters may be had for 2*d.* each, and turbot for 1*s.* 6*d.* Geese are 10*d.* each; and they and fowls abound all along the road. A fine dairy of cows wends its periodical way to the settlement. There seems no reason why the island, now so fairly brought under the notice of the friends of the Irish, should not support, in comfort, its present number of inhabitants, and twice as many as it has ever had. It will be a dreadful scandal if its prospects are broken up in the name of religion.

The wilds of Erris

September 11, 1852

WE HAVE crossed the wilds of Erris – the wildest district of Ireland, and the scene of the worst horrors of the famine. Of the horrors of the famine we shall say nothing here.[1] It is more profitable to look at the present state of the district, to see if future famines cannot be avoided.

The district of Erris extends north of a line drawn from the two great mountains, Nephin and Croagh Patrick, or the Reek – a holy mountain, to which the people make pilgrimages. Few but sportsmen and poor-law officials know much about Erris. Snipe and trout abound among its blue lakes and ponds, and grouse among the heather, which extends as far as the eye can reach. Police barracks, brilliantly whitewashed, glitter here and there; and near them may be seen a shooting-box, a public-house, and a few cottages. But in one place, at least, and probably more, the high road passes through wilds where no dwelling is seen for miles. The traveller must amuse himself with the vegetation, the various heaths, the exquisite ferns, the marsh willows, the bog-cotton waving in the wind, and the bog myrtle; or with the cranes, fishing from a stone; or with the moor game, poking up their heads from the heather; or with the snipe, swinging on a bulrush; or he may feast his eyes on the outlines and shadowy hollows of the distant mountains; for of human beings he will see none for miles together. When he does, it will be a policeman buying apples of a brown-faced countrywoman; or a young lady, with a letter for the mail-car – a young lady dressed in a white muslin gown with flounces, with hair in ringlets, and no stockings or shoes; or it may be a Londoner, with gun and dog, seeking sport; or a merry peasant boy, with his donkey and load of turf. The sudden changes of scene are remarkable; for instance, the finding a fair going on at Bangor – a place of half-a-dozen houses. A company of constabulary are in the road, ready for the fray, which is sure to take place at nightfall, when the people have drunk enough to be quarrelsome.

Women in scarlet and yellow shawls are tripping hither over the bog, carrying their shoes and stockings. Maudlin men are swearing eternal friendship, and shaking hands with the landlady of the only public-house, which is so crowded that the poor woman does not know which way to turn herself. Amidst all the noise and signs of drink, and sights of folly, the stranger cannot but remark that he never saw such health in his life before. Throughout this part of the country the old maxim will recur to him, however he may abhor it – 'the fewer the better cheer.' Our business is to tell of things as they are, and not to sentimentalize about how they might be expected to be; so we state that where one cottage remains inhabited among half-a-dozen that are unroofed, there may romping be seen before the door, and loud mirth be heard from within. Many a laughing party may be seen round a huge pile of smoking potatoes, in a dirty cabin. The pig is cordially invited to the fire-side, and a great potful of potatoes is emptied before him. Boys and girls show splendid rows of teeth as the car approaches, and, with grins and antics, shout and race after it, putting to flight all the traveller's preconceptions about the melancholy left behind by the famine.

Another kind of change occurs when he draws near Belmullet. He suddenly observes that the rude fences are apparently built of marble – of glittering and veined blocks of the purest white. He has entered upon a new limestone district; and he knows he may now look for verdure instead of brown heather. He enters the pretty little valley of Glencastle, and finds its sides bristling with wood, and its slopes carpeted with green. On the upland is a fine harvest of oats, standing in shocks. As he advances, the scene opens finely, the great Blacksod Bay being on his left hand (sometimes hidden by sloping fields), and on his right the beautiful bay of Broadhaven, like a great lake shut in by yellow beaches and mountains of most varied outline. Presently the town of Belmullet comes in sight, with its public works, its wharfs, its drawbridge, and cutting, and all the apparatus of a commerce which does not exist. This town, where a coast-guard inspector resides, is remembered as the head-quarters of the famine,[2] where the clergyman and the inspector and their assistants were almost killed with toil and sorrow, – the toil of serving out the meal, night and day, and the sorrow of seeing the dead and dying heaped before their doors.

The dead and dying were brought from all places round: but chiefly from the Mullet – the remarkable peninsula which obtrudes itself into the sea beyond the town. It was this peninsula that we traversed Erris to see – that we might be sure that we had witnessed the worst of the wrecks left by the famine. Few have seen them, but those whose business lies among them. The waiter at the inn testified his pleasure at having guests to make welcome, so very few go there; and when we left he wished we could have stayed longer. In the centre of the town there is an air of some pretension, and some look of comfort; but the outskirts are miserable enough. All this is forgotten however on approaching Binghamstown, the most shocking wreck that we have seen, except perhaps one other village in another part of Mayo. We found more inhabitants remaining than we had expected, and they did not look personally miserable at all. But the lines of ruin where there was once a street, the weeds and filth about the deserted hearthstones, or (what seemed almost worse) the crops of potatoes and cabbages grown on the floors where dead neighbours lived so lately, made our very hearts sick. The Catholic chapel is not considered at all in a ruinous state in comparison with other places, yet its windows are half boarded up, its walls are mouldy, and half the cross on its roof is gone. The large white house near was the seat of a gentleman, of one of the ancient families of Ireland. After a long struggle with embarrassments, he was too weak to bear the stress of the famine year. He let his house for a workhouse, and was thankful to be made its master. In those ancestral rooms he ruled as master – not of his own house, but of the workhouse! He soon died. One of his sons is, we are told, there now as a pauper. His widow and daughters live in an ordinary labourer's cottage near. One such tale is enough, and we will tell no more.

The soil is considered excellent all along the Mullet; and, near Belmullet, the rising grounds were covered with harvests, bristling with 'stooks' of fine oats. Further on, there were enclosures everywhere, showing what the cultivation had been; but there was little growth of anything. Some of the fields were lapsing into mere waste; in others, cattle were grazing. On either hand the most lovely bays ran into the land – bays always alive with fish. Yet we saw only one net, in our drive of fourteen miles and back again. The usual declaration is, that the people cannot fish, for want of boats and nets, which they are too poor to obtain; but we saw a sight to-day which told a worse tale than even this. Seeing something like a deserted windmill without its sails, we inquired what it was, and found it was a curing-house, going to ruin. An Englishman had come here to establish a fishery.[3] He knew his business; but he did not know the people who were to do it. He was right about the fitness of the place for a profitable fishery; but he was wrong in supposing that his fishery must therefore be profitable. The people ruined his project, the success of which would have made their fortune, as well as his. They asked for advances of wages – one half-a-crown – another eighteenpence, and so on; and then they went off without doing their work. His money melted away, and he departed, leaving the curing-house to rot on the shore of the bay which swarms with fish.[4] And still we are met with the plea that the people are too poor to have boats and nets; and with complaints that capitalists do not come and settle, to develop the natural wealth of the district. Once more we ask why 20,000 Irish capitalists invest nearly £40,000,000 in the English funds, while such natural riches remain to be developed at home; and, again, we have to pause long for a reply.

We have said, in a former letter, that English settlers appear to be heartily welcome in the west of Ireland. Yet, since we wrote that, we have been where an English gentleman found, one morning lately, that the tails of all his horses were cut off. An English clergyman found, another morning, that one ear of his saddle horse had been cut off in the night. This last act is probably ascribable to theological hatred. As to the other, it appears that the good feeling towards settlers does not always extend to those who make the rearing of stock their object. They buy up or lease land for a sum or rent nearly nominal, when, as in the case of Lord Sligo's lands, the depreciation in value is excessive. They graze their cattle for almost nothing, employing next to no labour, and make vast profits. There is nothing really unfair in this. They give what the land, in a season of adversity, will bring, and they use it in a way most profitable to themselves. Nobody has a right to complain of this as dishonest. But we cannot wonder if the suffering neighbours are quick to feel the difference between this method of settling and that of men who come to till the ground and employ labour. Men see cattle growing fat among the enclosures where their neighbour's homes used to be. Their neighbours are gone – over the sea or into the grave – for want of work and food, and one herd of cattle succeeds another, to be sent away to England, and fill English pockets with wealth, while the Irish peasant remains as poor as ever. And within sight, perhaps, there is another English settler, who employs all the labour round him, and who says that if the land were made the most of, the country would be found to be much under-peopled. The peasantry cannot but draw comparisons between the two orders of settlers. That they should cut off horses' tails is horrible. That they should feel that the graziers could not be making such fortunes, if calamity had not, for the time, annihilated the value of land, is natural and unavoidable. That the extension of tillage will in time restore the value of depreciated lands, and rectify the balance between grazing and cultivation, is the issue to which we must look, and for which we would fain persuade the people to wait with patience. But what patience is needed! In answer to our inquiry, whether the condition and prospects of the people on or near the Mullet were improving, the constant answer was – 'In comparison with the famine years, yes, of course. In comparison with the years before the famine, no. We have no trade – no resources. Where is the improvement to come from?' And truly when we had passed through a few more of the depopulated villages on the Mullet, and seen the mere remnant of people that hang about that tract which might be so fertile, we could not but echo the question, 'Where is improvement to come from?' Yet, we cannot but feel that it will come, so rich are the means which Nature has laid there, ready to the hand of man.

Castlebar – Paupers – Emigrant Family

September 12, 1852

BALLINA IS the most prosperous-looking town we have seen for some time. The reason, no doubt, is, its good situation on the Moy, and its fine salmon-fishery, which is next in importance to that of the Bann. As we drew near to it, we observed signs of a brisker industry. We passed a really good farm, with a comfortable house upon it; with an orchard full of fruit, rows of well-grown trees pleasantly shading the road without damaging the fields. We passed a stock-master, who inquired of us about a stray bullock. He had purchased about three hundred head of cattle, at an average of £5 each, and was removing them home, in the north. We saw spinning in the cottages, and a cart full of ropes made of the bent, or coarse grass, which grows on the shores. In the town, the people were walking about as if they had business to do: and there was a look about shops and offices which showed that they really had it to do. Having read that Ballina was the third town in Mayo, while Castlebar was the first, we thoughtlessly expected to find Castlebar yet brisker than Ballina, – forgetting that Castlebar has no manufacture, and no facilities for trade, – forgetting, also, the singular letter of Lord Lucan,[1] as Chairman of the Board of Guardians, about the repayment of the advances made by England at the time of the famine. When we saw the state of the town, and found that we were close by the gate of Lord Lucan's park, all this flashed upon us; and we set about seeing and learning what we could of this noted place and its condition. Before we thus put ourselves on the watch, we were struck by the number of one-eyed people we met in the streets – three in a trice, on our entrance into the town. We had seen none such in the wilds; and we have learned to regard these remains of ophthalmia as a token of misery endured in the workhouse, or some other crowded receptacle of destitution. We have heard from an eminent surgeon,

105

entreated to advise what was to be done, when guardians were at their wits' end, what a spectacle it was to see 300 poor creatures down in ophthalmia, on the floor of a low-ceiled malt-house – one of the auxiliary houses of a union down in the south-west. In all workhouses, eye complaints seem to be the besetting ailment.[2] In some of the Irish, they are not found at all; in others, their virulence is dreadful. 'You must buy a green field,' said the gentleman; 'and you must get a large airy house.' They would do anything – anything in the world. 'Yes,' replied he; 'you had better, for (adapting his appeal to the supposed quality of his hearers) if a man dies it will cost you only 3s. 6d. to bury him; but if these people live blind (and blind people always do live), it will cost you £4. 15s. per annum each to maintain them as long as they live.' We are sorry to see by the last report of the Poor Law Commissioners that the disease was still on the increase at the date of that report, the number of cases during 1851 amounting to nearly 46,000. Of these above 40,000 were cured; but 263 persons lost both eyes, 656 lost one eye, and 754 sustained otherwise more or less injury to sight. Many more must have suffered out of the workhouses; and indeed, considering the healthy appearance of the people in other respects, the number of one-eyed persons in the towns is a striking circumstance to a stranger.

While within the town of Castlebar there is a general air of poverty and negligence, there are in the neighbourhood a good many unfinished roads – those melancholy roads which have occasioned so much controversy and ill-will. It is strange to mount painfully up a hill, by a newly-mended road, in order to go down again on the other side, overlooking all the while a grass-grown road winding round the base of the hill, and to hear that that shut-up way is one of the famine-roads, which has never been finished. It is as sad as strange to see how many of these have never been finished. Though nothing can excuse the language of the repudiating guardians, it is impossible to be on the spot without sympathizing in their mortification at the way in which the money from Government was spent, and their remonstrance against being made answerable for it.[3] There are persons – calm and benevolent observers – who say that an infinity of good might have been done where now the insult will never be forgotten of applying a labour test to men who dropped fainting or dying on the road. The men who were to earn their meal by working on the roads, could not work on the roads for want of that very meal. It was a pity to think of tests at all, under the peculiar circumstances of the time. The right way would have been, according to these authorities, to say to the landlords, 'No, you must not eject your tenants; that will ruin everybody. Government will secure you against your tenants, under certain conditions. Good farming must go on, or be begun where as yet unknown. Good teaching and due means shall be provided; your sustained rental will repay our advances; or, if not, we shall repay ourselves in kind. Thus will the value of the land be supported; our advances will be reproductive; the horrors of eviction will be avoided; and the rates will be kept moderate.' It is believed that such a scheme could not have cost more at the time than the plans actually adopted; and now . . . But there is no need to describe again the condition of the land and the people, with unfinished roads running in among them, as if to mock the deterioration of the land, and exasperate the temper of the people.[4] Lord Lucan has taken into his own hands large tracts of land round, we might almost say in, Castlebar, and is raising stock at a great rate.[5] The people do not like it: that is, they had rather see the land under tillage; but then, much of it is under tillage, for the use of the stock. We saw many acres of turnips, which looked well. Like other landlords in the distressed districts, he has, no doubt, suffered bitterly; and no one can wonder that he makes the most profitable use of his lands. It was an agreeable surprise to us to find that he was doing so; for certainly nothing can well look more forlorn and neglected than the estate on which he lives adjoining the town. Its untended woods and lumpy grass, and mouldy appearance altogether, would never suggest that its owner was a great stock-breeder. Meantime, the workhouse – the scene of his lordship's exploits as chairman and addresser of the Government – is in a more hopeful state than formerly, inasmuch as there are now only (if we remember right) 550 inmates instead of 3000.

There is much controversy there, as in many other places, about what should be done with these paupers. The ratepayers complain that hundreds of persons whom they feed and shelter are idling away their time, doing absolutely nothing, within the walls. They ask why the land which Lord Lucan once let for the purpose was not tilled by the labour of these people, and why Lord Lucan has taken it back into his own hands. The reply is, that the labour of the paupers cannot be made to support the institution, or they would not need to be there. In fact, the number of able-bodied men in the workhouses is now very small; and the women are usually not more than suffice, under the apathy of compulsory labour, to do what is wanted in the house. The greater number of the inmates are aged, sick, or children. If they are idle, that is really a fault of somebody's. If, by being idle is meant only that they do not support their workhouse by their own labour, that cannot be helped. The spirit of the controversy has however entered the house itself. A number of young women, who declare themselves healthy and active, have sent up their petition to the Board of Guardians to be aided to emigrate. Their letter bears, to our eyes, strong marks of having been composed for them; but, on examination by the Board, they have confirmed all that it declares about their indignation at their compulsory dependence and idleness, and their claim to be placed where they can work for their own support. So the guardians declare in their favour, and steps are to be taken to get them sent away.[6]

The population of Castlebar was, if we were correctly informed, 6000 before the famine; and it is now between 3000 and 4000. Many have gone to the grave; but more have removed to other countries. Large sums are arriving by post, to carry away many more.[7] We were yesterday travelling by the public car, when, at the distance of a few miles from Castlebar, on approaching a cluster of houses, we were startled – to say the truth, our blood ran cold – at the loud cry of a young girl who ran across the road, with a petticoat over her head, which did not conceal the tears on her convulsed face. A crowd of poor people came from – we know not where – most of them in tears, some weeping quietly, others with unbearable cries. A man, his wife, and three young children were going to America. They were well dressed, all shod, and the little girls bonneted. There was some delay – much delay – about where to put their great box; and the delay was truly painful. Of all the crowd, no one cast a momentary glance at anybody but the departing emigrants. The inquisitiveness, the vigilance, the begging, characteristic of those who surround cars, were all absent. All eyes were fixed on the neighbours who were going away for ever. The last embraces were terrible to see; but worse were the kissings and the claspings of the hands during the long minutes that remained after the woman and children had taken their seats. When we saw the wringing of hands and heard the wailings, we became aware, for the first time perhaps, of the full dignity of that civilization which induces control over the expression of the emotions. All the while that this lamentation was giving a headache to all who looked on, there could not but be a feeling that these people, thus giving vent to their instincts, were as children, and would command themselves better when they were wiser. Still, there it was, the pain and the passion: and the shrill united cry, when the car moved on, rings in our ears, and long will ring when we hear of emigration. They threw up their arms and wailed. When a distant turn in the road showed the hamlet again, we could just distinguish the people standing where we left them. As for the family, – we could not see the man, who was on the other side of the car. The woman's face was soon like other people's, and the children were eating oatcake very composedly.

There were no signs of affliction in them. It is denied here that the people are eager to go, as the newspapers assert. They go, we are told, because they must. Our own impression is that the greater number go without knowing much about it, because others have gone, or because they are sent for, or because they have a general idea that it is a fine thing for them. Many, of course, are more fully aware what they are about; but we do not see reason to suppose that political discontent has anything to do with it. We saw at Castlebar a print of O'Connell (as we had once before), but it was soiled and torn, and poked into a damp corner out of the way. If any ill-feeling towards the English has come under our notice at all (amidst much good-will towards British settlers), it is merely in connection with Protestant proselytism – and of that there is likely to be plenty more if the Protestant zealots go on doing as some of them are doing now.[8]

Irish Landlords and Irish Potatoes

September 17, 1852

WHEN WE chance to pick up an English newspaper, here in the west – a thing which does not happen often – we usually meet with some remark on the discrepancy between the various accounts of the state of the potato-crop. Nobody knows, by reading the newspapers, what to believe or expect. There are more reasons than one for this variation of accounts. No doubt the disease is worse in some parts of the island than in others; and no doubt many scores of acres of potatoes have turned out good for something, after they had been despaired of. But a new light on this matter has dawned upon us since we have come down from the wilds of Erris, and from the districts where English and Scotch settlers may be found, to a more thoroughly Irish part of the country, where there is less religious animosity, and more of the landlord and tenant strife. We are coming into the regions of landlord-hating; and very sad and terrible are the evidences we have met of the state of feeling existing towards the landlords, on the part of – not the peasantry, for of that we know nothing substantial as yet, but of the middle class. You may wonder what this has to do with the variety in the reports of the potato failure. Thus it is. The poor people keep up their *furor* for the potato, – though they will, because they must, eat Indian meal, more or less. But you may see, by the roadside, or sitting on walls, or crouching by the threshold, children munching raw potato[1] as English children munch apples. The mother pares and quarters a raw potato, and indulges the children with it. These people will not believe, till the last minute, that the potato will fail. They are saying now, after those above them, that we have had the seven years of famine, and that next year plenty will come again. The landlord is just as slow of belief. He watches the growth of the potato with the keenest anxiety; he holds his tongue about any reports of its failure that he may hear;

and, when the failure cannot be concealed, he makes the least of it, and is certain that it is owing to this or that accident, and that it is not likely to happen again. It is not that he is thinking about the prospects of the winter and spring, and of his rates. He is thinking not of his rates, but of his rents. There seems to be no doubt that the landlords are virtually in league with the peasantry, to keep up the dependence of the labouring classes on the potato, for the sake of their rents, which are very much higher under potato-cropping than they can be under any other management. While the most enlightened friends of the Irish people are hoping to see the peasantry weaned from this exclusive diet, and are heard to say that even the famine may be a benefit if it introduces cereal food as their main dependence, and while this view is earnestly held and enforced by the farming and shop-keeping class (who are rate-payers, but not rent-receivers), the landlords (in great numbers, we fear) are doing all in their power to foster the prejudices of the people, because only under the potato system can there be the excessive competition for land which affords them rents like those of times gone by. It is melancholy, we can assure you, to meditate on this as we travel along. For years past we have, like most other people, said 'Ah, it is very sad – this visitation; but it will bring in a better time than Ireland has ever known yet. It will compel a vast emigration, and thus clear the land for improved management; it will bring over British settlers to "plant" the lands which will be deserted. It will break up the wretched relations between landlord and tenant, and substitute a system of smaller holdings than the largest, and larger than the smallest, with a parliamentary title, freedom from incumbrance – freedom, in short, to begin afresh, with the advantage of modern knowledge and manageable numbers.' It was this view which consoled us during many a day's journey through an almost unpeopled country, and through districts where the unroofed cottages outnumbered the occupied. It was this which kept up our spirits under the stories we have heard in workhouses, and the sight of crowds of orphans within and without the walls. And now, after all this, we find the landlords trying to bring back the old state of things – the potato diet – the competition for land, the sub-letting, and all the consequent deterioration of land and people. We know of one instance in which a sensible and educated man, who is fond of farming, if he may do it well, was asked by a proprietor to undertake a certain farm, on the ground of his inclination to improve. He did so, and improved the estate by expensive preparations for very superior tillage. He fenced it thoroughly, and began to drain and plant. His landlord wanted him to grow potatoes largely, which he refused to do, for reasons which he assigned. At the end of two years, when he was about to drain a great deal more (encouraged by his success so far), he asked his landlord, at whose express request he had undertaken the enterprise, to give him the security of a lease, or other method of repayment for his improvements. The landlord refused all security whatever; and, of course, his tenant gave up the job. Whatever may be the landlord's difficulties, legal and conventional, in giving such security, he cannot but be an unpopular man while such refusals are sustained by improving tenants; and a new cause of discontent is becoming more serious every day.

It has been mentioned before that some British settlers have become graziers on a great scale, on lands which have sunk to an almost nominal value. If they are unpopular, much more so is the Irish landlord who follows the same course on lands which were under tillage only the other day. Some landlords are taking fright at the rise of wages consequent on the departure of multitudes of labourers for America. In despair of cultivating their land profitably, under a higher rate of wages, they are throwing their farms together for grazing purposes, spending their money in buying cattle instead of paying wages, and employing, perhaps, on half-a-dozen farms, a couple of herdsmen. They have, of course, a perfect right to do this, and many of them may have no other course open to them; but it does not tend to enhance their popularity. They would obtain love and honour by selling their land to men who have capital wherewith to cultivate, or by letting it to improving tenants, where now they are cursed by the remaining peasantry, who see fat cattle on lands where, as they think, half a hundred men ought to be earning a shilling or eighteen-pence a day. Tenants say that landlords' 'word and honour' are not to be depended on; and labourers say that they may go to the workhouse if those who should be their employers can only make vast profits by stock farming. And thus there is much landlord-hating, while the landlord may have many hardships to bear, on his part, from law and circumstance.

After all, we must come to the conclusion that the grand practical point is, that the land shall be made the most of. Wherever the fault of past failures may lie, this is the thing that must be provided for in the future. Now, in order to do this, one of three things must happen: – Either the landlord must make improvements (repaying himself, of course, for the expense); or the tenant must make them, for which purpose he must, of course, be securely compensated for his outlay; or the landlord's interest must be purchased by the tenant, in which case the tenant becomes the virtual proprietor. Here are three methods. There are no others. If the landlord agrees to none of them, he sets himself up against the great principle that the land must be made the most of. If he does so (and it is too certain that a great number of landlords decline all three propositions), it must inevitably follow that the land will pass out of his hands into those which can render it profitable. It must be so, by the immutable natural laws under which all social changes proceed. Meanwhile, he has no right to wonder at his personal unpopularity, nor to scoff at any nonsense, nor to defy any sense that is talked under the heading of 'tenant right.' At the cry of the labourer capital will come, and settle down upon the great man's land, paying him off, and dismissing him, as he has dismissed others, and taking on his neighbours, the labourers, in his stead.

It is believed here that this process would go on more rapidly but for the disappointment of some English purchasers, who find themselves deceived about the rental of the estates they have bought. It seems strange that men of business should buy land on the faith of any printed valuation, without close investigation. Sometimes three valuations are printed which differ so widely as to make English inquirers ask what the discrepancy can possibly mean. Sometimes it means that the rental is taken at what it was when potato-plots were let three times over; sometimes it means other things, which it would take too much space to explain now. The practical matter is that men who think of purchasing should test the particulars of the rental themselves, if possible, and on the spot. It would be a pity that the best hope for Ireland – that of the settlement of improving capitalists – should be impaired by the disappointment of a few too easy purchasers. There is, we rejoice to say, one other particular to be now considered by those who contemplate farming or fishing in Ireland – the rise of wages. There can be no doubt whatever that the people now on the land (throughout the west and south of Ireland) are insufficient for its thorough tillage; and new comers must no longer reckon on getting labourers, in any numbers, for 6*d*., and we hope not even for 1*s*., a day. And the people are still going away in crowds.

What a pity it is that the Quakers cannot purchase in the Incumbered Estates Court! Everybody is sorry; they would make so admirable a class of purchasers! But the arrangement about tithes precludes their buying those estates. Can nothing be done about this? It has been very striking to us that the one opinion in which we have found sensible, benevolent, well-informed, practical men most earnestly agreeing, throughout the length and breadth of the land, is this – that the best hope for Ireland lies in the settlement of British capitalists, who shall pay wages in cash, make no inquiry into any man's religion, do justly, lead a quiet life, and leave others in peace and quiet. This is the very description of the Quaker settlers already here.[2] Must the passage hither through the Incumbered Estates Court be closed against them alone?

Landlords, Priests, and Voters

September 21, 1852

THE WESTERN coast of Ireland is very beautiful – most striking in its wild magnificence. It is full of interest, too, from its noble capabilities, and from the spectacle of the modes in which the inhabitants keep themselves alive. But a few days are enough. A few days of observation of how the people live, merely by our going to see them, are sad enough to incline one to turn away, and never come again. From Galway we have travelled by the unusual route of the coast of Clare, where tourists being, as we supposed, out of the question, we hoped to discover how the people lived. From Galway to Ballyvaughan, and thence on to the borders of Mr. O'Brien's estates, was the most desolate region perhaps that we have traversed – almost as unpeopled as the wilds of Erris, without the curious charm of its having never been peopled. It was some relief to find that the unroofing of houses is not all recent. We were grieving over one mass of good-looking houses, when our driver told us that was the memorial of an old landlord quarrel; that a whole village population – thirty or forty families – all decamped in one night, about thirty years ago, in fear of their landlord. Some good-looking houses on heights and promontories were deserted at an older time; but the dozens and the scores of humble dwellings still have the soot hanging about their gables. The traveller on the admirable road which winds with the heights of the coast looks out anxiously to sea for fishing-boats; but there are none, – only the savage canoe or curragh is to be seen by good eyes, tossing near the shores. A woman here and there climbing barefoot over the rocks in search of bait, or of that seaweed which people eat to give a taste to their meal or potatoes; a boy and girl digging potatoes from out of the stones of limestone fields, are nearly all the people that are to be seen at any one place. There seem to be too few to beg. A very large number of men are gone to England for the harvest, or to America; the wives and children are in the workhouses; and the roofs then come off their abodes. While on the part of the coast of Clare which is almost entirely limestone, we hoped and believed that the excessive subdivision of the land was owing to its stony character. We saw vast heaps in the middle of little fields; and we hoped that the innumerable fences were merely a method of getting rid of the stones. But, since we have come down upon a more fertile district, where there [are] no stones in the middle of the fields, we find the enclosures no larger. Rank and ruinous hedges or turf-banks occupy a large surface, and divide fields which are mere plots, like the sluggard's garden. The first revival that we were sensible of was when the whitewashed dwellings of Mr. O'Brien's tenants began to glitter before our eyes. 'Corny O'Brien,' as his neighbours call him, is considered a kind landlord; and is not, we were assured, the less beloved in that capacity for being 'an apostate' – as people here call a Protestant whose parents were Catholic. The care and expense that Mr. O'Brien has lavished on making the Moher cliffs accessible, safe, and attractive to strangers, have made his name popular along the coast. The great number of men that we saw employed in getting in his crops of hay – such a quantity that we could not conceive how it was all to be eaten – was an explanation, quite satisfactory, of the affectionate tone in which we heard him spoken of. It is true, there is little more doing in his neighbourhood, in the way of permanent employment of industry, than elsewhere, – no regular scientific farming, no manufactures, no fisheries; but there is something done to attract strangers, and to keep the labouring class from starving. You will wonder at all this detail. It is not given for nothing, but as introductory to what we have to say of the affair of Six-mile Bridge.[1]

You are aware of the exasperation of the priests about Lord J. Russell's[2] letter to the Bishop of Durham,[3] and about the Ecclesiastical Titles Bill.[4] You understand how the theological strifes of Ireland, – and especially of the west, where the less-informed priests are sent, – have been aggravated by the proceedings and debates in Parliament about Catholic affairs. And you will see in a moment that the temper of the priesthood is not likely to be improved by the pressure of the poverty to which they are subjected by the emigration of a multitude of their supporters. The subsistence of the priests is derived mainly from the poorest and most ignorant class of their disciples; and there is no doubt of the severe poverty under which many of them are labouring. Their political action becomes vigorous in proportion to their adversity; and you do not need to be told what it was in the late elections.[5] The Six-mile Bridge affair is just one of the landlord and priest quarrels which are taking place all over Ireland; and when the trials come on, they will be worth observing, as an illustration of the politics of the whole island.

Colonel Vandeleur is the proprietor of the greater part of Kilrush.[6] Kilrush, with all its great cornstores, and its quay, and its good streets, and preparation for trade, is in a sadly stagnant condition. Colonel Vandeleur is not employing labour to such an extent as to satisfy his neighbours; but they are taught to believe that if he was in Parliament the trade of Kilrush would improve, and all would go well. There is much contradiction on the spot as to whether the eighteen voters escorted by the soldiers would, if voting by ballot, have voted for him or for 'Corny O'Brien.' The probability seems to be that they would, if not interfered with, have voted for Vandeleur, as a matter of course, 'because tenants are always understood to vote for or with their landlords.' One incident seems to show this. These men were 'cooped,' as we say in England, by 'the Liberals' – some of O'Brien's party, moved and led by priests;[7] and then they were released by some of the Vandeleur party; whereupon, seeing Colonel Vandeleur, they cried out, 'Oh, master, we knew you would not leave us prisoners. We knew you would come.' We think it may be understood that these eighteen voters voluntarily adhered to their landlord against the priests, though the Liberals (or some of them) insist that they were coerced by their landlord. Either way, what a farce is the suffrage in their case!

Forty-two soldiers were required to escort these eighteen voters. 'And not one too many,' we are told: 'you have no idea of the ferocity of an Irish mob, led by priests, who hope to get rid of the Ecclesiastical Titles Bill, or to carry any electioneering point whatever.' The party had entered a narrow lane, fenced by high walls on both sides. The magistrate, Mr. Delmege,[8] was at the time some way behind, talking with the two officers who were in command of the soldiers. A mob, among whom three priests were seen to be busy, gathered on the other side of the walls, and began to pelt the party with stones. More and more rushed to the spot, and the stoning became more dangerous; and at last the mob collected at both ends of the lane, to hem in their victims. It is said that not a man of the party would have escaped alive if the soldiers had not fired. The magistrate says he made no request that the soldiers might fire. The officers say they gave no orders to their men to fire. The soldiers say they had no orders to fire, and that it was as citizens that they did so, in the exercise of their citizen right of self-defence. How these statements will be supported when the trial comes on, we shall see. Meantime, eight men, if not nine, have been killed; and we understand that the three priests are to be brought to a legal account for the transaction, as well as the magistrate and the military. Colonel Vandeleur lost his election by two votes only; and people are wondering whether Mr. O'Brien will keep his seat or lose it.[9] Nobody has the least idea (as far as we can gather opinions) that the wishes of the electors can be judged of, in any degree whatever, by the state of the poll. This is the conclusion in which all acquiesce, whatever they may have to say of Vandeleur or O'Brien – of priest or landlord – of magistrate or military – of voter or escort.

From the first word we have heard about electioneering matters in Ireland, to the last, one thing has been plain to us, – that if we cannot get the ballot, we had better give up the absurd and cruel sham of popular election. There is no need to point out that the ballot is equally necessary, whether, in any particular case, the tenants vote according to their own opinion or against it. That their wishes are argued about is enough. That they are the subject of conflict is enough; that they are 'cooped,' and released, and escorted, is enough. That cry, 'Oh, master, we knew you would not leave us,' is worthy of negro slaves appealing to their owners, rather than of electors exercising a right of citizenship. It is mournful enough to compare the actual working with the ideal of most institutions; but when we hear how this Six-mile Bridge affair is talked of in Clare and Kerry, it seems to us that we have never – except, perhaps, in the slave States of America, or in the proclamations of Louis Napoleon – heard such a spouting of farcical tragedy. Let the advocates of the ballot keep their eye on the trials for this affair, which are to come on a few months hence.[10] If the evidence brought forward should be anything like what is communicated to us now, it will be the business of all honest Liberals to repeat it incessantly – to din it into all ears, till the Irish tenant-voter is either blessed with the ballot or released from the injurious burden of the suffrage. There can be no question which alternative should be insisted on in his behalf.

The Workhouses

September 22, 1852

BEFORE ENTERING an Irish workhouse, the English visitor is aware that the people to be seen within are altogether a different class or race from those whom he has been accustomed to see in workhouses at home. In England, the pauper population, domesticated in those abodes by legal charity, are, for the most part, a degraded order of people. The men and women have either begun life at a disadvantage, or have failed in life through some incapacity, physical or moral; or they are the children of such that we find in workhouses; and we expect therefore to see a deteriorated generation, – sickly or stupid, or in some way ill-conditioned. In Irish workhouses it is not this sort of people that are to be found. Indeed, the one thing heard about them in England is that they are ready to die rather than enter the workhouse. They are the victims of a sudden, sweeping calamity, which bore no relation to vice, folly, laziness, or improvidence. In the first season of famine, the inmates were a pretty fair specimen of the inhabitants at large; and they are now the strongest and best-conditioned of those original inmates. They are now the people who lived through the famine which carried off the weak and sickly. The visitor therefore enters the workhouse gates without that painful mingling of disgust and compassion in his mind which is one of the most disagreeable feelings in the world. From afar he sees the great building – solid and handsome, not at all dull or dreary-looking, but lightsome, with plenty of windows, and generally in an airy and cheerful situation. Again and again have we asked one another whether, if we had been hungry peasants, we should have been otherwise than eager to go to those refuges, where food was known to be certainly procurable. We can understand the dislike to the supposed confinement, to the diet, to the cleanliness, to the total change, in any ordinary times, but we should have thought that there had been nothing here that hunger would not have made almost inviting. We have inquired a good deal into this matter; and we have

119

visited several workhouses. With regard to the well-known fact that many thousands died immediately after admission, it is asserted by some persons that a large number had applied days or a week before they could be admitted; but it seems more widely true that admission was at the worst period regarded as a sentence of death; and that, at all times, there is a dread of food in the first place, and of the confinement and new ways afterwards, so that the request for admission was delayed till too late.

What we have seen now is nothing like what we should have seen in the famine years. The first workhouse we visited was that of Newtown-Limavady, in Londonderry. In the centre of the estates of the great Companies is little distress; and in the harvest season we saw only groups of children, healthy and playful, clean and bright; and women and girls spinning, washing, or cooking; and infirm old men and boys, much fewer than the house would hold; and benevolent agents going in very often, to see that they were comfortable. Matters are not so pleasant everywhere, of course; but still they are a vast improvement on what 'S.G.O.'[1] and others saw awhile ago.[2] For instance, we stopped at Ballyvaughan, on Galway Bay. In the course of our afternoon walk, we were struck by the situation of a farm-house on an eminence, with a green field before it, stretching down to the bay. Entering the field, we saw below us a number of women washing clothes, evidently from the workhouse. This house was an auxiliary to the auxiliary house of Ballyvaughan. The prevalence of ophthalmia in the house caused this field and dwelling to be hired for an infirmary. Forthwith we went to the larger house, an assemblage of whitewashed buildings, arranged as a workhouse, for the relief of the overcrowded establishment at Ennistymon.

This Ballyvaughan house was prepared to contain 900 inmates. On the day of our visit – at harvest-time – at the most prosperous season of the year, and in a neighbourhood where there is an admirable employer of labour, the number was no less than 667. It was inconceivable to us, when we heard this, what the people could have done when there were no houses nearer than Galway and Ennistymon. People who had to come above thirty miles for relief perished for want of it in great numbers – some at home, and some by the roadside. It will not be so again, for there is to be a proper workhouse built at Ballyvaughan, and the question of its precise situation is now under debate. A proprietor in the neighbourhood is draining his lands largely, and with funds borrowed from the Improvement Commissioners, one of whose stipulations is that the labourers' wages shall be paid in cash.

10. Head of the Killeries, Connemara.

11. Errive,
Mayo and
Galway.

12. Pass of Sailruc, Galway.

13. Protestant missionary settlement, Isle of Achill.

14. Ballina, Co. Mayo.

15. Derrynane Abbey, the seat of Daniel O'Connell.

16. Entrance to Dingle harbour.

17. Black Rock Castle.

18. Waterford.

If we remember rightly, as many as two hundred men are thus employed regularly, and for sufficient pay. How, then, were there 667 in the workhouse in the harvest month? How many were able-bodied men? One official said twenty, but on inquiry it turned out that they were not able-bodied at the moment. Ophthalmia, or other ailment or infirmity, had incapacitated these twenty. Of children there were 300. That was a fact only too easily understood: they were orphaned by the famine. There were many widows and 'deserted women;' the 'desertion' being that their husbands had gone to England for summer work, leaving their families to the union.[3] The expectation was that most of these men would come back, with more or less money. Some would probably go from Liverpool to America, leaving their families where they were till they could send funds to carry them out to the United States. We heard here again of a scandal which we have since encountered more than once. Some of the guardians have turned out young women, all alone, to shift for themselves. In each case the clergyman and the great man of the neighbourhood have rebuked this practice, and put a stop to it: and it is well; for there will be an end of the well-grounded boast of the virtue of the Irish peasant women, if scores of girls are thus set adrift by their so-called guardians. In one case the excuse given was, that there was no particular notice of their being young women, but that they were included among the able-bodied, and ordered off with that class. Twenty were thus got rid of at Ballyvaughan, and thirty at Kilrush, besides many at other places. We heard with much more satisfaction of the efforts made to enable young women to emigrate to Australia. From Kilrush no less than 450 (some of our informants said more) have been sent across the Atlantic, chiefly to Canada.

On the shores of Malbay, in Clare, stands a little sea-bathing place, called Milltown, all glittering with whitewash; and the most glittering part of it is a large house full of thorough lights, which is described in the guide-books of a few years ago as a fine hotel, where sixty beds are made up for visitors. Travellers had better not go there now in expectation of a bed, for this house is at present a workhouse – another auxiliary of Ennistymon – and spoken of with pride for its healthy situation. Yet, on the way to it we saw a painful sight – a cart or truck, loaded very heavily with paupers – chiefly children, with some women, – the whole being guarded by three of the constabulary, carrying arms. These were runaways, we were told, who were being brought from gaol to Milltown workhouse. We know nothing of the merits of the case, but the spectacle was not a pleasant one. If the dread of ophthalmia causes any to abscond, we do not wonder at it. The story goes, however, that many put themselves in the way of the disease, actually try to catch it, to avoid work and obtain the superior diet ordered for the patients.[4] The Poor Law Commissioners believe this. We saw the patients at Ennistymon – dozens, scores of them – lying on clean comfortable beds, in rooms coloured green, with green window-curtains, their skins wholesome-looking, and the hair of the young people bright and glossy, but all alike suffering under that painful-looking disease, the consequence of over-crowding, and other predisposing disadvantages.[5]

The aspect of the other parts of the Ennistymon house is anything but depressing. The greatest number receiving relief from its doors at the worst time was 20,000. The house being built to hold 500, of course the chief part of this relief was out-door, of which there is now none. An incident of the time which happened here explains something of the horror with which the people regarded the workhouse. In order to prevent the sale of the meal given in relief it was wetted by order of the guardians. Much of it became as hard as mortar; and most of it turned sour and caused illness in the already enfeebled people. Popular reports of wholesale poisonings have often arisen from a less cause. Now, however, it is found that the meal and other food agree well with the inmates, whose average of health is high, exclusive of the prevalent ophthalmia. The resident officers spoke cheerfully of the change since last year. During the fever season last year there were deaths daily to the amount of from twenty to twenty-five in that crowded house, whereas there are now only about three in a week. The breakfast is porridge with milk; and the dinner, soup made of meal, with various vegetables; and an allowance of bread, which suffices also for supper. The people are hoping now to be allowed potatoes twice a week; and great is the pleasure with which they look forward to this treat. There is no regular agricultural instructor of the boys at Ennistymon, but some are promising weavers, under the teaching of a zealous Yorkshireman. The women spin and knit, and the sewing of the household is done by the girls, who are also taught fine work, by which they may make money hereafter.[6]

Long before we entered any Irish workhouse Mr. Osborne's name was uttered to us with blessings, as we find it still wherever we go. There are no two opinions about him, and the blessedness of his visit – as far as we have heard. Gentle and simple, Catholic and Protestant, Tory and Liberal, bid us believe all that he has said – assure us that his information was precisely correct – declare that he is the best of all the good friends of Ireland – and glow while they tell us that what he said was (in the words of a poor Catholic) 'religion, and charity, and truth, all in one.' We had not doubted this before; but this universal testimony strengthened our desire to see the Kilrush house.[7] We there heard, from resident officials, terrible accounts of the famine and fever times,[8] when people were brought in, and died between the outer gate and the door of the house; when they were laid three in a bed[9] (those beds which are comfortable and decent for one, but which still are made to hold two), and the dead and the living were found lying side by side every morning. But enough has been said about that.[10] There have been auxiliary houses opened to a greater extent than are now needed. Three have been lately closed. The house was built to contain 1100, and the sheds 416 more. The number in the house when we were there was 2735, and the deaths during the last twelve months have been 362. There is a farm of twenty-five acres, where the boys are taught to labour. It was Sunday when we were there; and we neither saw the people at work, nor met the master and matron. Colonel Vandeleur and a party of friends were there. After they were gone we went round. We thought the place very clean, and the people, on the whole, healthy-looking; but our impressions of the management, in the hands of subordinate officers (who seemed to us too young), were not very favourable. There was much confusion and inaccuracy in their statements; and the terms they were on with the people, and the manners of the household, did not seem to us so good as we had expected from what we had seen elsewhere.[11] There can be no doubt, however, of the improvement which has been fairly instituted in the Kilrush house, and which is still advancing.[12]

Here and there we meet with some one who wishes to see work-houses made self-supporting. Such persons seldom see any alternative between paupers being absolutely idle and supporting the house by field-labour. There is no need to tell you what we say when our opinion is desired – how we ask whether any industrial enterprise ever answers under corporate management; whether there are not, in the case of pauper labourers, peculiar disadvantages; and whether the whole principle of a legal charity for the helpless is not abandoned when the proposition is made to maintain them by the labour of the able-bodied. Of this we may have occasion to say more, if the subject should again be pressed upon our notice as it has been. Meantime, we have only to say now that we cannot conceive what would have become of the people without the workhouses; and that we cannot conceive what is to become of the workhouses unless some productive industry – farming, fishing, or manufactures – is ere long established in the west of Ireland.

Killarney

September 23, 1852

NO ONE WHO has seen the Killarney lakes can wonder that visitors bring away no very precise accounts of the condition of the inhabitants of the district. We hear a good deal about the swarms of beggars, guides, boatmen, and curiosity-sellers, because they have hitherto been a part of the scenery; but the charms of the scenery are so transcendent, and the visits of travellers are so short, that there is no room for wonder or reproach if we hear less of the people of Kerry, who yet see the greatest number of English, than of the rest of the Irish nation. Henceforward, less and less will be heard of the beggars and other persecutors of the traveller; for the nuisance has been found so intolerable, that the magistrates and gentry of the neighbourhood have taken vigorous measures to put a stop to it. For our part we have found it nothing worth complaining of, – nothing to compare with the importunity of the car-pursuers of Connaught. A few women with pitchers of goats' milk and bottles of potheen on the hill-sides; a few vendors of curiosities and arbutus wares; a few boys pretending to assist, when you want nothing but to be let alone: these are all, under the prodigious temptations of the place and season.

We are told that a million of money now enters Ireland annually, in the shape of tourists; and of these nearly all, of course, come to Killarney. We will not say what the profits of the hotel-keepers are said on the spot to amount to this season; because we cannot be sure that such reports are correct, and we have no means of verifying them. It is enough to say that each innkeeper is supposed to be making several thousand pounds between May and October. We have observed with pain, throughout the greatest part of the country, that there seems little for the Irish to depend on but the influx of visitors; the most precarious and demoralizing of all resources for subsistence. At this place, where the very springtide of this kind of resource is met with, we have looked about us to see what is the aspect of life, and what seem to be the prospects of the inhabitants.

The neat, trim, finished appearance of the approaches to Killarney is so striking to the traveller as to be known to all the world. Lawns that are mown, plantations that are fenced, walls that are not dilapidated, avenues of old trees, paths that are not grass-grown, are a treat to the eye. There are also turnip-fields that show at once what they are, instead of putting on all sorts of gay disguises of weeds. Of course, hands are required to do all this work. We find that Lord Kenmare and Mr. Herbert – the two great proprietors on the margins of the Lakes – employ many labourers, and pay them somewhat higher wages than we have been accustomed to hear of in Ireland.[1] Then there are the boatmen and guides. These men make money only from June till the middle of October. During the rest of the year they do not know what to do with themselves. Some make scanty and fitful earnings by fishing; but they utter mournful complaints of the neglect and helplessness under which they suffer during the winter, after having been made profit of during the summer. The boatmen's story – calmly and gravely told – is, that the innkeepers, who assume the whole business of employing and paying them, allow them only 1*s*. 6*d*. for a day's work in the height of the season – short as that season is – and give them no aid or countenance whatever during the rest of the year. If this is the case, and the whole of it, the evil will soon be remedied. The opening of the railroad before next year will enormously increase the number of visitors to the Lakes;[2] and the boat monopoly will no doubt be broken up and the men enabled to improve their earnings.

Seeing a great number of Kerry cattle on the hills, we inquired into the destination of the produce, and we found, as we expected, that a large quantity of butter goes to Cork for exportation. Here, again, we find the producers, for the most part, in a state of undue subservience to the merchant. The Cork butter-merchants come their rounds once or twice a year; and the needy dairy farmers bind themselves by a six months' contract to the price named by the merchant. Those who have capital hold themselves independent, and profit accordingly. One farm that we have seen to-day consists of forty acres, twenty of which are under tillage, eighteen or so in grass, and the rest bog, or required for the yards and bit of garden. Some wheat is grown, and, with the oats, sold, while Indian meal is bought for family use. A few Swedes [*sic*] and some mangold-wurzel[3] are grown for the cattle. There are ten cows, which yield a firkin, or half a cwt. of butter (value two guineas and a half) per week, for about half the year, and less for the other half. Much sour milk is sold in the town; and there are other advantages – such as plenty of food for pigs – wood out of the bog, turf, etc. The Cork market for butter and for pigs is an advantage to all Kerry and a good part of Limerick; and might be much more so, with good management, and a better investment of the capital which is certainly now flowing freely into the country. Of the bog-oak carving everybody has heard; but comparatively few know how vast is the quantity of wood exhumed from the Kerry bogs, and how great is its value. It has undergone a preparation which fits it for almost interminable wear; and it is impervious to insects. The manufacture of churns, milk 'keelers,' bowls, and even bedsteads for local use, is such as might be a broad hint to sensible men to make something more of such a resource. Whilst the finest black specimens are reserved for carving and knick-knacks, the rest might furnish a good industrial resource in the hands of an enterprising man. If the little Kerry cows are found grazing on the Nottingham meadows, and speckling the hill-sides of Yorkshire, Kerry churns, of a singular and indestructible wood, would find no difficulty in getting there if their value was understood.

Amidst these resources, what is the aspect of Killarney, apart from the lakes and their adjuncts, to the stranger? There is the grand Catholic cathedral, begun by poor Pugin,[4] and little likely to have been finished by him, if he had been alive and well. It is a melancholy sight, that half-developed edifice, standing on the bright sward, unused and unusable. It has cost from £9000 to £13,000, (there is no making out anything nearer than this,) and it would require, some say £6000, some say £10,000, to finish it; and nobody sees where the money is to come from.[5] Another great building is the workhouse, now, by the addition of wings after the famine, become indeed a very large building. It is one of the best managed houses in Ireland, strangely and mournfully populous, considering the aspect and resources of the neighbourhood; but, on the whole, one of the most satisfactory establishments of its class. The population of Killarney was somewhat under 10,000 before the famine. It is now under 7000; yet, thinned by death and emigration, it still yields a large workhouse population in the season when the harvest is gathered in from the fields, and opulent strangers are swarming on the lakes.

There is another prodigious edifice, more imposing still. We could not credit the information when told that it was a lunatic asylum. Looking from it to the styes in the outskirts of the town, where human families are huddled like swine, we could not but feel that to build such an establishment in such a place was like giving a splendid waistcoat to a man without a shirt. That pile of building a lunatic asylum! But for what lunatics, and how many? For the pauper lunatics of the county of Kerry only. It seemed to us an Irish bull of a melancholy sort; and especially when we heard that there is another asylum at Limerick, and another at Clonmel, and another at Cork; but we found that the affair is English altogether, – a parliamentary enterprise, at which the Irish are as much surprised as anybody.[6] We went over the building, which is nearly ready for occupation, and will be open for the reception of patients in two or three weeks. As we looked along its vast corridors, and our footsteps echoed under its vaulted roofs, it seemed to us like some of those grand old monasteries on the Danube or the Guadalquivir, which it makes one feel youthful and romantic to read of; and it is built to accommodate, in this land of hunger and rags, two hundred pauper lunatics! There are at present eighty Kerry patients at Limerick, and eighteen elsewhere. Let us hope that these are enough – reduced as the population of Kerry now is. It is incredible that the place can be half-filled by the people for whom it is built; yet there is nothing said, as yet, about appropriating any portion of it to the use of paying patients. It seems as if this must follow – so great as would be the advantage to such patients of a position expressly adapted to their needs, – and so important as it is, in the present state of Ireland, that institutions of this kind should support themselves, when the opportunity is fairly offered.

It should be added that this enterprise was ordered and begun before the famine. The report to Parliament, which lies before us, on lunatic asylums in Ireland, which contains the beginning of its history, bears the date of 1845.[7] A committee of the Lords (of 1843) had before reported on the neglect of the lunatic poor of Ireland, for whom no other refuge was provided than the gaols and a few cells in houses of industry. It is perfectly right that what the Irish legislatures had neglected should be done by us; but there is surely some medium between shutting up persons with diseased brains in gaol-cells and building palaces, and providing a rich dietary for them, before the very eyes of their houseless and hungering neighbours. The state of brain produced by fasting is a real and true insanity. By this process the building might too easily be filled. Otherwise, we must hope, it never will. If a stranger was told that such a building as that was filled from Kerry alone, he must needs think that the Kerry people answered to poor Swift's account of the human race in general.[8]

The interior arrangements of this institution are, on the whole, excellent, – not, perhaps, quite up to the mark of recent improvement elsewhere, but opening to the poor innocent prisoner of the gaol-cell and inappropriate infirmary a prospect of space, air, activity, and comfort, which it is pleasant to think of.

The Rival Churches

September 26, 1852

A s we have come down to the south, from Mayo and Galway, we have heard less and less about the Protestant conversions which make such a noise there. We find the Catholics and Protestants on better terms: but the comfort of this observation is spoiled by the reflection which accompanies it – that the Protestant Church has no business here as an establishment. The peace and quiet, wherever they are found, are solely owing to the number of Protestants being too small to make any stir. Wherever we go – whether we find the clergy of the two Churches in a state of deadly mutual hatred, or letting one another alone – we are driven back upon our old conclusion, that wherever the Church of England is more or less a missionary church in Ireland, there we find society torn to pieces with quarrels; and that, where there is tranquillity, she is not discharging the function of a missionary church, and has no right to her establishment over the heads of the majority, whom she assumes to be converting.

We have passed a church, here and there, with a little parsonage standing near it; the church new and spruce-looking, if not handsome; the parsonage perhaps a good white house, with a porch, and hydrangeas and fuchsias adorning the front; perhaps a mere barn-like cottage, with mud hovels standing directly before the windows. In any case, the answer to our question – how many worshippers attend the church? – is nearly the same: – 'four or five families;' – 'a score or two of persons, according to the season.' In one place, where the parsonage is a good house, the boast of the Protestants is that a hundred people attend the church. If we inquire about the income of the clergyman, we hear of £300 a year in one place; £800 in another; in a third, that the income, which was £1500, is now reduced to £400. In this last case it was that our Catholic informant (a great admirer of the Clergyman) told us of a guest of his from England who went with him to his chapel, and found it full of people on their knees, as full as it could hold; and how he, in return, went to the

Protestant church – a handsome church – with his guest; and how the
guest was surprised to find only four or five persons there. It is as well
to hear both sides about such matters; and we therefore were glad to
obtain a Protestant account of the number of attendants at that same
church. The Protestant account is that there are between twenty and
thirty in the whole. What can the Catholics think of an income of
£400 (after the reduction) for the care of under thirty souls, – and at
a time when their priests are becoming desperate from poverty? It
was in that neighbourhood that a Protestant clergyman, with high
preferment, but nothing that could be called a flock, received an
affecting testimony of the attachment of his Catholic neighbours, who
respect his character, and love him for his charity and liberality. A
tenant of his wanted to abscond without paying rent, and chose
Sunday for the feat, thinking himself secure of not being observed or
pursued on that day. He got together on Saturday afternoon everything
that he could make away with, and on Sunday morning he was off.
Some suspicion had got abroad among the peasantry, and he was
followed and brought back, with all his gear, and delivered up to his
clerical landlord. This is all very well as a transaction between Catholic
and Protestant neighbours; but it fills us with shame – only hearers of
the anecdote as we are – that the good landlord should be receiving
a large income as a clerical sinecurist, while the clergy of his grateful
neighbours are sinking so low in poverty, from the depopulation of
their districts, as to be showing more and more of the ferocity of
hardship. There are some residents – some of both Churches – who
have said to us that it would be a good thing if the Government
would repeat the offer to pay the priests. If it was done prudently, and
with some regard to their feelings, it is believed that they would
gladly enough receive it now. There was a time when we, not having
seen so much of Ireland as we have now, were in favour of such a
provision for the Catholic priesthood. Our present impression
(subject to change, if the existing crisis should develop new features
in the case) is that it would be a pity to spoil the process of testing the
priests which is now going on. There is no doubt that the most
mercenary of them are undergoing detection, by means of the distress
of their flocks at home, and the opening of the eyes of such of them
as have gone abroad; while the same circumstances are sure to bring
out, in full brightness, the disinterestedness of such of them as are
worthy of their professions. The really devoted will be supported
while their flocks have anything to eat themselves. The rest – we fear
we must say the large majority – will become known by their felt

rapacity and hardness much better than by any denunciations and canvassings by Protestant rivals. Glad as we should be to see the few apostolic priests placed at ease, we should be sorry to see the process of the probation of the whole stopped short in the middle. As the fleece is dropping off in tatters, and the wolf's hide is showing itself from within, we would not, if we could, patch up the rents, and so help to beguile again the suspicious flock. However, there is no hurry about this – no present need to argue it – for nobody supposes that the present Government will endow any Church but its own.

Our attention was long ago directed upon one matter which it is painful to think and speak about, but which it would be wrong to pass over in inquiring into the state of the Churches. It is easily conceivable that a Protestant clergyman in Ireland must find himself very unhappy in the position in which he is most likely to find himself. He comes over, probably, in a good spirit – devoted to a difficult duty – hoping to bring converts into his Church – longing to rescue the poor and ignorant from superstition, and to redeem them for this life and the next. He presently finds all this out of the question. There is no converting ignorant Catholics but by setting up in fierce opposition to the priests – but by setting up counter threats and promises; and in such a game – without bribery by food and work – the priest is sure to have the best of it. The gentle and peace-loving clergyman cannot enter upon, or sustain, such a warfare as this. He sinks into silence, except at certain hours on Sundays; and then, how should he speak with any earnestness, when he has scarcely a hearer beyond his own household? He finds little or nothing to do in return for the income he enjoys. He is taunted with the enjoyment of that income, or he suspects that he is. He meets with no sympathy, intellectual or religious. He lives in an atmosphere of storm or stagnation. Either every man's hand is against him, or no one regards him. Under such influences, who can wonder if his nature faints? Some men may, in such a position, be humble enough to bear the humiliation. Some may be heroic enough to stand unmoved, – a mark for obloquy and insult. Some may sincerely believe that they earn their maintenance as churchmen by their good deeds as citizens outside their empty churches. But there is a large number besides, who are but common men, and cannot hold so anomalous a position; and of these, too many fall into bad habits. Some are merely selfish, surrounding themselves with pet animals, or sporting, or dozing away their lives in mere laziness; but others drink. There is no need to describe the process of decline, or the painful spectacle which here and there meets the eye of the traveller, on the road or by the way-side inn. The sin and the fate are the same wherever seen. When we have mentioned this to Protestants – in order to inquire – the answer has been, repeatedly, an admission of the occasional fact, with the addition, 'But the priests do so too.' Some do. There are instances in both Churches, no doubt; and the priests have the disadvantage of comparative ignorance and depressing poverty. It is not our business (nor anybody's either) to make out how much drunkenness there is in either Church, in comparison with the other; but to point to the sad significance of its existence in the case of clergymen without flocks. If the sin and shame have arisen out of their false position, let the blame visit them lightly. If we had our wish, we would decline to waste time and energy in blaming anybody, but abolish the false position altogether.

The operation of the National Schools will be found, in the course of another generation, to be a curious one.[1] Wherever we go we find them attended almost entirely by Catholics, not only because of the paucity of Protestant children, but on account of the enmity of the Protestant clergy. Yet it is impossible for the Catholic priesthood to benefit by them. No boy would be received in college, to prepare for the priesthood, who had been educated in a National school. We watched the other day the countenance of an intelligent little lad of ten years old, destined for the priesthood, whose father was talking to us in perfect good faith of the O'Donohue's seven-yearly appearance on the Killarney lakes, and the other legends of which that giant is the hero.[2] The boy, brought up in this kind of faith, cannot go to the National school, though his father would like to send him, because it would be fatal to his prospect of the priesthood; and his sisters are sent to the nunnery school. At another place, meantime, the two schools are the National and a Protestant one. The parents in the neighbourhood would like to send their children to the Protestant school, because the teaching there is of a high order; but the priests compel them rather to fall back upon the National school, which is not well managed – or thought not to be so. It is clear, on the whole, that the clergy of both Churches, as a body, hold themselves, and would fain hold their people, aloof from the National school. If another generation finds that both clergies have sunk into powerlessness under the unavoidable operation of these schools, who but the clergy will be answerable for their fate?

The religion and morals taught at nunnery schools are rather remarkable – as far as we can learn. We were visiting one lately, when we saw and heard some curious things. A page in a copy-book (not an exercise-book, but a copy-book) gave a summary of evidences and precepts in favour of 'the unblody (*sic*) sacrifice of the mass,' from the Old and New Testaments, which showed that the pupils were supposed to know nothing of either Testament. In the fruitful garden was a fierce dog, formidable, even when chained up, to all but the sisters. Sister A. explained that the dog was placed there to protect the vegetables from being stolen 'by the parents,' said she, 'of the children we are supporting.' She went on to say that though 'it would not do to say so to the people themselves,' there was no sin in such theft, because the people were hungering, and, added she, 'God himself put these things in their reach; so there is no sin in eating them on the spot, though there would be in carrying them away. But of course it would not do to tell them so.' We longed to ask why the nuns put a dog there to keep the people from touching what God put in their way; but the question might have been too puzzling. Again, the little burial-ground was quite filled with the half-dozen graves; and the simple question was asked, whether it was to be enlarged? The eager reply was, when it was wanted, and not before. 'Why anticipate death? Evil comes soon enough: why anticipate it?' This way of talking might have been adopted as suitable to world's people [*sic*], but it is not very like the ordinary notion of convent views of life and death. We should like to know how the children in the school are taught to regard death. In the case both of nuns and children, the more they are led to dread death, the greater is their dependence on the priest, whose offices alone can bear them safely through it: and this may account for the difference between the nuns' and what is commonly called the Christian view of death.

From Killarney to Valentia – Dingle Bay – Cahirciveen

September 28, 1852

THERE IS hardly a more interesting day's journey in all Ireland than that from Killarney to Valentia – the most westerly port in Europe, and the station from which the O'Connell estates may be overlooked. By the way, we omitted to mention, in speaking of the unfinished cathedral at Killarney, that, close by, a large monastery is rising from the ground. In answer to our observation that the money which is building the monastery (the 'monkery,' as the inhabitants call it) would have finished the noble cathedral, our Catholic companion observed that the monks cared most for their own affair, and had no thought of letting the money be spent on any other object. The boarded windows and truncated tower of that church were a melancholy spectacle, as we left Killarney, – so little hope as any one seems to have that poor Pugin's design will ever be wrought out. For several miles the road lies in that tract of country which appears to be enclosed between Macgillicuddy's Reeks (the loftiest mountains near Killarney) and the Dingle mountains – Dingle Bay being yet unseen. At length marks of improvement occur, which at once arrest the traveller's attention. The pastures are really and truly green: the hay is not half rushes; the oats are well stacked, and the stacks near the farmsteads are plentiful. There is a little barley, too. There are orchards, with apple-trees bending with fruit. The bye-roads are in tolerable order. Up the skirts of the hills, and over a considerable extent of the bog, there are inclosures which prove that a vigorous and sustained reclamation has taken place. The chief drawback is that the children are all but naked, and very impish-looking in their filth, with their hair on end, and no clothing whatever but a rag of blanket round their bodies. On inquiry, we find that this improved region is the property of Lady Headly, – the same lady who has built a church at Killarney, and pays a curate £200 a year. She is called a generous employer; and the reclamations are believed to answer extremely well. The people on her estate are said not to be poor at all, – nothing that can be called poor, – as they are paid such good wages – five shillings a week. We asked how it was that the children were so naked; and the answer was one which showed that clothes are not here thought, in the case of children, a necessary of life at all. After the treat of seeing this improved tract, came that of emerging from the valley, and winding round the base of the Drung mountain, above the glorious expanse of Dingle Bay, – here seven miles across at its narrowest part. We were swept along one of Nimmo's noble roads, with our feet overhanging the fence of two feet high, and a heathery precipice plunging down 200 feet into the blue sea below, – at such a depth that the gulls and curlews are like white specks floating in mid-air. Nimmo evidently carried the true artist spirit into his profession. It is impossible to travel along the western coasts of Ireland, as we have done, without feeling towards him as towards a great artist, watching the manifestations of his creative faculty, and sympathizing in the boldness, the skill, and the grace of his works as in the beauties of the sculpture, the painting, or the architecture of masters of another kind of art. Every traveller who knows this road vaunts its beauty; and some have said that the scenery is equal to any on the coast of Italy. It is not so; but it is wonderfully beautiful, in such weather as we have now. But in all that expanse, so many miles in breadth, and stretching away as far as the eye could follow, – even from that height there was not visible a vessel of any kind whatever. The blue waters lay absolutely unbroken, but by the dip of the sea-bird. No comment can strengthen the impression of such a fact.

The road retires at length into a valley, where the moorland becomes wilder with every mile. The turf, where cut, is of great thickness. There is no drainage, and scarcely any attempt at cultivation. A few patches of wet potato-ground, and weedy and scanty oats, occur; but, for long distances, there is nothing to disturb the crane at his pool, or the hawk, hovering aloft, with his eye on the young kids perhaps, which look very white, as they repose themselves on a peat-bank; or on his proper prey, the chicks and ducklings which appear here and there, as if it were spring. Where there are kids, there is probably prey for the hawk and eagle near. The interest now is, that we are entering upon O'Connell's property – approaching Cahirciveen. Among some green fields and plantations stands a neat abode: it is the dwelling of his agent. On the other hand, on the brink of the inlet below, stand the ruins of a country house, the roof and windows gone, and the chimney and gable grown over with ivy. This is the house in which O'Connell was born. At every step one becomes more able to sympathize with his love of his Kerry mountains, with their long stretches of heather, peopled with moorfowl and four-footed game, and separated by noble bays and lovely inlets, where an evening sail must be a charming contrast with the nights spent in the House of Commons. We grow milder about his personal extravagance – more genial about his sports with his beagles, and his open house – more sympathizing, till – we enter Cahirciveen. After that, all is over; and we return to our deliberate estimate of his character.

We need not describe that place. It has been done by the *Times'* Commissioner in such a way that no one who cares about the matter at all can have forgotten it.[1] There is little to add, after the lapse of six years. Mr. O'Connell's receipt of hundreds of thousands of pounds from the Irish people seems not to have done any good to his tenantry at Cahirciveen.[2] The greater part of that property he rented from Trinity College, Dublin, and sublet to tenants, from whom he received a large income. The existing embarrassments are known to be very great, notwithstanding the efforts which have been made by the Catholic bishops to clear them away. And there seems to be no feeling left about the man who was so idolized so very short a time ago! A few years since the traveller heard of him at every step – never by his own name, but by the title of 'the Liberator' – uttered as if it were a sacred name. Now, it is evidently understood that he never did anything, nor ever could have done anything, to justify the promises by which he gained the people's confidence, and the wealth which they yielded him out of their want. 'The people liked to be under him,' we are told, and he never wanted tenants. Perhaps he should not be severely blamed for the fatal over-peopling of his estates, which – a prevalent evil everywhere – was aggravated in this case by the affection, the pride, and the vanity which urged the competition to live under the Liberator. But the penalty remained when the feeling was gone. When the news of his death arrived, there was grief 'for three or four days,' and then he seemed to be forgotten. He is seldom or never heard of now: his portrait (a good painting, we are told) was lately sold for two shillings. His sons are thought not to inherit his ability, and they excite no interest. The remarks of the *Times'* Commissioner are found to have been very true, and to have done great good – first, by causing a grand cleaning and mending all through Cahirciveen, and afterwards by opening a good many eyes to the great man's personal extravagance and forfeiture of his promises; and the people should not be taxed with ingratitude if these are the things that are heard of now. Ever since we entered the country, our impression has been growing stronger, that the people are not now in the habit of attributing their woes to political injuries: and in this centre of O'Connell's influence, where, ten years ago, every man was his worshipper and his slave, it certainly appears now as if politics occupied no part of the people's thoughts. During the famine 2200 of the 3000 inhabitants of the island of Valentia received relief at the soup-house; and a very large number has since emigrated from the whole country round. They know very well that O'Connell's promises were of no value against such visitations as they have suffered under, and they are thinking of getting food, and not of a separation from England. Whatever the priests in Achill and elsewhere may say, the people do look to the English for their redemption in this world, knowing that from the English alone has any effectual aid been derived. The aspirations, desires, prayers (whatever you may call such earnest wishes), that we have met with, are two, from all sorts of people – that they could emigrate, and that the English would come and settle and pay good wages. Of Repeal we have not heard one word, nor of any political agitation whatever, but that which relates to the great ecclesiastical quarrel of the day.

The most implacable enemy of O'Connell could not but be touched and softened by a visit to Derrynane Abbey at this day.[3] There can hardly be a more affecting spectacle than that house, where so much of the politics of our century has been conceived and discussed. The situation of that old seat of the O'Connells is finer than description can give an idea of. Seen from above, in its green cove, embosomed in woods, guarded by mountains, whose grey rocks are gaudy with gorse and heather, and facing a sea sprinkled with islets, it looks like a paradisiacal retreat. The first glimpse of it from the Cahirciveen road (the road by which O'Connell passed from one mass of his large property to another) shows his yacht riding in a sound in front of his grounds; and that sea-view suggests the remembrance of the old days when the O'Connells of both families – Dan's uncles and father – were understood to do as others did who lived in situations so favourable for those commercial enterprises which are conducted by night. In the wild times of the last century, when defiance of law was rather a virtue than otherwise, and communication with France was an Irish privilege, gentlemen who had houses among the bays and sounds of the west coast were under every inducement to make their fortunes by smuggling. The wild ruin of the house where Daniel was born stands in an admirable situation for smuggling; and so does the Abbey; and the legend runs, that the facility was abundantly used. Smuggling is quite over now, as the coast-guard tell with a sigh. And Agitation is over too. So the one house stands a ruin, and the other is rotting away, in damp and neglect. It is inhabited; it is even filled with company at times; – it is to be so to-morrow. But not the less forlorn is its appearance, when seen from a nearer point than the mountain roads, choked by its own woods, which grow almost up to the windows, stained with damp, out of joint, unrepaired, unrenewed, – it is a truly melancholy spectacle. Melancholy to all eyes, it is most so to the minds of those who can go back a quarter of a century, and hear again the shouts which hailed the advent of the Liberator, and see again the reverent enthusiasm which watched him from afar when he rested at Derrynane from his toils, and went forth to hunt among his hills, or cruise about his bays. Now, there is his empty yacht in the sound, and his chair in the chapel covered with black cloth. All else that he enjoyed there, in his vast wealth of money, fame, and popular love, seems to be dropping away to destruction. When we were there, the bay, whose full waters must give life and music to the whole scene, was a forlorn stretch of impassable sand – neither land nor water. The tide was out. It was too like the destiny of him whom it neighboured so nearly. His glory swelled high; and grand at one time was its dash and roar: but the tide is out. And it can never return – could never have returned, if he had lived; for there is going on, we trust, a gradual upheaving of the land, giving some promise of that reclamation which he never would allow.

Valentia

September 29, 1852

THERE ARE various reasons why Valentia is interesting. Its Spanish name catches the ear, and reminds one of the Spanish legends which exist all down the coast from Galway hither; and of the wrecking of two vessels of the Armada in Malbay; and of the friendly intercourse which existed here between the continental pirates and the Irish, in the time of war, in consequence of the representations of a Catholic bishop that the value of all depredations was levied on the Catholics by the English. Valentia is interesting from its position – so favourable to smuggling,[1] invasion, and other sea tricks (from its enabling such tricksters to slip out on one side while their pursuers came in at the other), that Cromwell erected forts at both its north and south entrances.[2] It is interesting as overlooking O'Connell's town of Cahirciveen, yet being never visited by him. It is interesting as being a sort of little kingdom of the Knights of Kerry – the Fitzgeralds – who would not exchange that old title of Knight of Kerry[3] for any that the Queen could bestow. It is interesting as being one of the places named for a packet-station – its port being the western-most in Europe; and 'the next parish,' for which an official gentleman was one day inquiring, being in America. A packet-station however it is not to be. Passing over other causes of interest, we come to that which is, at the present moment, of the deepest significance in our eyes. Valentia affords the broadest hints of any place we have visited of the importance of the settlement of the English in Ireland. And the present moment is the time to point this out, as the island is in the Incumbered Estates Court, and is to be sold (the inhabitants believe) in October.

The island is five miles long, by two and a half broad. Of its noble scenery, this is not the place to speak. Before the famine, its population was 3000. Now, in spite of the highly favourable circumstances we shall speak of, the population is only 2500. The Knight of Kerry has a house there, in a fine situation, with some woods about it,[4] and a capital dairy of Kerry cows. A good deal of butter is made for exportation, and the cattle, a small and pretty breed, are an ornament to the hills and fields. The cabins of the rural population are wretched. The thatched roofs are rounded, and have no eaves; and the dwellings are usually set down one before another; so that a hamlet has the appearance, from a little distance, that we noticed in the fishing villages in Achill, of a cluster of Hottentot kraals. In our eyes they are less respectable than Indian wigwams, because of their darkness, and the infamous filth surrounding them, in the hollows in which they are sunk. The squaws in Wisconsin throw skins and fish-bones about; but their wigwams are pitched on dry sand or the wholesome grass of the prairie, and are shifted when the stench begins. Throughout the rural districts – elsewhere as well as here – we have been struck with the laziness of the people about beginning the day. Daylight is precious now, and we are abroad early. After a couple of hours' travelling, we see the housewife sitting down to milk her cow (by her own fireside, literally), and the donkey putting his head out of the cottage door, going forth for his morning meal: he has waited till the dew is off the grass. The children, still hot and heavy with sleep, in their rags (the same that they have slept in), are a disgusting sight to the traveller who is some miles on his road. This is not digression, though it looks like it.

You ask anybody at Valentia whether there is no fishing going on. The answer is that you may get any fish you please. 'But *does* anybody get it?' Two or three nets may be seen drying on the grass in the space of five miles, and a man on the road wanders about with two crabs to sell. You are told that there is a fishing station about a mile and a half from the port; a curing-house, where there were to have been boats and nets and employment for many people; but, from one thing or another happening, the place has never been opened. You find that one of the Fitzgeralds designed this fishery; that then it was sold – not yet in operation – to a gentleman who hoped great things from it; that he, in his turn, parted with it to the Irish Fishing Company, who talk about opening it; but that it is still only talk.[5] If you look in upon the people, you find them at dinner, perhaps; or rather, you find them eating; for regular meals seem not to be liked. They prefer salt fish to fresh, and sour milk to sweet: so you find them turning out their potatoes and salt fish (dried on the roof or the fence) upon the floor, – or a board, if they happen to have one, – there being no utensil whatever in the house but the big pot the potatoes are boiled in, and the bogwood keeler or beaker that the cow is milked into; for this discomfort is not from poverty, but occurs in a dwelling where the man possesses a cow, pigs, geese, and chickens, as readily as where he is worth nothing. The doctor cannot find any sort of utensil in which to administer medicine in cabins which shelter as many farm beasts as children, and where the owner farms twenty acres! This is enough. It will show you one aspect of life at Valentia, – which is much like that life at Cahirciveen with which everybody has been made familiar. Now for the other.

At the little port there is a preventive station, a station of constabulary, a little inn renowned for its 'fragrant cleanliness,' and a large establishment of slate-works, in connection with the splendid slate-quarries up in the hills. These slate-works have been in operation five-and-thirty years, sustained by English capital, and conducted by English skill and care.[6] The workpeople however are Irish, every man of them, except the overlooker, who is Welsh.[7] At present there are 120 men employed at the quarries and works; and the difference between this part of the population and the rest is so striking that the blind might be aware of it. It is not only that the men and boys, even those at the roughest work, can scarcely be called ragged at all; there is a look and tone of decent composure and independence about them which seems at once to set one down among a company of well-paid English artisans. These people are all well-paid: and, by good training, they get to work very well in time. Their ideas rise with their position: and then occurs the difficulty – what to do for wives; for men thus improved in their tastes do not exactly like to pick up wives out of the stench of the cabins.

We have mentioned the little inn. It has been kept for nineteen years past by an Englishwoman. When a window is broken, she has the glazier over to mend it. There are no holes in the floor, nor stains of damp on the walls. The carpets, carefully mended, are so bright that you see there is no dust in them. The forks and spoons shine. The white bed-curtains would show every speck: but there are no specks to show. There is not even a cobweb anywhere; and this is the first time we have missed cobwebs in an Irish inn. The kitchen is as clean as the bedrooms. We questioned the sensible old lady closely as to how she managed to get her house kept in this way, for she could not, if she were half her age, do all this work herself. She told us that she has taken the most likely girls into her service, shown them how she chose to have things done, seen that they were done properly; and, if she met with resistance or laziness, sent away the recusant in a trice. Such was her account. Elsewhere we were furnished with an appendix to it. She cannot keep her servants. However short a time the girls remain with her, they become superior to other girls in their domestic habits, so that they are sought by the men at the slate-works. The superiority is, in most cases, still very small; and there is often a sad falling back after a little while; yet their destiny, as wives to the most prosperous men on the island, shows what would be the effect of an improved training of the women. Again, the proprietor of the slate-works lives beside them. He and his lady are English; and they bring over English servants, for their own comfort. They also lose all their servants immediately. The best men at the works marry them, as surely as they see their neat ways and their English industry.[8]

And how was it with this marked population at the time of the famine? We have said that out of a population of 3000, no less than 2200 received relief. We have now to add that, out of the remaining 800, no less than 600 were maintained by the slate-works. There were actually only 200 who were not either slate-workers' families or paupers. Such a fact speaks for itself.

There has been a great emigration from Valentia, as from everywhere else; and some people on the mainland told us that they thought all the Irish would go away: and certainly it seems as if all connected with the land, or with precarious employments, earnestly desired to go. They talk to us eagerly about it, and look wistfully in our faces, as in some hope that we might possibly help them away – car-drivers, waiters at inns, and shop-people, as well as the peasantry. But we hear nothing of this from men who are earning regular and good wages. The evident sense of insecurity among people who see what is the present dependence upon tourists is, while very touching, a good symptom. There is no need to explain how earnest is the desire among such for more and more English to come and settle. Valentia is called the next parish to America. We do wish that the Americans who are sympathizing with Repealers, and acting and speaking on the supposition that all Irishmen are praying day and night for release from English oppression, could step into this 'next parish,' and thence on, as far as Derrynane Abbey, and hear for themselves how much the Irish are thinking about Repeal, and what is their actual feeling towards the English, on the one hand, and, on the other, towards their own landlords, who would have composed their 'Parliament in College Green' long ere this, if the Liberator had had his way.

Priests and Landlords – New Features of Irish Life

October 5, 1852

A S WEEK after week passes away, and we travel from moorland to village, and from coast to city, the old state of Ireland comes out to the eye more clearly from the new innovations upon it; and the innovations themselves become more distinct in their operation as the old state of things reveals itself to the vigilant observer. At first, there is a confusion, as in a dissolving view, when a new scene presents itself before another is gone; but, by degrees, the two separate themselves into a background and a foreground, and are equally clear at their respective distances. Day by day now we watch with more interest the movements of the two great background figures – the landlord and the priest – observing how they are themselves watching each other, and the innovations proceeding before their eyes. This jealous watchfulness is the only thing in which they agree – unless, indeed, it be in their both being very unhappy.

Very unhappy they both are. The landlord has for centuries been a sort of prince on his own territory. His lands spread along the sea and over the mountains, and include the rivers, like a royal dominion. A man who calls mountains and rivers his own cannot but feel himself a prince; and princely is the pride of the Irish landlord. His word has been law, and there has been no one to call him to account till within a quarter of a century. First, his old enemy, the priest, was emancipated; and now, one attack upon his prerogative after another has driven him to desperation. He believes himself the object of legislative persecution – he is called to account about the letting of his lands – he is rated for the support of his poor – his solvent tenants throw up their farms and leave the country – and he is not allowed to evict in his own way those who cannot pay rent. His rents fail him; and, when he cannot pay his debts, his estates are sold for the benefit of his creditors; and he finds himself stripped of lands, power, and position, with little (perhaps too little)

142

solace of sympathy and indulgent construction. Those who have sunk are, for the most part, quiet – as beseems their dignity. Those who are sinking, or in fear of sinking, are very far from being quiet. They scold and vituperate the priest, as if both were in rivalship about rising, instead of being both under the same doom of fall. There is nothing more painful than landlord language about the priests; unless it be the ever-strengthening suspicion in the observer's mind of the part borne by the priests in the destruction of the landlord.

The priest is as far from peace and prosperity as his great rival. He is in deep poverty, from the depopulation of the rural districts, which were his bank up to the time of the famine. He is reduced to follow the Protestant zealots from house to house, and set up his sacerdotal threats against the promises and praises of the emissaries who are seducing his flock from him. He is confronted with rustics who hold up their Bibles before his eyes; and little children are lifted up in his path to spit Scripture texts in his face. He is not allowed to manage his duty in his own way, and to take care of his own position. It is clearly understood, among both his friends and his enemies, that he is controlled 'from head quarters,' so that he is compelled to do what he knows to be rash, and forbidden to do what he believes to be best. About the Ribbon Societies, those may speak who have knowledge. We have none, beyond that which is possessed by all the world, – that the priests know all about them; and that the priesthood have unbounded power over them. Whether it is true, as many believe, that the matter is managed by an authority above that of the resident priesthood – whether the resident priests are willing or unwilling participants in a system of secret and bloody conspiracy, is a matter of which we know nothing. All that we can say is, that there can be no conspiracy against the property and life of the landlords that the priests are not fully informed of.[1] Which is the more unhappy class of the two, there is no need to estimate. The landlord struggles, protests, or silently mourns, and sinks. The priest goes about with an unpleasant countenance – significant, discontented, suspicious; in his unreserved moments confiding to a friendly ear his regrets that Irish affairs are misunderstood 'at head-quarters;' – that he is compelled to obey orders which he thinks ignorant and rash; – and that the Wiseman[2] movement was prematurely made: and while he thus unburdens his mind, he is sinking perhaps as fast as his rival.

As for the innovations – the modern features of Irish affairs – they are curiously connected with each other, and with an older time. Down in the O'Connell part of Kerry, where Repeal was the cry which once echoed from every mountain steep, we saw some noticeable things. There was a fair at Cahirciveen the morning that we left the neighbourhood. We set out very early; and for five hours we met the people going to the fair. For a distance of fifteen Irish miles we saw almost the whole population on the road, or crossing the bogs towards it. We were agreeably surprised by their appearance on the whole, though the produce they were carrying was small. Many of the women rode – each behind her husband (not on pillions) – on good horses; and men and women were well dressed. The number of mules was surprising; and there were not a few carts. The walkers usually carried shoes, and were substantially clothed; and we scarcely saw a beggar that whole morning. Out of some of the most wretched hovels came men in new blue cloth coats (of the country homespun), and women with silk handkerchiefs, and here and there an artificial flower in the cap; affording another evidence that the condition of the people is not to be judged of by that of their dwellings. The last party we saw going to the fair was a group of three women, coming down a mountain path near Derrynane Abbey. Among this population there is now no talk – and most people think little remembrance of any talk – about Repeal. And why? Some miles further on we came to the beautiful Dromore, the seat of Mr. Mahony, whose estates extend far away over the mountains towards Cahirciveen and Killarney. We were struck with the prosperous appearance of the whole neighbourhood; and when we reached the wretched Kenmare, we heard a good deal about Mr. Mahony and his property, which explained some things that we had seen. We were told that Mr. Mahony was 'fortunately circumstanced' about his property: that he is never disappointed in his rents; that everything grows well on his lands; that he had not more than ten or twelve paupers on all his property in the famine time; and that, moreover, though he is a Protestant, he is a very good man, and his neighbours love him. When we inquired how he came by all this good 'fortune,' we learned that he and his father before him (who was a clergyman) fixed very moderate rents, and were very strict about getting them; that they allowed no sub-letting on any pretence whatever; and that good tillage was encouraged in every way. The tenants are well off; pay their rent as a matter of course; and have proved themselves able to bear the stress of such misfortune as can scarcely visit them again. They do not want Repeal; being naturally content as they are. But Kenmare! – what a spectacle it is, even now, when the streets are not strewn with dead and dying, and young men are not employed as they were in famine time, to carry the dead to the parish coffin, which held six corpses.[3] The Kenmare Union is 'the most distressed union almost in Ireland,' we were told on the spot. It is many thousand pounds in debt; and there is 'a great wish to shut it up;' 'but,' said more than one informant, 'the commissioners will stand by the poor.' It was pleasant to hear that expression so near Derrynane Abbey; to find that the Imperial Government, in this one form in which it is known to the poor, is regarded as their refuge and their hope. Kenmare is, as everybody knows, chiefly the property of the Marquis of Lansdowne,[4] and so is that part of the neighbourhood which is the most terribly reduced. He is a good landlord as far as intention goes; has made roads here and there all through Kerry, and has enabled six hundred of his tenantry to emigrate.[5] But there must be fault somwhere to cause so strong a contrast between his tenantry and that of his neighbour, Mr. Mahony. Some told us that he had not been there for fourteen years; and others said that everything had begun to improve since his present agent superseded the former. The former agent (a Scotchman too) 'had an object,' as an advocate of the potato told us (one who, from his position, ought to know better), in encouraging the utmost possible growth of the potato: he thought, by that means, to reclaim mountain land. So he let small patches of it to all comers: and they sublet it, and – . But it is the old story, which we may spare ourselves the pain of telling again. There were sixteen or twenty families on one farm, the lessee of which would 'walk about with his hands in his pockets, while the poor paid his rent;' and on the smallest plots there were as many mouths as could be fed in the best seasons. Hence the horrors about Kenmare in the famine, when half the population of the town died; and in the country, many roofs were tumbled in upon dead families whom there was nobody to bury. Even now some persons who are not landlords hesitate to admit that this method of 'reclamation' was a bad one. They still encourage the culture of the potato, as 'the finest crop after all,' while seeing what good consequences are arising from the new agent's practice of attaching the plots to neighbouring farms, as fast as the holders emigrate. In Kenmare there seems to be no trade, and scarcely any productive industry; while there is more depression than in almost any other town we have visited: yet there, quite as evidently as in the more prosperous neighbourhood, the people do *not* want Repeal, but rather look to British institutions for 'standing by the poor.'

Since we were there, this subject has been more than once brought to our minds – and in ways not a little touching. We were standing, the other day, on a grassy terrace above the glorious river near Cork, when our host pointed out to us, very high up on the wooded hill which forms the opposite bank, a white house, just visible among the trees. We admired the beauty of the situation: but it was not that. That was the house where Robert [*sic*][6] courted poor Sarah Curran.[7] There he went, day after day, with his head full of those schemes of repeal of which she knew nothing. If it is touching to us to connect these young people and their fate with that gay scene of activity and beauty, what must it have been to them – to him before his violent death, and to her in her slow decline? Not many hours after, we were traversing Tipperary, looking out in vain for human beings, for miles together, – though the cattle and the tillage in the fields showed that there must be inhabitants. Except about the towns we saw nobody. Where there are people they always come out to look at the railway train; but we swept through an almost deserted country, for scarcely any appeared. As we entered the valley of the Suir, and drew near Clonmel, we were observing a long slope of tillage, ending in a mountain. The mountain was Slieve-na-mon, the place of meeting of the Executive Council of 1848. In the private parlour of the inn at Clonmel hung two prints and a medallion. The prints were portraits of Smith O'Brien[8] and Meagher.[9] The medallion was Mitchell [*sic*].[10] In the course of some conversation with a resident, we observed that these men, if they had succeeded at first, must presently have come to ruin, because they were Protestants, as Protestants cannot hold rule in a priestly movement. The answer was, that Ireland is very wretched; that Ireland has more wretchedness than she can bear; that a good Protestant is better than a bad Catholic to raise Ireland out of her wretchedness. This was the first time that we had met with anything approaching to a vindication of Repeal or an interest in it; and in this case the plea was simply 'wretchedness' – meaning poverty. As we passed down the rest of the valley of the Suir, we thought that its loveliness and fertility (for it is full of promise) must rise up before the eyes of the exiles, much as that river scene at Cork certainly did within the prison-walls of Robert Emmet, when he wrote his last letter to his beloved.[11] Among the recent phenomena of Irish life, we hope we may recognize this – that the lovers of their country have more knowledge and less presumption than those who have failed before them; and that they see that patriotism requires that they should not endanger the peace of their country, and the lives of their countrymen, without well knowing what are their own aims and resources.

Of other new features of Irish life I have no room to speak to-day.

Emigration and Education

October 7, 1852

AMONG THE new features of Irish life, none is more striking than the emigration that is going on almost the whole year round. We have met with scarcely anybody who does not lament over this departure of the people as an unmitigated misfortune, – it being the middle-aged and young who go, and the aged and children who are left behind. You do not need to be told that we do not share this regret, though we can easily understand and cordially respect it. The clearance of the land by a method which secures the maintenance of the inhabitants seems to us a very great good.[1] The aged are more safe and comfortable in workhouses than they could have been amidst the chances of Irish cabin life in these times: and as for the children, the orphans and the deserted, they are the hope of the country. From the workhouse schools, a large body of young people will be coming forth, very soon, with new ideas, good habits, and qualifications which will make of them a higher order of peasantry than Ireland has ever yet known.[2] But the landlord watches with pain the autumnal emigration which we see going forward from Cork, Waterford, and Wexford. It is the respectable farming class that goes out in autumn. Hundreds of farmers – each with his family party – are, this month, paying away for passage-money the cash they have received for their crops; and day by day they are sailing: here, a middle-aged father and mother, with a son of twenty, and four young daughters, paying £112 for their passage to Australia; there, a younger couple, with three or four infants, bound for the Mississippi valley. Tempted by no lease, – detained by no engagement with the landlord, such men as these sell off their crops and go, paying their rent if they can, and if they think proper; but too many, not thinking it proper – saying that the landlord has had much more than his due out of them, on the whole, and that they can't spare him the cash which will take their children to a better country. We do not speak of this as a general case; but it is too common a spectacle. Of course, the landlord does not like it.

The spring emigration is equally distasteful to the priest. It is in spring that the poorest people go; and they are the priest's peculiar people. But the priests are becoming, more and more, one of the heaviest of the burdens of the poor. They are raising their charges for their offices as their flocks diminish; and this does not add to the inducements to the remainder to stay. The marriage fee is established at 10s. The priest now demands £1. Even at this price, his gains are much diminished; for the custom of handing round the plate used to yield from tenfold to a hundredfold what is got by fees from the married. A priest used to get sometimes a hundred pounds from the plate, – in the days when the priests kept horses and cars. Young couples now have frequently to borrow money to pay the priest his fee. A Quaker lady was lately so struck by the extortion in the case of a couple who were thus borrowing, that she wrote to the priest. He made an evasive answer to her, and to the young people insisted on his £1. The lady called on his bishop. The bishop said that the fee was 10s., 5s. for himself, and 5s. for the officiating priest. The priest, however, would not give way, and he got his £1. Such men do not like to see the spring emigration of peasantry and impoverished farmers, escaping from their control to a country where they will find no fairies, will hear no denunciations from the altar, will incur no sacerdotal curse, and will either turn Protestant in a little while, or will write home how much more easy and comfortable an affair Catholicism is in America than in Ireland. The tradesmen do not like the emigration – regarding it either as a sign or a threat that productive industry has ceased or will cease, and dreading the time when there will be no exportation of produce, except the landlord's cattle, and no home demand for what tradesmen sell. The remaining farmers do not like it, because it raises wages. They will soon have to give their labourers three six-pences a day, instead of one; and they do not yet see that their labourers will then be worth three times as much as they are now. Some people are asking them now, 'Would not you go away if you could get only 6d. a day?' – 'When you pay a man 6d. a day, are you not bribing him to lie down on his back in the sun as soon as you are out of sight?' But the farmer does not yet see this. He talks of the lazy nature of the labourer, and pays him so little that he has not strength for severe toil, and needs to lie down in the sun as soon as his employer's back is turned. The very few who do like the emigration – through all its sadness – are the managers of the workhouses, and men who can look forward to the time – not very distant – when the aged who are left behind shall have gone decently to their graves, warmed and fed meanwhile – and the children shall have come forth as a new race of labourers – and the lands which are now thrown together for grazing shall have recovered their fertility, and be again fit for tillage – and a hundred burdened estates shall have been divided among a thousand unburdened proprietors – and new sources of industry and profit may be opened up, as in a new colony; when, in short, this fine country shall have renewed its youth, through the removal of its worst irritations and pains, and the infusion of fresh nourishment.[3]

And here is another innovation. It is pleasant to be informed and reminded, in almost every house we enter, that the purchasers in the Incumbered Estates Court are almost all Irish. Everybody seems to know exactly how many English and Scotch there are, and to be pleased that there are so few, even while hoping that more English capitalists will come, and telling what good has been done by those who are already here. They believe, and hope, in fact, that the Irish purchasers (who cannot be, to any considerable extent, of the old landlord class) will bring an English mind, so to speak, to their new enterprise, – conducting it, not according to feudal prejudices, but to sound economical principles. For our part we cordially sympathize in this gratification, and say that we hope the new purchasers are some of the 20,000 Irish capitalists who have been investing nearly £40,000,000 in our $3^1/4$ per cents. Our informants and we join in being glad that Mr. Ashworth[4] has (if the newspapers say true) bought the salmon-fishery at Galway, and that the people about Carrickfergus are associating to work the great salt-mine there; and that the 'slob' lands reclaimed from Wexford harbour are rewarding the enterprise of their reclamation; glad, in short, of every exposure to the sunshine of daylight and of hope of the great natural wealth of Ireland.

Though the difficulty about the tenure of land is an old one, the tenant-right agitation, as a way to a remedy, is a new feature. It is enough to say now that the agitation cannot die away fruitlessly; that it surely cannot end in the confiscation, avowed or virtual, of the landlord's property; and that no one will be more benefited than himself if, through this movement, he finds himself released from legal restrictions which, though called privileges, are as baneful to himself as to his tenants, by impeding the improvement of the soil. It is a movement as yet too indeterminate to be accepted as more than the expression of a great need. Viewed in that way, it is – however unacceptable to the landlord and (as a sign of progress) to the priest – full of interest and of promise. We have seen, for the last few days, what the country looks like in a part where the landlords cannot be so feudal as elsewhere – in a part where free-trade has poured in food, and kept the population alive, and where commerce is too firmly established not to have made its benefits felt through all the distresses of the last seven years. In travelling from Waterford to Wexford, the traveller's spirits rise, however sad are some of the roadside spectacles that meet his eye. Over and beyond them he sees the ranges of farmyard stacks, the flourishing dairies, the shipments of produce from the long quays – the signs of mingled agricultural and commercial industry which denote and promise a social welfare that the landlord and priest in league could not overthrow. While this evidence is before the world's eyes, in any part of the island, the landlord cannot uphold, or return to, his feudality; and the great question of tenure is on the way to a settlement, whether by tenant-right associations or by other means.

It is grievous to see one new feature of Irish life disappearing before the echo of the world's admiration has died away. At Cork there stands a chapel, conspicuous in its situation, and meant to be so for its beauty – Father Mathew's[5] chapel – built as a monument of Temperance reform.[6] Its pillars are truncated, its arches stop short in their spring, its windows are boarded up; it stands a sad type of the Temperance Reform itself – a failed enterprise.[7] The relapse of the people into intemperance is indubitable and very rapid. Everywhere we are told that the temperance, begun in superstition and political enthusiasm, was maintained only by the destitution of the famine time; and everywhere we see but too plainly that the restraint was artificial and temporary. 'Now that they are better off,' we are told, 'they are taking to drink again;' and so it seems, by what we see in the towns and by the roadside. We never believed that such a process as that of self-government could come, complete, out of such an act as a vow, or such an impulse as social sympathy. And it seems that the further safeguard of experience of the healthfulness and comfort of sobriety – an experience so lauded before the famine – is not enough. Once more, and as usual, we must look for hope and help to that power which will never disappoint us – to education. Of all the new features of Irish life, this is the most important. It is too important a subject to be introduced at the end of a letter, if it could come in amiss anywhere. But its name tells everything: explains its nature, and asserts its value. It is a *leading out of*. Education will lead the Irish people out of their woes; and it will lead them up to the threshold of a better destiny.

The People and the two Churches

October 10, 1852

IN CASTING back a last look upon Ireland as her shores recede, the traveller naturally thinks of that remarkable island as she once was, in contrast with what she has been since, and with what she is now. There was a time when Ireland gave light – intellectual and moral – to the nations of northern Europe; when she was the centre of the Christian faith, whence apostles went forth to teach it, and where disciples of many nations came to learn it. She had a reputation for scholarship and sanctity before England and Scotland were distinctly heard of. Few nations then stood so high as the Irish; and few have ever sunk so low as she has since sunk. Her modern state has been a mournful burlesque upon the ancient one. Instead of the ancient apostles, we have seen her modern priests; instead of the old chiefs, her modern landlords; instead of the ancient orders and guilds, her recent secret societies of rebels against the Government, conspirators against the landlord, and slaves of the priests. Instead of the ancient feasts, feuds, and forays, we have seen modern famine, and an escape from home far more awful to witness than any exodus from a land of bondage.

Though this last movement proceeds, it is clearly true that Ireland has entered upon a new period – upon a new life which is full of hope. We ought not to be surprised if the people are slow to see this – if the emigration should go on as at present, for some years to come. The people cannot be expected to forget what they have seen in ghastly years just over. While waste lands lie round about them, and roofless cottages stare them in the face, wherever they turn, and the churches quarrel, and priest says that all is going to ruin, the peasant and the farmer cannot be expected to see that there is 'a good time coming;' and they may have reached a foreign shore, and have looked homewards thence for a long while before they perceive that the good time has actually set in. But that it is so, is clear to the less-interested observer.

There is nothing the matter with the original structure of the country. The land is good enough: the sea is fruitful enough; and there is plenty of it, all round the indented coasts; and, under the soil, there is almost as much wealth as its surface could yield. There is nothing the matter with the country. And there is nothing the matter with the men in it, but what is superinduced. There is no need to speak of the fine qualities of the Irish character; for they are acknowledged all over the world. As for the rest, employ them at task-work – at secure work – and they soon show themselves as industrious as anybody. Pay them regular wages, and pay them in cash, and they immediately show themselves as provident as anybody. Not as skilful in depositing and investing – that is another matter, but as capable of looking forward, and of providing for the future. Let them alone about their religion, and obviate competition for land, and they are as peaceable as anybody. We cannot yet point out the circumstances in which they are found as truthful as other people; for, in sad fact, we have met with few signs of that virtue, except among some educated and in rare cases besides; but we can see how the vice has grown up, how it has been encouraged, and, we trust, how it not only may be, but will be, outgrown. Lying is the vice of slaves; and the extraordinary and extreme inaccuracy of statement that everybody meets with all over Ireland is the natural product of the fear and hatred in which the people have lived for centuries, with such a priesthood as theirs for their moral guides. One of us observed to the other, a few days since, in talking over the testimony of a poor man on an important matter, that it was the first time since we entered the country that information given by anybody had been confirmed by the independent testimony of anybody else. To us, one of the most mournful spectacles in the country is that of the courts of justice, – those platforms on which lying on the largest scale, and perjury the most audacious, are ostentatiously exhibited to the world. To see for one's self how strong is the Irishman's natural sense and love of justice, and then to observe him as witness or counsel in a court of law, is one [of] the strangest experiences we know. We believe the virtue to be constitutional and permanent; the vice, induced and temporary. The Irishman has had too little occasion to see that law has any sort of connection with justice. When the connection is more extensively established than even now, great as are the recent improvements in the law, the Irishman's love of justice will make him an ally of the law, instead of its quizzing and cunning foe. We have had frequent occasion to regret the high walls which surround all the pretty places in the neighbourhood of the towns we have last visited. While walking or driving between such walls, with nothing but the sky to look at, we have been told the reason – that the people have so little idea of the law being instituted for just and mutually protective purposes, that trespass and damage are preventible only by such defences as these walls. If we should live to come again, some years hence, we shall hope to find railings in the place of these walls. We should like to see what is within; but we should like much more to see the people learning that the law is meant to be every honest man's friend, and guarding it accordingly. As to the practical failure of trial by jury meanwhile, we see nothing to be done but to educate the people up to it. The deepening adversity of the Catholic priesthood on the one hand, and the spread of education through the National Schools on the other, afford such promise of an improvement of the national character in regard to veracity, that, in our opinion, the effect of such improvement upon the administration of justice must be waited for. Great as is the evil of a vicious or insecure administration of justice, it appears to us to be less than that of altering the principle and form, in condescension to a vice of national character which may be in course of cure.

Up to a very recent time – probably up to this hour – there has been discussion among English political economists as to whether, in consideration of the Irishman's passion for land, there might not be, in his case, some relaxation of established rules, some suspension of scientific maxims, about small holdings of land; whether the indolence, improvidence, and turbulent character of the Irish peasantry might not be changed into the opposite characteristics of the Flemish and Saxon countryman, by putting them in the same position. We have borne this question in mind throughout our survey of the country. We presently saw that the habits of slovenly cultivation, of dependence on the potato, and of consequent idleness for the greater part of the year, were too firmly associated in the peasant mind with the possession of land to allow the peasant to be a safe proprietor at present. A course of discipline was obviously necessary to fit him, in any degree, for the possession of land: and this discipline he could never have while on the land, and especially with the priest at his elbow, whose business it is to prevent his obtaining knowledge and independence. By degrees we discovered how the necessary discipline was being received precisely by those men who

are not on the land. And a very pleasant discipline it is to them, –
being that of a growing prosperity under work for wages. The chief
reason of the passion of the Irish peasant for land is that land has
always been, to him and to his fathers before him, the symbol of
power, independence, and dignity. Recent years have shown him great
landowners stripped of their lands, and, in many cases, glad to be so;
– and men of power, independence, and dignity, whose possessions
are in some other form than land. He feels something of this himself,
when, remembering his hungering family on his putrid potato-plot,
he now looks at the money he has laid by since he began to work for
wages. He cannot but feel the comfort of his present state in
comparison with the former. We have said before how great is the
readiness, the eagerness to work for fair wages, paid regularly and in
cash. It would be absurd now to interfere with this process, for the
labourer's sake. It would be grievous too for the sake of society. No
one who has observed the isolated Irishman on his solitary potato-
ground, and the Irishman at work on some social labour which
requires an observance of hours and rules, can fail to be struck with
the difference of social quality. Ireland would be as quiet a place to
live in as any other if regular and punctual labour went on there as
elsewhere; labour requiring, as manufacturers and public works do,
a certain degree of combination of regular labourers. This combining
and quieting process is advancing now; and it will spread with every
extension of scientific industry. By it men may be fitted, in the course
of generations, for the proprietorship or other holding of small pieces
of land; but the process is only beginning as yet. While emigration is
going on, wages must rise. The more they rise, the less will the
peasant think of having land. When the present rage or necessity for
grazing is moderated, and high farming is begun on the estates which
are changing hands, the peasant's notions of the uses of land will alter
prodigiously. If then – after having seen and learned how land ought
to be used – he once more wishes for a bit, to see what he can make
of it, he will then be more in the condition, as to fitness, of the
Flemish or Saxon cultivator, and may possibly be safely trusted with
a field. But this time is far off; and it will be a future generation which
sees the change, if it ever happens.

The miseries of Ireland, it has been often and long agreed, proceed
from economical and religious causes. The worst economical
mischiefs are in course of extirpation by a method of awful severity,
but one which discloses unbounded promise. The old barriers are
thrown down day by day; the country is opened to occupation and

industry by the process which clears it of those who could not find a subsistence upon it. And, while emigration carries away, to prosper elsewhere, more than a quarter of a million people yearly, the National Schools are training and sending forth, to be Irish residents, half a million at once of the youth and childhood of the country. Many good laws have been passed, breaking down the land monopoly, and precluding the old agitation about landholding. The agitation that exists is about ecclesiastical matters; and emigration may be found to act as favourably upon this kind of agitation as upon the other. The late census shows the population of Ireland to be one-third less than under ordinarily favourable circumstances it would be. Those who have gone away are Catholics – of the class that sustains the priesthood; and the children that will be born to those emigrants in their new country would have been the support of the Romish church at home. Of those who are to fill up the gaps in the population, some will be Protestants from England and Ireland; more will be educated Catholics out of the National Schools; and others will be the children of the Catholics now and hereafter educated at the Queen's Colleges, in disregard of the discouragement from head-quarters. Religious animosities will be allayed, rather than fomented, by these two last classes of rising citizens. They will never be the slaves of such a priesthood as that of the Ireland of to-day. That priesthood is obviously destined to decline. It may become more noisy and quarrelsome as it declines, but its power for mischief would soon be over, if it were not for the establishment in the land of the Church of the minority.

This Church of England in Ireland is the most formidable mischief now in the catalogue of Irish woes.[1] This church, as we have said before, either does nothing or breaks the peace. If she continues in place, wealth, and artificial power, she may set about numbering her days; for it is clear to all dispassionate inquirers that awakened Ireland will not long tolerate a slothful Church; and that the strife she provokes, here and there, with the other Church, will and must issue in the popular rejection of both. The world sees, and Ireland feels, an express education of the young spreading from shore to shore, and a virtual education of the adults proceeding under the influence of events – both alike independent of both Churches. The world sees, and Ireland feels, that all her peace and progress (and it is not premature to speak of peace and progress now) are owing to influences quite apart from both Churches; while the obstacles, the discouragements, the dissensions with which she has to contend, are owing to the faults of the one or the other Church, or their mutual strife. What is to become of these Churches or of religion, if it is to be insisted upon in the form of either, in a country which has begun to taste of peace and progress, no ghost need come from the grave to tell.

Endnotes

EDITOR'S INTRODUCTION

1 'There are few areas of Victorian life which she did not take within her scope and on which she failed to leave her mark. She is easy to mock but it is not so easy to emulate her talents and the conscientious and on the whole beneficent use she made of them'. Joan Rees, *Writings on the Nile: Harriet Martineau, Florence Nightingale, Amelia Edwards* (London, Rubicon, 1995), p. 21.

2 R.K. Webb, *Harriet Martineau: A Radical Victorian* (London, Heinemann, 1960), p. 43.

3 *Ibid.*, p. 45.

4 Although the following should be remembered: 'No one who knew her considers that she did herself justice in the Autobiography. It is hard and censorious; it displays vanity, both in its depreciation of her own work, and in its recital of the petty slights and insults which had been offered to her from time to time; it is aggressive, as though replying to enemies rather than appealing to friends; and not one of either the finer or the softer qualities of her nature is at all adequately indicated. It is, in short, the least worthy of her true self of all the writings of her life'. F. Fenwick Miller, *Harriet Martineau*, 1884, (New York, Kennikat, 1972), p. 175.

5 It should be borne in mind, however, that these illnesses, and later the fear of death, were to provide Martineau with considerable material for publication. See T.L. Broughton, 'Making the most out of martyrdom: Harriet Martineau, autobiography and death', *Literature and History*, 2 (1993), pp. 24–45, for further discussion.

6 Harriet Martineau, *Autobiography*, vol. I, (London, Smith, 1877), p. 70.

7 *Ibid.*, p. 19

8 *ibid.*, p. 160.

9 Harriet Martineau, *Ireland: A Tale*, 1832, R.L. Wolff (ed.), (New York, Garland, 1979), pp. vi–vii.

10 Timothy Foley, 'Public sphere and domestic circle: gender and political economy in Nineteenth-century Ireland' in M. Kelleher and J. Murphy (eds), *Gender Perspectives in nineteenth century Ireland: Public and Private Spheres* (Dublin, Irish Academic Press, 1997), p. 21.

11 Among the vulgarisers of Classical economic theory Harriet Marineau holds a position of undisputed pre-eminence. The monthly sales of her *Illustrations of Political Economy* exceeded 10,000 in the 1830s whereas a decade later Mill's *Principles* could only achieve a sale of 3,000 copies in four years'. A.J. Taylor, *Laissez-Faire and State Intervention in Nineteenth-century Britain* (London, Macmillan, 1972), p. 27.

12 For an assessment of Martineau's commitment to political economy, see A. Hobart, 'Harriet Martineau's political economy of everyday life', *Victorian Studies*, 37 (1994), pp. 223–51.

13 *Quarterly Review*, 49, (1833), p. 151.

14 'The Tales are very heavy going. Characters speak like the embodiment of stiff Principles that they are, the creation of settings is toilsomely mechanical, and even without an awareness of Martineau's method of composition, the reader cannot miss the fitting of doctrinal pieces into a prearranged ideological outline'. D. David,

Intellectual Women and Victorian Patriarchy: Harriet Martineau, Elizabeth Barrett Browning, George Eliot (Ithaca, Cornell University Press, 1987), p. 42.

15 For a detailed assessment of Martineau's American travels, see G. Thomas, *Harriet Martineau* (Boston, Twayne, 1985), pp. 32–59, and S. Hunter, *Harriet Martineau: The Poetics of Moralism* (Aldershot, Scolar, 1995), pp. 148–95.

16 Alison Blunt, *Travel, Gender, and Imperialism: Mary Kingsley and West Africa* (London, Guilford, 1994), p. 19.

17 Harriet Martineau, *Eastern Life, Present and Past* (London, Moxon, 1848), preface.

18 See D. Porter, *Haunted Journeys: Desire and Transgression in European Travel Writing* (Princeton, Princeton University Press, 1991); D. Spurr, *The Rhetoric of Empire: Colonial Discourse in Journalism, Travel Writing, and Imperial Administration* (Durham, Duke University Press, 1993); N. Thomas, *Colonialism's Culture: Anthropology, Travel and Government* (Cambridge, Polity, 1994); and E.A. Bohls, *Women Travel Writers and the Language of Aesthetics 1716–1818* (Cambridge, Cambridge University Press, 1995), in addition to M.L. Pratt's *Imperial Eyes: Travel Writing and Transculturation*, (London, Routledge, 1992), for an overview of some of the issues raised here.

19 For an informed, if lighthearted, appraisal, see G. Trease, *The Grand Tour* (London, Heinemann, 1967).

20 For a discussion of the development of nineteenth century anthropological and ethnological institutions, particularly their relationship to the formation of Empire, see Christine Bolt, *Victorian Attitudes to Race* (London, RKP, 1971).

21 *Quarterly Review,* 76, (1845), pp. 98–9.

22 Shirley Foster, *Across New Worlds: Nineteenth-Century Women Travellers and Their Writings* (London, Harvester, 1990) p. 8.

23 *Ibid.*, p. 406.

24 Harriet Martineau, *Selected Letters,* V. Sanders (ed.), (Oxford, Oxford University Press, 1990), p. 125.

25 Harriet Martineau, *Ireland: A Tale*, p. xiii.

26 Harriet Martineau, *Autobiography,* vol. 2, (London, Smith, 1877), p. 407.

27 *Westminster Review,* 3 (1853), p. 35.

28 Harriet Martineau, *Autobiography* vol. 1, G. Weiner (ed.), (London, Virago, 1983), p. xv.

29 Harriet Martineau, *Society in America*, vol. 1 (London, Saunders, 1837), p. 199.

30 V. Sanders, *Reason Over Passion: Harriet Martineau and the Victorian Novel* (Sussex, Harvester, 1986), p. 168.

31 Interestingly, although parts of the census were published throughout the early 1850s, the *Comparative Table of the Census of Ireland* was published on 13 October 1851.

32 *Fraser's Magazine,* 44, (1851), p. 223.

33 In an article for the *Westminster Review,* published in April 1854, Martineau declared her admiration for the census along similar lines. However, an important aspect of the article is the manner in which she looks at census figures, indeed the accumulation of statistical information generally, as inherently beneficial, a classificatory gesture that was to be replayed throughout much of the nineteenth century.

34 'Ultimately, Martineau's "solutions" to the situations in Ireland and India centered on education and entrepreneurial capitalism, which she thought the British had a responsibility to promote in both countries. It was the rationalist argument that science, knowledge, and disciplined economic behaviour would save inhabitants in both cases from the crises and conflicts generated, she thought, by traditional culture'. S. Hoecker-Drysdale, *Harriet Martineau: First Woman Sociologist* (New York, Berg, 1992), p. 122.

35 Little psychoanalytic effort is necessary, I believe, to follow the trajectory in Martineau's mind between the colour green, slime, and an unfettered Irish peasantry.

HARRIET MARTINEAU'S PREFACE

1 The *Daily News* started in 1846, and ran until 1943. From its inception it was always known as a liberal newspaper: The 'principles advocated by "The Daily News",' Dickens wrote in the introductory article, 'will be principles of progress and improvement, of education, civil and religious liberty, and equal legislation – principles such as its conductors believe the advancing spirit of the time requires, the condition of the country demands, and justice, reason, and experience legitimately sanction'. H.R. Fox Bourne, *English Newspapers: Chapters in the History of Journalism,* (vol. 2) (London, Chatto, 1887), p. 141. Martineau's connection with the newspaper was to last for over twenty years.

2 The Dublin Statistical Society was established in Dublin in 1847 in order to promote the study of statistical and economical science. Academics and economists from Trinity College and later, the Queen's Colleges, were members: 'The men who founded the Dublin Statistical Society undoubtedly assumed that statistics meant social statistics, not a branch of mathematics, and they regarded the subject as a form of applied economics'. Mary Daly, *The Spirit of Earnest Inquiry: The Statistical and Social Inquiry Society of Ireland 1847–1997* (Dublin, Statistical and Social Society of Ireland, 1997). The Great Famine (1845–52) prompted a series of investigations by the society.

3 The Belfast Social Inquiry Society was established in December 1851 for the purpose of promoting the scientific investigation of the sciences of statistics, political economy, and jurisprudence. It was linked to the Statistical Section of the British Association for the Advancement of Science.

4 William Neilson Hancock (1820–1888). Whately Professor of Political Economy at the University of Dublin, later Professor of Political Economy at Queen's College, Belfast. President of the Dublin Statistical Society (1881–2), and Secretary of the Belfast Social Inquiry Society.

LETTER ONE

1 Although cross-channel traffic between Derry and British ports such as Glasgow and Liverpool was well-developed by the mid nineteenth century, a more natural point of arrival for Martineau would have been Belfast. However, the significance of Derry, with its history of plantation and siege, seems to have been the additional attraction. More specifically, although the work of the 'great London corporations' clearly impress Martineau, the fact that Catholic Irish still reside on Company lands opens up an interesting set of economic conditions. These lands, she tells us, 'have for centuries been managed by Englishmen, and largely peopled by Scotch', yet 'quite enough of the Catholic peasanty' still remain. Evidently, it is the opportunity to compare apparently differing ethnic and economic groups in the north of Ireland with each other, as well as with the larger economic unit, that really inspires.

2 'Although legally a city, throughout the seventeenth century Londonderry was never larger than a very small town. In 1616, 102 families were living there and by 1620 this had increased to 121, although the size of each family is unknown. The population was smaller than Coleraine at this stage but quickly began to

overtake its "sister" town and by 1628 it was estimated that there were 305 able-bodied men in Londonderry. Initially the population was made up of some of the old Derry settlers, the workmen and officials sent over from London, and young people such as the Christ's Hospital boys. Slowly, with the arrival of new settlers and the birth of children, the population began to rise'. B. Lacy, *Siege City: The Story of Derry and Londonderry* (Belfast, Blackstaff, 1990), p. 101.

3 The 'great London corporations' refers to the twelve London Companies, descended from medieval guilds, who invested in the plantation of Londonderry at the beginning of the seventeenth century. Surveys and building work began in earnest in 1611, particularly at Coleraine, with the walls and gates of Derry completed by 1618. The twelve Companies consist of the Mercers, Grocers, Drapers, Fishmongers, Goldsmiths, Skinners, Merchant Taylors, Haberdashers, Salters, Ironmongers, Vintners, and Clothworkers Companies.

4 'Mere Irish' refers to the 'pure' or aboriginal Irish and has a distinctly sixteenth century connotation, as well as an obvious resonance for Martineau as she travels the Londonderry plantations. Usually employed as an ethnic marker, it became a way of speaking about those Irish who followed the Catholic faith. One of the better-known planters who 'popularized' its use was Edmund Spenser, in *A View of the Present State of Ireland*, written in 1596 but not published until 1633: ' . . . and conspiring with the Irish did quite cast off their English names and allegiance, since which time they have ever so remained and have still since been counted mere Irish'. E. Spenser, *A View of the Present State of Ireland* W.L. Renwick (ed.), (Oxford, Clarendon, 1970), p. 65

5 T.W. Moody's *The Londonderry Plantation: 1609–41*, (Belfast, Mullan, 1939) still stands as the authoritative account of the plantation of Derry. However, for a more recent, if somewhat valorific account, which relates the business of the Companies until the outbreak of the First World War, with a particular focus on their architectural achievements, see James S. Curl, *The Londonderry Plantation, 1609–1914* (Sussex, Phillimore, 1986).

6 Although Portrush might have been one of the more visible landmarks as Martineau approached Lough Foyle, her true point of entry would have been through the channel at Magilligan Point.

7 The salmon-fishing industry has been an important source of revenue in the Derry and Coleraine areas from the sixteenth century onwards. Following the Plantation, fishing rights in the Foyle, along with other rights of ownership, became the property of various London Companies, including the Fishmongers, Drapers, Salters, and Mercers. Today the area supports a thriving salmon and general fishing industry, and is protected by two, virtually identical Acts of parliament, namely the Foyle Fisheries Act 1952, and the Foyle Fisheries Act (Northern Ireland) 1952, which were simultaneously enacted in Dáil Éireann, Dublin, and Stormont, Belfast.

8 From the Irish, *slab*, meaning soft mud on a sea-shore.

9 At this point, Martineau appears to be struggling with the name of the city of Derry: 'Derry, from the old Irish *daire*, modern Irish, *doire*, means "oakwood" or "oakgrove". From the beginning of recorded history this word, in a variety of versions and associations, has been used as the name of the hill on which the centre of the modern city is built. The placename element "derry" is very common in Ireland, recalling the widespread oakwoods of ancient times. Frequently, it was used to denote an island of high, dry land totally or partly surrounded by peat bog'. Lacy, *Siege City*, p. 8.

10 Although Martineau hints at the successes of the company at land reclamation, Curl suggests that although 'Positive steps to reclaim the slob-lands were taken in 1838', and that land 'that was reclaimed from the slobs was drained, planted,

and fenced with thorn quicks', he also suggests that the 'whole question of the redemption of the slob-lands went on for many years, and was bedevilled by the claims of the Irish Society on the waters of the Foyle and the Bann'. Curl, *Plantation*, pp. 247, 271.

11   'The linen industry in Derry was in relative decline by the third decade of the 19th century, as the nature of the linen industry changed. These changes being the increasing size of bleach greens and the application of power to spinning. Derry did introduce power spinning, but it was not sustained . . . [and] by 1860 flax spinning was no longer carried out in Derry'. Brian Mitchell, *The Making of Derry: An Economic History* (Derry, Genealogy Centre, 1992), pp. 26–7.

12   Unlike Belfast, which processed pigs into bacon and hams, the city was a major pre-Famine exporter of live animals. In 1835, for example, Derry exported 11,000 live pigs to England, as well as over 1,000 tons of eggs, over 20,000 tons of corn, and 855 head of cattle, the result of the development of steamships in the 1820s. See W.H. Crawford, 'The evolution of Ulster towns, 1750–1850' in P. Roebuck (ed.), *Plantation to Partition* (Belfast, Blackstaff, 1981) for a fuller discussion of the economic development of the north-western region.

13   Martineau's claims for the advantages of Indian meal are a little misleading. Yes, the Irish peasantry devised methods for consuming the new food, by mixing it with oatmeal to make it more palatable. However, there was also resistance, even for a period within the workhouses, towards its introduction. More importantly, the suggestion that it improved the health of its consumers is less than entirely accurate. Kinealy suggests that 'especially when mixed and diluted with water, [it] may have appeared to fill stomachs, but nutritionally [it] did little else. By engineering this change of eating habits upon some of the Irish people, the government inadvertently was increasing the vulnerability of those people to nutritional deficiencies and diseases'. C. Kinealy, *This Great Calamity: The Irish Famine, 1845–52* (Dublin, Gill and Macmillan, 1994), p. 48.

14   St Finlough's Church, Oghill, Ballykelly, completed in 1851.

15   The 1641 Rebellion: 'From 22 October 1641 an attack was launched on Ulster settlers by their native neighbours, especially directed at those outside the walled towns. Possibly 4,000 were killed, not counting those who died from their sufferings as refugees. Retaliatory attacks on Catholics soon accounted for nearly as many'. Roy Foster, *Modern Ireland, 1600–1972* (London, Allen Lane, 1988), p. 85

16   Jonathon Bardon suggests that the thirty manuscript volumes held in TCD 'filled with the sworn statements of survivors of 1641' were usefully employed to 'justify massive confiscations of land held by Catholics'. (p. 137) So thorough were the confiscations that by 1688 'less than 4 per cent of counties in the province [Ulster], other than Antrim, was owned by Catholics. Once more men who had lost everything withdrew to the woods and the hills and stood "upon their keeping."' *A History of Ulster* (Belfast, Blackstaff, 1992), p. 143. A parallel with the confiscations of Catholic lands after the 1641 Rebellion, particularly the ideological opportunities it afforded, may be found with the 1622 'massacre' at Virginia: 'The "massacre" provided what had proved to be most necessary for the colony to survive: a huge infringement of Natural Law which left its victims free to pursue any course they wanted, unregenerate savagery having forfeited all its rights, civil and natural. The zealousness with which the English ideologists drew the consequences of the "massacre" indicates something of the relief that was mixed with the horror at the news. Edward Waterhouse, who wrote the most detailed account, finds an appropriate image: "Our hands which before were tied with gentlenesse and fair vsage are now set at liberty by treacherous violence of the Sauges: not vntying the Knot, but cutting it."'

P. Hulme, *Colonial Encounters: Europe and the Native Caribbean 1492–1797* (London, Methuen, 1986), p. 172.

17 A reference to Ulster Protestant emigration to America in the eighteenth century, in many instances the result of the Penal Laws which affected Presbyterians as well as Catholics. The effect of Ulster Protestant emigration was to have as much of an effect on those who remained as those who departed: 'Protestant emigration caused near-panic among the ruling classes . . . [Their] main concern in connection with the 1718 emigration was that "No papists stir. The papists being already five or six to one, and being a breeding people, you may imagine in what condition we are like to be in'. R.J. Dickson, *Ulster Emigration to Colonial America 1718–1775* (1966) (Belfast, Ulster Historical Foundation, 1988), p. 35.

18 Curl suggests that the 'Fishmongers' Company in the first half of the 19th century was closely associated with progressive, liberal forces, and with the Evangelical movement within and without the Church of England, and so its members were particularly concerned with reform, with education, with universal literacy, and with the revival of devout Christian observances. It is therefore not surprising that so much effort was expended on school building'. Curb *Plantation*, p. 271. Although a number of schools had been built on the Fishmongers' estates, at Sistrakeel and Greysteel, for example, it is reasonable to presume that Martineau is referring to the school at Ballykelly. The large Lancastrian school at Ballykelly, completed in 1830 to a 'stripped-down Neoclassic[al]' model (and now a special needs primary school), would have been the likely venue for Martineau at that time. *Ibid.*

19 See the National Board of Education below.

20 The traditional version of the Bible among English-speaking Roman Catholics.

21 Secret agrarian oath-bound societies which went under different names in the various counties. They emerged in the eighteenth century, but had a particular appetite for 'agrarian outrage' in the nineteenth: 'The early nineteenth century saw the proliferation of rural protest movements, the "banditti" or "Whiteboys" of contemporary accounts, who can be categorized, often according to locality, as Whitefeet, Threshers, Terry Alts, Rockites, Carders, Caravats, Shanavests or Ribbonmen – the last term applicable to an organization with a more generalized political view than many of the others'. Foster, *Modern Ireland*, p. 292. The Whiteboys appear as a shadowy paramilitary presence in Martineau's Irish *Political Economy* volume, *Ireland: A Tale*. Another society, the Orange Order, appears to be of less interest to Martineau, a surprising omission given its particularly Ulster inflection. See T. Desmond Williams (ed.), *Secret Societies in Ireland* (Dublin, Gill and Macmillan, 1973), and S. Clark and J.S. Donnelly (eds), *Irish Peasants: Violence and Political Unrest 1780–1914* (Wisconsin, Wisconsin University Press, 1983), for a fuller discussion of the growth and influence of Irish secret societies, including the Orange Order.

22 A reference to the personal donation by Arthur Sampson, agent to the Fishmongers, of a stained-glass window at St Finlough's church, Ballykelly, as a mark of respect to the Catholic tenantry.

LETTER TWO

1 Martineau's description of a wasted crop, albeit in relation to Co. Londonderry, is probably accurate enough; 'The Famine has been customarily referred to as having taken place in 1845 to 1847. However, there is evidence to suggest that signs of the potato blight lingered in Co. Antrim until the early 1850s. On 21 December 1850 "it was resolved by the Lisburn Board of Guardians that

stirabout should be distributed for dinner instead of potatoes on Tuesdays . . ." Exactly one year later, in September 1852, "The relieving officers reported that so far as they have been able to ascertain the potato blight appears to be more extensive and severe throughout the Union at present than in any year since 1846"'. C. Dallat, 'The Famine in County Antrim' in C. Kinealy and T. Parkhill (eds), *The Famine in Ulster* (Belfast, Ulster Historical Foundation, 1997), p. 34.

2 The village of Muff (now Eglinton) had seen an extensive building programme since the 1820s by the Grocers' Company. Curl suggests that 'in February 1823 there was much building activity in Muff' (p. 168), and that 'six houses and shops, with allotments behind, had been completed' by 1827 (p. 165). However, by the 1830s the attention of the company was more emphatic: 'to remove the uninhabited "cabins" that disfigured Muff, and to carry out new works. The unfinished state of the town had a "bad moral effect with reference to English controul"'. Curl, *Plantation*, p. 168.

3 'Of a great part of this district the London Companies are landlords – the best of landlords, too, according to the report I could gather; and their good stewardship shows itself especially in the neat villages of Muff and Ballikelly, through both of which I passed'. W.M. Thackeray, *The Paris, Irish and Eastern Sketches* (1842) (London, Smith, 1883), p. 537.

4 Martineau has been either misled or misinformed on this point. Timber for Westminster Abbey and Westminster Hall was English sourced: 'Meanwhile Master Hugh Herland and his carpenters had been shaping the timbers of the [Westminster Hall] roof at a place near Farnham called "the frame." The oak timber for the roof had for the most part been obtained before the period covered by the surviving "particulars", but it is known from the enrolments that some of it came from the royal woods at Odiham and Aliceholt in Hampshire, and that 200 oaks to make rafters were bought from the abbot of St. Albans' park at Bervan, or Barvin, near Northaw in Hertfordshire'. R. Allen Brown *et al* (eds), *The History of the King's Works*, vol. 1 (London, HMSO, 1963), p. 529. I am indebted to Richard Mortimer of the Westminster Abbey library for this reference.

5 Arthur Sampson was appointed agent to the Fishmongers' Company in 1824, when his father, George Vaughan Sampson, had resigned. Given the great interest shown by Martineau in statistics and the new sciences and societies then instituted in Ireland, Sampson junior would have been a natural ally (and very possibly a guide) during her visit to Derry. Moreover, George Vaughan Sampson was the author of *A Statistical Account of the County of Londonderry* (Dublin, 1821), one of twenty-three statistical accounts initiated by the Dublin Statistical Society. He was also behind 'the formation of the North-West of Ireland Agricultural Society that was set up to improve the knowledge of husbandry throughout the region' (Curl, *Plantation*, p. 163), and he helped establish the Templemoyle seminary: 'Sampson's ideas appear to have been influenced by the experiments of Phillip Emmanuel von Fellenberg (1771–1884), who founded an agricultural college at Bern in Switzerland in 1799. Subsequently he established another college in Prussia in 1806, and it was this that commended itself to enlightened persons in Ulster as a model for the Templemoyle Seminary'. *Ibid.*

6 The Templemoyle Agricultural Training School was established in 1826. The 'Grocers' Company, with resident gentry of the area under the aegis of the North-West of Ireland Society (which raised about £3,000 towards the costs of erecting the buildings), founded the Agricultural College at Templemoyle'. Curl, *Plantation*, p. 170. Over 800 agricultural students were trained there up to 1850, but the school went into slow decline after that date. It closed in 1866.

7 Thackeray's *Irish Sketches* was published in 1842. His ten-page account of the school is both detailed and generous, as Martineau suggests: 'Before quitting Templemoyle, one thing more may be said in its favour. It is one of the very few public establishments in Ireland where pupils of the two religious denominations are received, and where no religious disputes have taken place. The pupils are called upon, morning and evening, to say their prayers privately. On Sunday, each division, Presbyterian, Roman Catholic, and Episcopalian, is marched to its proper place of worship. The pastors of each sect may visit their young flock when so inclined; and the lads devote the Sabbath evening to reading the books pointed out to them by their clergymen'. Thackeray, *Irish Sketches* p. 543.

8 George William Frederick Villiers, 4th Earl of Clarendon (1800–1870). Began an international diplomatic career at the age of twenty, was involved in Irish affairs from the late 1820s. A political liberal, he supported Peel's reform of the Corn Laws, was appointed Lord Lieutenant of Ireland in 1847, a position he held until 1852. In his attempts to administer impartially he alienated most factions within Irish politics, and is described in the *DNB* as being 'almost a prisoner in Dublin Castle' because of the constant threats on his life from all quarters. After his sojourn in Ireland, he went on to negotiate the Peace of Paris in 1855.

9 'Thirty noblemen and gentlemen followed Lord Clarendon's subscription of £50 with various sums amounting to about £1000; and when Lord Clarendon found that the subscription only amounted to something short of £1500, he at once guaranteed £1000 more. With these means twenty-nine or thirty practical Instructors were immediately despatched into as many of the most distressed districts of the West and South – and with, as far as we can at present judge, the happiest effect, and at no greater expense than in 1847, of £340; and in 1848, of £498'. *Quarterly Review*, 85, (Sept. 1849), p. 546.

10 The National Board of Education had been established in 1831 (following a Commons' select committee report in 1828) to supervise Irish elementary education. Two-thirds of the costs of establishing, staffing and maintaining schools were paid from public funds, and the state retained a certain control over the syllabus and teaching, as well as regulating schools through an inspectorial system. All the Irish Churches had objected to the attempted exclusion of religious instruction, but the initiative was nevertheless extremely popular. By 1845, 4,000 schools had been established, catering for over 400,000 pupils throughout the country.

11 The *Quarterly Review*, as Martineau suggests, took a much less enthusiastic view of the Templemoyle seminary: 'The idea was admirable, and the interior management seems to be excellent; but the result, though considered brilliantly successful in Ireland, where even half successes are rare, seems to us, as plain men of business, not quite so satisfactory'. The reviewer took particular exception to figures, from 1826 to 1843, which revealed that little more than half of the students 'have in any degree fulfilled the original object of the institution. And here we have a remarkable instance of that unfortunate peculiarity of the Irish character which we have so often had to regret – and which it seems even the most intelligent and sober-minded men (even in grave and cautious Ulster) cannot escape – of palliating and defending mistakes and failures, instead of endeavouring by an honest confession and vigorous resistance to check and correct them'. *Quarterly Review*, 85, (Sept. 1849), p. 541. The figures for those students actually leaving the country to take up employment elsewhere, which Martineau was most concerned about, are as follows: of 497 students qualified between 1838–1843, 93 emigrated to either America, the West Indies or Australia.

12 'In addition to reading, writing, and arithmetic, the syllabus included Latin, Greek, and Hebrew. The students lived and were given their academic training' as well as in all departments of agriculture. Curl, *Plantation*, p. 170

13 'We trust also that, this being the season in which Irish laziness is most remarkable as well as most injurious, Lord Clarendon will be enabled to make a large addition to the number of his thirty Instructors, whose timely and little-costly intervention may save in the next year thousands of lives and millions of money. But whether this incomprehensible people can be persuaded to work for their livelihood or no, we trust that we shall hear no more of the vile cant about "hereditary bondage and the accursed tyranny of England". The bondage was and is no other than the bondage of obstinate ignorance, and the tyranny, the tyranny of inveterate sloth'. *Quarterly Review*, 85 (Sept. 1849), p. 562.

14 'As the carman had no other passengers but myself, he made no objection to carry me a couple of miles out of his way, through the village of Muff [Eglinton], belonging to the Grocers of London and thence to a very interesting institution. It lies on a hill in a pretty wooded country, and is most curiously secluded from the world by the tortuousness of the road which approaches it'. Thackeray, *Irish Sketches*, p. 537.

15 Martineau is, of course, alluding to the Siege of Derry of 1689, particularly the Protestant defence of the city which contributed to the defeat of James II by William of Orange.

16 Queen Victoria had in fact visited Ireland, but some years earlier: 'The visit had originally been planned for 1846, but had been postponed due to the potato blight. In recognition of the continuation of distress in some parts of Ireland, the Queen's visit in 1849 was not to be a state visit, and the need for economy was stressed. Significantly also, her visit was to be brief, well orchestrated, and confined to the east of Ireland, that is, Cork and Dublin. Although there were criticisms of the expense which the visit would entail, overall the government considered that the benefits would outweigh the disadvantages'. Kinealy, *This Great Calamity*, p. 264.

LETTER THREE

1 'The new system of public works [designed to provide work for Famine victims] had been devised by Trevelyan back in August 1846. The works could not be "reproductive" – that is, they must not profit individuals or compete with capitalist enterprise – and were therefore largely confined to building walls, roads, bridges, causeways and fences. Unlike Peel's scheme, where the Government accepted much of the cost, the new relief works were to be financed entirely out of the county cess [tax], though the treasury would advance loans. Irish property must pay for Irish poverty'. Bardon, *Ulster*, p. 283.

2 Although Martineau's response to Famine and post-Famine relief work is motivated by pragmatic concerns, as always, her reaction is interesting. Less concerned about the inhumane nature of such works – 9*d.* or 10*d.* per day for work on the construction of frequently unnecessary roads – Martineau draws a sceptical veil over their purpose.

3 Construction of the railway between Derry and Coleraine had been authorized on 4 August 1845, but by the end of 1852 the line was operating only as far as Limavady. It was not until the following year that it eventually reached Coleraine. What appears to have 'marred the beauty' of Martineau's view across Lough Foyle was the sight of Irish tenantry, working in draining and reclaiming land, either as part of the Public Works scheme or as employees on the lands of the Fishmongers' Company.

4 Although the navigation of the Bann from Lough Neagh to Coleraine was a less than successful venture, it appeared to many as a viable engineering and commercial enterprise. Following a special Act passed in 1842 – which Martineau seems to have been aware of – the Board of Works began to improve navigation in the Lough Neagh basin. However, the labour shortages (due to the Famine), as well as the costs and physical obstacles encountered generally, ensured difficult times ahead: 'The cost effectiveness of the whole scheme was therefore very dubious and, although there was some reduction in flooding, the fact that it was a combined drainage and navigation scheme made it fall between two stools, with neither interest satisfied'. Ruth Delany, *A Celebration of 250 Years of Ireland's Inland Waterways* (Belfast, Appletree, 1986), p. 167.

5 Martineau is stretching a point here. The line from Belfast to Carrickfergus was opened on 11 April 1848, well in advance of her visit, and the spur from Lisburn (rather than Belfast) to Antrim was in operation also. But to get from Carrick to Antrim one had to travel via Belfast, and not directly as Martineau implies.

6 It was precisely the development of the railway system, and its spectacular success, that forced canal developments between Lough Neagh and the sea into recession: 'Whether this programme of rapid railway extension was directly influenced by potential competition from the proposed navigation along the Lower Bann and on Lough Neagh is difficult to say, but it had the effect of severely blighting the prospects of the Lower Bann as an artery for traffic from the inland sea to and from the north coast'. W.A. McCutcheon, *The Canals of the North of Ireland* (London, MacDonald, 1965), p. 130. The River Bann was bridged, at Coleraine, in 1859.

7 'Possibly the least efficient if not the most dangerous railway ever to operate in Ireland was the Londonderry and Enniskillen. This began its disastrous career in 1845 with misguided authority to build the 60-mile line between the two places in its name. Its troubled history is a catalogue of routing squabbles, legal battles (invariably lost), low receipts, shoddy track, derailments, absence of maintenance, canal competition, untrained staff and poor management'. Fergus Mulligan, *One Hundred and Fifty Years of Irish Railways* (Belfast, Appletree, 1983), p. 91.

8 'In 1838 parliamentary powers were given to embank the slob lands from the mouth of the Faughan to Magilligan Point. The reclaimed land was to belong to the undertakers for 300 years. The plan was to reclaim 25,000 acres, but from the enormous expense of the undertaking the parties were only able to reclaim about 4,000 acres at a cost of about £50,000. Nearly £100,000 was spent in trying to reclaim the remainder; but the parties failed before the embankment was completed. The Ballykelly reclamations were completed between 1838 and 1845. In October 1845 a contract was signed by the railway company to make the Foyle embankment and the Downhill tunnels'. T.H. Mullin, *Limavady and the Roe Valley* (Limavady, Limavady District Council, 1983), p. 81.

9 Martineau is a little casual in her choice of terms here. Flax is always pulled, never cut. It is pulled from the ground to keep the fibrous stems as long as possible (a metre or so). Her reference to the smell given off from soaking flax, however, is apparently accurate. Story has it that it was so offensive that only married men could be persuaded to retrieve it from the 'dams', single men regarding it as a severe hindrance to their social lives.

10 'Of the other London companies who adopted this policy of clearance by stealth, the Fishmongers' estate at Ballykelly provided for some 60 tenants to emigrate with their families. The Grocers' estate nearby also contributed to the removal

of 80 families in the period 1849–51 as a means of helping their policy of consolidation of farms'. T. Parkhill, 'The Famine in County Armagh' in Kinealy and Parkhill (eds), *The Famine in Ulster,* p. 165.

11   Thomas Drummond (1797–1840). Scots engineer and administrator. Inventor of the limelight, and an improved version of the heliostat. Was part of the Ordnance Survey team involved in making a trigonometrical survey of Ireland between 1824–33; appointed Under-Secretary at Dublin Castle in 1835. Reformed the Irish police, and opposed the excesses of the Orange Order. Believed that peace in Ireland would come only through prosperity, and attempted to modernize the country through widespread employment and use of natural resources. See J. Andrews, *A Paper Landscape: The Ordnance Survey in Nineteenth-Century Ireland* (Oxford, Clarendon, 1975) for the definitive study of the work of the Irish Ordnance Survey.

12   The personal element of these lines is confirmed by Webb who describes Drummond as 'one of the most charming and impressive of her [Martineau's] regular visitors', and goes on to cite a letter in which Martineau declared, 'As his [Drummond's] business then lay in Downing Street, & I lived in the next street, Fludyer Street, he used to come to my study from Lord Althorp or Lord Grey when they wanted my opinion on measures they were then preparing'. Webb, *Harriet Martineau,* p. 126.

13   'Relatively short of administrative experience Drummond had the definite advantage of knowing a good deal about the Irish countryside and its people, having worked during 1825–30 with Colby on the Irish Ordnance Survey. He was deeply committed to the improvement of Ireland. Indeed when in mid-1835 there were rumours of his appointment as Under-Secretary, his mother wrote to him saying that she hoped he would have the chance to satisfy his "partiality for Ireland". He was unbelivably conscientious, attending to every detail of administration and more besides. Drummond's health eventually proved unable to bear the weight of work which he undertook, and when he died in April 1840 he was mourned throughout the country for having 'won the affections of the masses of the people by his love of justice, his hatred of oppression, his sympathy with poverty and suffering, his unfaltering championship of right'. M.A.G. Ó Tuathaigh, *Thomas Drummond and the Government of Ireland 1835–41* (Dublin, National University of Ireland, 1977) p. 6.

14   A very fragrant, essential oil obtained from the petals of the rose.

15   'The Proportion of the Clothworkers' Company and its Associated Companies contained 13,450 acres, or some 2.64 per cent. of the total area of the County. It was situated in the half Barony of the town and liberties of Coleraine'. Curl, *Plantation,* p. 375.

16   It is possible that this particular tirade – against the Clothworkers' Company, the railways, the lack of sound husbandry – was prompted by something which Martineau found personally, rather than philosophically, disagreeable. According to Curl, the Clothworkers were overseeing considerable developments and improvements throughout the 1830s and 1840s: 'The Clothworkers, like the other Companies, gave £25 each to the Coleraine Parish church rebuilding fund, and provided liberal grants for educational and charitable purposes. Support was given to a number of schools, and distressed tenants were helped with small donations. Many plantations had been established by 1849 at considerable expense: nearly a hundred thousand trees were planted at Dartress and Ballywildrick plantations alone. The Company also contributed to the costs of improving the channel from Coleraine to the sea for navigational purposes'. Curl, *Plantation* p. 390.

LETTER FOUR

1 The Edict of Nantes was promulgated at Nantes on 13 April 1598 by Henry IV of France. The edict upheld Protestants in freedom of conscience and permitted them to hold public worship in many parts of the kingdom. The edict also restored Catholicism in all areas where Catholic practice had been disrupted. On 18 October 1685, however, Louis XIV revoked the Edict of Nantes and deprived the French Protestants of all religious and civil liberties. Within a few years, between 200,000 and 400,000 Huguenots emigrated from France (mainly to America, England and Holland), thus depriving the country of its most industrious commercial class. Although around 10,000 Huguenots settled in Ireland (mainly Youghal, Portarlington and Lisburn), a significant number settled in Hampshire and Norfolk (including the Martineaus), with a particular concentration in the town of Norwich, Martineau's hometown. Indeed, after London and Canterbury, Norwich had the greatest number of Huguenots for much of the seventeenth century, and Robin Gwynn estimates that in the 1630s Norwich had a combined French and Dutch Huguenot constituency of around 760, with London showing 2,240, and Canterbury 900 communicants each. Robin Gwynn, *Huguenot Heritage: The History and Contribution of the Huguenots in Britain* (London, Routledge, 1985), p. 32. Martineau's reference to 'ingenious foreigners' emigrating to 'our islands' refers as much to her own inheritance as it does to the settlers at Lisburn.

2 Although the linen industry had been perilously close to collapse in the 1830s, and although the 1850s, when Martineau was touring, was a turbulent decade also, the industry boomed in the 1860s. By the 1870s, suggests Bardon, Ulster was 'firmly established as the greatest centre of linen production in the world.' Bardon, *Ulster,* p. 328. Although the benefits of such industry was greater and more regular employment, it was not without its dangers: 'No mention was made of the damaging effect of deafening noise caused by whirling power belts, clashing Jacquard cards, flying shuttles and banging sleys, nor of the danger of passing on tuberculosis by "kissing the shuttle" to suck out the end of the yarn'. *Ibid*, p. 332.

3 The Flax Improvement Society 'was established for the promotion and improvement of the growth of Flax in Ireland, and during an existence of eighteen years, it having been dissolved in 1859, it did good service in the cause for which it was started. The Queen and Prince Albert were patrons of this Society, and the Lord Lieutenant vice-patron. Government granted £1000 a year to assist in defraying the expenses, and local donations, and noble patronage and support, were accorded to it; but, notwithstanding these advantages, it came to an end, and the void created by its dissolution has not yet been filled up'. A. Warden, *The Linen Trade, Ancient and Modern* (1864) (London, Cass, 1967), p. 405

4 'When war was declared by her Majesty's Government against the Emperor of Russia, it was at once apparent that the interruption of our commercial relations with that empire might seriously affect the supply of the raw material of the British and Irish linen manufacture, as well as of the seed which has hitherto been obtained from Riga, for sowing in Ireland . . . of the yearly import of flaxseed for sowing in Ireland, from two-thirds to three-fourths come from Riga'. *14th Annual Report and Transactions of the Royal Society for the Promotion of Flax* (Belfast, Simms, 1854), p. 8.

5 The society also apparently shared Martineau's faith in the financial benefits of flax production: 'The objects for which that Society was established have an intimate connexion with our national prosperity, involving, as they do, the interests of the great classes who are the medium for the circulation of capital, – the agriculturalists, manufactures, and landed proprietors'. *Proceedings of the*

1st Annual General Meeting of the Society for the Promotion and Improvement of Flax (Belfast, Clark, 1842), p. 13.

6 The Flax Improvement Society, founded in 1842, underwent a change of name and patronage in 1845 and became the Royal Flax Society: the '[Marquis of Downshire, President of the Society] was happy to be able to notify to them . . . that last week he received a letter informing him that her Majesty and Prince Albert had kindly consented to become joint-patrons of the Society . . . her Majesty wished her name, and that of his Royal Highness, to be added to the Society, as joint-patrons, with a view of making the Society better known and extending its usefulness'. *6th Annual Report and Transactions of the Royal Society for the Promotion of Flax* (Belfast, Simms, 1846), p. 10.

7 Martineau has basically misunderstood the process of flax growing and harvesting. If flax is to be harvested for spinning it has to be pulled before the seed has ripened. If it is grown for its seed, then it has progressed beyond the point where it can be harvested for spinning. Her misunderstanding is particularly surprising given the moderate linen industry of Suffolk and Norfolk. See Nesta Evans, *The East Anglian Linen Industry: Rural Industry and Local Economy, 1500–1850* (Aldershot, Gower Pasold Research Fund, 1985) for an account of the importance of the linen industry to towns such as Norwich, Martineau's birthplace.

8 Literally, 'beating' the flax.

9 Schenck's system, described by Martineau in the following pages, aimed at hastening the time required for steeping. Its contribution to the flax economy drew mixed reviews: 'I have already said that without the flax-factorship be established in this country, the farmer will never feel strongly inclined to grow flax; but let factors establish themselves, and the farmers will extensively grow the crop; but as the conveniences of water for steeping the plant (although numerous) are not perhaps exactly so general in England as in Ireland, Schenck's system will in many instances be preferred by the factors, and will undoubtedly be the means of increasing and accelerating the flax culture in this country'. E.F. Deman, *The Flax Industry; Its Importance and Progress* (London, Ridgway, 1852), p. 98.

10 'The Committee believes from the partial evidence which they have been able to collect, that there is no ground for supposing this process to be so advantageous, either to the producer or to the consumer, as Schenck's system'. *10th Annual Report and transactions of the Royal Society for the Promotion of Flax* (Belfast, Finlay, 1850), pp. 14–15.

11 After being soaked in stagnant water and weighed down with boulders for about ten days, the flax was removed, drained, and spread out to dry for about three weeks. It was then ready for the scutching process, a procedure which removed the brittle outer part of the flax stems. The scutching-mills, many of which were erected in the eighteenth century, prepared the flax for weaving: 'The scutching process consisted of smashing the outer shell of the stalks with a heavy roller and the recovery of the soft internal fibres. In the hackling process these fibres were drawn through graded combs in order to separate fibres into bundles of equal length and quality. From the mid-eighteenth century onwards, and especially from the early nineteenth century the scutching process was generally performed in a small local mill but prior to that flax was hand-scutched by the growers themselves'. W.J. Smyth, 'Flax Cultivation in Ireland: the Development and Demise of a regional staple', in W.J. Smyth and K. Whelan (eds), *Common Ground: Essays on the Historical Geography of Ireland* (Cork, Cork University Press, 1988), p. 237.

12 'According to instructions, received from your Secretary, containing directions to inspect the principal flax retteries, working under Schenck's process, in

France, Belgium, and Holland . . . I now submit the following report: . . . I do not, however, consider myself justified in communicating what I ascertained on the latter points, but shall merely state that the commercial prospects of these concerns are generally favourable'. Mr De Cock's Report in *16th Annual Report of the Royal Society for the Improvement of Flax* (Belfast, 1857), p. 49.

13 'Since 1851 I have visited many retteries worked under Schenck's process, both in the United Kingdom and on the Continent; and, strange to say, I never found any two working on an identical principle. To this diversity and confusion may, I think, be attributed the non-success, to the present time, in many instances, in the working of Schenck's system'. Mr De Cock's Report in *17th Annual Report of the Royal Society for the Improvement of Flax* (Belfast, 1858), p. 42.

LETTER FIVE

1 Tenant Right centred on what were known as 'the 3 Fs' – Free Sale, Fair Rent, and Fixity of Tenure – issues of tremendous importance for the small farmer. Foster suggests that the Tenant Right issue 'began appearing on political platforms in the 1830s, and came to general attention after 1850', and he points out that 'Some Tenant Righters called for the breaking up of grazing farms, though more were themselves graziers. Like other agrarian issues of nineteenth-century Irish politics, it knitted together a number of incompatible grievances by identifying the landlord as enemy'. *Modern Ireland*, pp. 380–1. Although undoubtedly seized upon by several as a convenient strategy to pursue other agendas, there was much to celebrate in Tenant Right agitation. Bardon, for example, emphasizes the non-sectarian, pluralistic nature of certain aspects of the Irish Tenant League, formed in August 1850: 'For [Gavan] Duffy this was "The League of North and South", bonding Catholic and Protestant farmers in a common cause, and for a time his passionate hope seemed justified. At Ballybay, on the top of a hill close to the Monaghan road, a platform to take five hundred was put up, together with a flagstaff flying a banner of blue, white, green and orange, designed to represent all creeds. That evening a soiree, attended by several priests and Presbyterian ministers, was held on the platform, while bands played a medley of tunes including "Saint Patrick's Day", "The Protestant Boys", and "The Boyne Water". *Ulster,* p. 315. See also, Martin Dowling, *Tenant Right and Agrarian Society in Ulster 1600–1870* (Dublin, Irish Academic Press, 1999).

2 John Frederick Hodges (1823–1899). Professor of Agriculture at Queen's College Belfast, Director of the Chemico-Agricultural Society of Ulster, taught medical jurisprudence in a career spanning fifty years at Queen's. Even before the Famine, Hodges was urging the introduction of more scientific methods in agriculture, as may be found in his eerily prophetic pronouncements of 1844: 'Never was there a more urgent necessity, than exists in this country at the present time, that some great effort should be made by all classes to advance its too much neglected agriculture. In consequences of the changes which have taken place in the laws regulating the importation of grain, and the rapid increase in our population, it becomes absolutely necessary, that . . . we should adopt some means of increasing the produce of our fields. In Agricultural Chemistry we are offered the only rational means for this purpose'. John F. Hodges, *What Science can do for the Irish Farmer: Being an Introductory Lecture on Agricultural Chemistry* (Dublin, Curry, 1844) p. 4.

3 The Chemico-Agricultural Society of Ulster was established in Belfast on 18 August 1846. At its first general meeting, Hodges declared that 'For a country circumstanced as Ireland was, with such natural resources, such a large

population to be employed, such a need for employment, and such capabilities, the establishment of any society, with such objects, must be of the very utmost importance. A Society had been formed in Scotland, for the purpose of bringing science to bear on the pursuits of the farmer, and the most important benefits had resulted from it. Witnessing the results which followed in the train of the workings of this Society, the gentlemen here had asked themselves whether they were not in a position to effect equal or similar good for this country; and the consequence was, that they were led to originate the Chemico-Agricultural Society of Ulster'. *Report of the Proceedings at the 1st General Meeting of the Chemico-Agricultural Society* (Belfast, Finlay, 1846), p. 4.

4　A journal, as such, does not appear to exist. It therefore seems likely that Martineau is referring to occasional publications on behalf of the Society, such as Hodges's *Lessons in Chemistry* (below).

5　Hodges was a foreign Member of the Royal Academies of Agriculture of Sweden and Turin, and of the Imperial and Central Society of France. The text to which Martineau refers was still being approved at least ten years after her visit: 'The sale within a few months of a large edition, and the adoption of the work by the Commissioners of National Education in Ireland, for the use of their rural schools, prove that a large class of the farmers of this country are alive to the advantages to be derived from an acquaintance with the nature of the materials upon which they operate'. John F. Hodges, *The First Book of Lessons in Chemistry, in Its Application to Agriculture* (Belfast, Simms, 1863), 2nd ed. preface.

6　'This great increase of the quantity of work which, in consequence of the division of labour, the same number of people are capable of performing, is owing to three different circumstances; first, to the increase of dexterity in every particular workman; secondly, to the saving of the time which is commonly lost in passing from one species of work to another; and lastly, to the invention of a great number of machines which facilitate and abridge labour, and enable one man to do the work of many. A common smith, who, though accustomed to handle the hammer, has never been used to make nails, if upon some particular occasion he is obliged to attempt it, will scarce, I am assured, be able to make above two or three hundred nails in a day, and those too very bad ones. I have seen several boys under twenty years of age who had never exercised any other trade but that of making nails, and who, when they exerted themselves, could make, each of them, upwards of two thousand three hundred nails in a day'. Adam Smith, *The Wealth of Nations* (1786) (London, Dent, 1975), pp. 7–8.

7　Encumbered estates were those with large debts or mortgages, which could not be sold without discharge of those debts. Landowners were therefore saddled with estates which they could neither sell nor improve. In July 1849 the government passed the Encumbered Estates Act, a radical piece of legislation which allowed certain estates to be sold (those whose annual charges and interest payments exceeded half the net yearly income of the estate), and included the power of compulsion of sale. Creditors were entitled to bid, and received a degree of protection in their new property through a parliamentary title to the land, safe from the claims of any previous creditors.

8　A precise, formal, old-fashioned person; one having strict or narrow ideas of conduct.

9　Martineau appears to be referring here to the Landlord and Tenant Act (of 1851, not 1850), which recognized the tenant's right to remove agricultural and trade fixtures and buildings on the expiration of a lease, provided the land was undamaged.

10　Sir Joseph Napier (1804–1882). Born in Belfast, educated at Trinity College Dublin. Actively opposed to Catholic Emancipation, he professed staunch Tory politics and an Evangelical Protestantism. He argued against any changes to the land laws in Ireland in favour of tenants, stating in the House that tenant grievances lay in their indolence and fondness for sedition, rather than in land laws or landlord greed. Attorney-General for Ireland from 1852–3, he did, however, introduce four Bills in 1852 to amend the Irish land tenure system.

LETTER SIX

1 'On 6 April 1830 O'Connell had founded a Society of the Friends of Ireland of all Religious Persuasions to fight for a number of causes of which one was repeal of the union. For him repeal, to be achieved with liberal Protestant as well as Catholic support, meant what he defined himself in 1833 as "an Irish parliament, British connection, one king, two legislatures". Basic to his anti-union politics was the avoidance of all physical-force methods and a total reliance on parliamentary democracy'. J. Lydon, *The Making of Ireland: From Ancient Times to the Present* (London, Routledge, 1998), p. 292.

2 Daniel O'Connell (1775–1847). 'The Liberator'. Educated at Cork and the English Colleges of Saint-Omer and Douai. He left France in 1793, but his brief experiences of the revolution there had a lasting impact upon him, and determined his pacific approach to politics. He was called to the Bar in 1798, and set up the Catholic Board in 1811. In 1823 he founded the Catholic Association, and was elected MP for Clare in 1828 (re-elected 1829). His most famous campaign was for Catholic Emancipation (granted in 1829), following which he devoted himself to the repeal of the Union. He subsequently founded the Repeal Association in 1840, but clashed with more militant nationalists such as Thomas Davis and Charles Gavan Duffy, who forged the Young Ireland movement. Elected Lord Mayor of Dublin in 1841, he remained active until his death for Catholic rights.

3 'The trick was never to define what Repeal meant – or did not mean. Later, in the Home Rule era, Repeal came to be shorthand for the unacceptable face of nationalism; "We all declare against Repeal," remarked one moderate, "and then put whatever meaning we like upon the declaration".' Foster, *Modern Ireland*, p. 308.

4 William Reginald Courtenay, 11th Earl of Devon (1807–1888). Politician and philanthropist. Secretary to the Poor Law Board (1850–9); headed an investigation into the Irish land system (popularly known as the Devon Commission): 'On the 20th November 1843 five gentlemen – earl of Devon (chairman), Sir Robert Ferguson, George A. Hamilton, Sir Thomas Redington and John Wynne – were directed by Royal Commission to inquire "into the state of the law and practice in respect to the occupation of land in Ireland".' D. Armstrong, *An Economic History of Agriculture in Northern Ireland, 1850–1900* (Oxford, Plunkett, 1989), p. 85.

5 'A more militant approach was soon demanded by younger members of the Repeal Association. Dissensions tore the movement asunder and by the time of O'Connell's death in 1847 it was obvious that his methods of winning repeal had failed utterly. New ideas became dominant, not least those propagated by the group known as Young Ireland, led by Thomas Davis'. Lydon, *The Making of Ireland*, p. 296.

6 From 1850, the Irish Tenant League, and others associated with land reform, had sought the establishment of independent tribunals which would determine fair rents for properties. It was not, however, until Gladstone's Land Act of 1881 that such a system was developed.

7 The Ulster system of Tenant Right gave greater economic benefits to the outgoing tenant than in other parts of the country; namely, he could expect to be properly renumerated for any improvements he had made during his tenancy: 'Concerted action against landlord power began not with wretched evicted smallholders but amongst more substantial tenants, many of whom had come through the potato harvest failures largely unscathed. Their aim was to defend the Ulster tenant right – a custom long accepted in the north that there would be no eviction if the rent was paid and that a tenant giving up his holding could demand a lump-sum payment (often as high as £10 an acre) from the incoming tenant. The 1845 Devon Commission had criticised this practice, which seems to have prevailed over most of Ulster, and several northern landlords had recently disregarded it. The problem was that tenant right was merely a custom, variously interpreted in different areas (in some places it gave no protection from eviction), but it was a valuable form of insurance, providing the outgoing tenant, for example, with enough cash to take his family to America. Such a right was worth defending'. Bardon, *Ulster,* pp. 313–14.

LETTER SEVEN

1 Robert Jocelyn, 3rd Earl of Roden (1788–1870). Elected MP for Dundalk in 1810, created a peer of the United Kingdom in 1821. An ardent Conservative, for many years he took a prominent part in Conservative and Protestant gatherings in the north of Ireland and elsewhere. Religious societies, such as the Hibernian Bible Society, the Sunday School Society, the Evangelical Alliance, and the Protestant Orphan Society, found in him a warm supporter. In the Orange Society he became a grand master. On 12 July 1849 an affray took place between Orangemen and Roman Catholics at Dolly's Brae, near Castlewellan, Co. Down, in which a number of lives were lost (30–50; all Catholics). A commission of inquiry appointed to examine into the matter censured Lord Roden for his conduct in connection with this affair, and he was deprived of his place on the commission of the peace.

2 'The turmoil of the century [seventeenth] and the large scale confiscation which followed the war against Cromwell brought in new proprietors who saw in the trees a rapid road to wealth. An era of confiscation did not favour tree preservation and a succession of owners, uncertain of the permanency of their stay, utilised their period of possession to turn their trees into cash and the woods fell at an alarming rate'. H.M. Fitzpatrick, *Trees and the Law* (Dublin, Incorporated Law Society of Ireland, 1985), p. 2.

3 Augustus Frederick Fitzgerald, 3rd Duke of Leinster (1791–1874). Educated at Eton and Oxford, he succeeded to his title young, and quickly established a reputation as a liberal Whig. He supported Catholic Emancipation and the Reform Bill, and was an attentive and highly regarded landlord.

4 Sir Robert John Kane, (1809–90). Studied medical and practical science both in Dublin and Paris. In 1831 he was appointed Professor of Chemistry to the Apothecaries' Hall, Dublin, a position he retained until 1845. In 1842 he was appointed Secretary to the council of the Royal Irish Academy. Kane paid much attention to the development of industries in Ireland, and delivered a course of lectures on the subject in Dublin in 1843. In 1844 he collected his material in a volume, entitled *Industrial Resources of Ireland*. The work met with much success, and a second edition was published in 1845. In 1845 Kane received the appointment of President of the Queen's College at Cork. He was knighted in 1846, and elected President of the Royal Irish Academy in 1877. In 1880 he was made Vice-Chancellor of the newly created Royal University of Ireland.

5 'That the country was some centuries ago remarkable for its extent of forests, as it is now by the reverse, appears from all our histories. Many causes conspired for their destruction. In some districts they were extirpated to increase the arable surface. In others in order to destroy the shelter which bands of outlaws found in their recesses. During all this time, no one planted; all sought their immediate profit and cared not for the future'. R. Kane, *The Industrial Resources of Ireland* (Dublin, Hodges, 1845), p. 3.

6 'An Act for the Preservation of Shrubs and Trees: 'Whereas the several acts passed from time to time in this Kingdom for the encouragement of planting, cannot attain the great and desirable ends proposed by them . . . be it enacted . . . That no person whatsoever holding . . . or by will or sufferance, shall cut down, grub up, lop or top any tree, wood, or underwood'. *Irish Statutes*, vol. xv (1790–1).

7 'An Act for Encouraging the Planting of Timber Trees: 'Be it enacted by the authority aforesaid, That . . . any Tenant . . . for years exceeding twelve years unexpired, shall plant sally, ozier, or willows, the sole property of such shall during the continuance of the term vest in the tenant, [and he] shall be entitled to the said trees or the value of them according to the directions hereafter mentioned'. *Irish Statutes*, vol. ix (1763–7).

8 'An Act to Amend the Laws for the Encouragement of Planting Timber Trees: 'Any tenant for life or lives, by settlement . . . or any tenant for years, exceeding fourteen years unexpired, who shall plant, or cause to be planted, any timber trees of oak, ash, elm, beech, fir, alder, or any other trees, shall be entitled to cut, fell, and dispose of the same . . . at any time during the term. Provided always, That any tenant so planting or causing to be planted, shall, within twelve calendar months after such planting, lodge with the clerk of the peace of the country . . . an affidavit'. *Irish Statutes*, vol. xii (1781–4).

9 Although the two eighteenth-century acts referred to by Martineau constitute efforts by government to redress the depletion of Irish woods, there were several reason why Irish woods were decimated in the first place. Woods, as McCracken suggests, 'were profitable to the new settlers [, but] they had their drawbacks. They offered shelter to dispossessed Irish and they harboured wolves'. E. McCracken, *The Irish Woods Since Tudor Times: Their Distribution and Exploitation* (Newton Abbot, David and Charles, 1971), p. 32.

10 'My landlord did not wish to take my trees, nor did he wish to pay me for them, and he could not give them to me. Suppose he had said your only alternative is to cut them down, I must then destroy the place I have been making for forty years in order to get my rights – and this because the law so wills it. My Lord, its monstrous! Will the face of this country improve under such a law? . . . No. I may grow furze or heath, or brambles, but I won't grow timber [A Sufferer]'. *Paper on the State of the Law Relative to the Registry of Trees. Cork, October 31, 1844*, PP, vol. xxii, 1845, appendix no. 59.

LETTER EIGHT

1 George Berkeley (1685–1753). Philosopher, Bishop of Cloyne. Born near Thomastown, Co. Kilkenny, and educated at Trinity College Dublin, where he became a Fellow in 1707, and a Tutor from 1707–24. Published *Treatise concerning the Principles of Human Knowledge* (1710), and was elected junior Dean in 1710 and junior Greek lecturer in 1712. Published *The Querist* (1735–7), a series of detached maxims in the form of queries: [Q 512] 'Whether our natural Irish are not partly Spaniards and partly Tartars; and whether they

do not bear signatures of their descent from both these nations, which is also confirmed by all their histories?' A.A. Luce and T.E. Jessop (eds), *The Works of George Berkeley, Bishop of Cloyne,* vol. 6 (London, Nelson, 1953), p. 147.

2 Berkeley sailed from Greenwich on 4 September 1728, and landed at Newport, Rhode Island, the following January. He remained in America until autumn 1731, whereupon he departed for London, arriving in Britain in February 1732. Berkeley continued to take an interest in the colonies, particularly in educational matters – his original plan had been to establish a college in the Bermudas – and in addition to leaving books for the universities of Harvard and Yale, founded scholarships at Yale.

3 The *Report from Her Majesty's Commissioners of Inquiry into the State of the Law and Practice in respect to the Occupation of Land in Ireland* (the Devon Commission) was presented to both Houses. Well over one thousand individuals gave evidence, and a wide range of land issues were addressed, including rents, use of land, evictions, and landlord-tenant relations. PP, vols XIX–XXII, 1845.

4 No reference to the Society for Protecting the Rights of Conscience exists in Thoms Directory for 1852–3.

5 Richard Whately (1787–1863). Born in London, educated at Oriel College Oxford, Whately was consecrated Archbishop of Dublin on 23 October 1831. In Trinity College, of which he was *ex officio* visitor, he founded in 1832 a chair of Political Economy. In 1833 he took his seat in the House of Lords. A member of the Royal Irish Academy (nominated Vice-President, 1848), Whately presided over the statistical department of the British Association at Belfast in 1852 and at Dublin in 1857: 'There was an orchestrated attempt in the nineteenth century to assimilate Ireland to England by, in effect, changing the perceived national character of the Irish to a robust, hard-headed, progressive, modern, in a word, masculine mode. The conductor of the orchestra was Archbishop Richard Whately of Dublin and his chosen instrument was a particularly swashbuckling macho version of the 'science' of political economy'. Foley, 'Public Sphere', p. 21.

LETTER NINE

1 Mary Leadbeater (1758–1826). Quaker and author. Published *Cottage Dialogues* (1811), *The Landlord's Friend* (1813), *Tales for Cottagers* (1814), and *Cottage Biography* (1822). Her most successful publication, *Cottage Dialogues,* was a quasi-fictional account of peasant life in Ballitore, Co. Kildare, intended to instruct the poor in good husbandry: ' . . . the characteristic of the book is good sense. Prudence and economy, morality and religion, are judiciously and liberally diffused through the whole, without touching upon particular tenets, without alarming party prejudice, or offending national pride'. M. Edgeworth, Preface, in M. Leadbeater, *Cottage Dialogues among the Irish Peasantry* (London, Johnson, 1811), p. iv.

2 The notion that O'Connellite politics were responsible for the declining critical interest in Leadbeater's texts is provocative. Another interpretation is that, quite apart from its inappropriateness at a time of famine, the didactic form became simply unpopular: 'An attack upon the whole concept of didactic fiction was made in 1845 in the *Dublin University Magazine,* the Irish Protestant and Tory periodical, by Sir Samuel Ferguson. The impression gained from reading this review . . . is that while there was a convention that such instruction should exist and that authors and readers alike followed the convention, the professional critics were in something of a quandary. They could not object to sound moral

teaching, either in their own personae or as visible literary figures but they were uneasy about the artistic damage that such teaching might do'. M. Keane, *Mrs. S.C. Hall: A Literary Biography* (Gerrards Cross, Smythe, 1997), p. 48.

3 Regarding ophthalmia, Kinealy suggests that it 'was caused by a vitamin deficiency resulting from a prolonged absence of fat in the diet. Prior to the Famine, the Irish diet traditionally included Vitamin A in the form of milk, but this tended to disappear as the traditional potato diet was replaced by a far less nutritious grain-based diet'. Kinealy suggests that during the three-year period between 1849 and 1851, 1,352 people admitted to workhouses alone lost the use of one or both eyes. 'It was not until the spring of 1852', just before Martineau's arrival, 'that some signs of recovery were apparent in these unions, and the levels of distress and mortality began to decrease'. Kinealy, *This Great Calamity*, p. 294.

LETTER TEN

1 The Trustees of Maynooth, meeting in June 1795, considered several sites for the seminary, although the lands around the Duke of Leinster's estate became fairly quickly the preferred option: 'they invested in about sixty acres of land, on a lease for lives renewable for ever granted to them by the Duke of Leinster . . . Maynooth in those days could hardly be described as being 'in the vicinity of Dublin'. What induced the Trustees to move so far out was undoubtedly the active good will of Ireland's premier nobleman, the Duke of Leinster . . . The 'Catholic college' does not appear to have been very welcome in other places, so the patronage of the Duke, a liberal according to his friends, a radical according to his enemies, was an important factor'. P.J. Corish, *Maynooth College, 1795–1995* (Dublin, Gill and Macmillan, 1995), p. 13.

2 William Thomas LePoer Trench, Earl of Clancarty (1803–1872). Educated at St John's College, Cambridge, he was a Conservative in politics. His administration of his Galway estates found less favour with his tenants than Martineau suggests.

3 Clancarty was deeply involved with the Evangelical movement in the west of Ireland: 'Evangelism did not claim the abiding attention of most Protestants, but it did sweep into its fold the Trench family, an event which was to be productive of much strife and ill-feeling in Ballinasloe for well nigh a hundred years. As the principal landlords in the parish, using all the influence of their position, they became patrons of the various efforts to win proselytes from Catholicism'. P. Egan, *The Parish of Ballinasloe* (Dublin, Clonmore, 1960), p. 178.

4 'The point may technically be made that the Cromwellian settlement affected "only a small part of the population": in fact, at most 2,000 families (and their retainers) were actually moved. But to this must be added the psychological displacement of changes of ownership, even where *residence* remained unaltered. The salient fact was that Catholics held about 60 per cent of Irish land in 1641; about 9 per cent in 1660; and about 20 per cent after the Restoration settlement'. Foster, *Modern Ireland*, pp. 115–16.

5 'Connaught and Clare were the designated areas for transplantation of proprietors who forfeited their lands elsewhere; they were to be settled within a cordon sanitaire imposed by the Shannon and the sea. The reasons for choosing this area were strategic, not economic; Ulster, not Connaught, was still considered the poorest province'. Foster, *Modern Ireland*, p. 110.

6 Martineau's exasperation with the Irish landscape is underlined by the fact that although many native Irish had 'left', their habitations, silent witnesses to despair, remain.

7 'Prior to the unlocking of the chemical reservoir stored in coal tar, there were some tentative efforts to exploit the chemical potential of turf. One of the pioneers in the field was a Welsh chemist named Rees Reece who patented a process for distilling peat in an air blast in 1849'. J. Feehan and G. O'Donovan, *The Bogs of Ireland* (Roscrea, UCD Environmental Institute, 1996), p. 102.

8 In 1849 a large plant 'was set up by Reece and his Irish Peat Company at Kilberry near Athy, the first of its kind in the world. The aim was to produce peat gas and tar, along with a range of by-products including calcium acetate, ammonium sulphate, methyl alcohol, paraffin wax, petroleum and lubricating oils'. However, despite the active participation of Sir Robert Kane (above), the venture failed, 'possibly because coal gas became a cheaper raw material for the manufacture of these products'. Feehan and O'Donovan, *The Bogs of Ireland*, p. 103.

LETTER ELEVEN

1 Edmund Ronalds (1819–1889). Lecturer in chemistry at St Mary's Hospital and the Middlesex Hospital, he was appointed Professor of Chemistry in Queen's College Galway in 1848. He resigned the chair in 1856 to take over the Bonnington chemical works in Edinburgh, retiring in 1878. He operated a private research laboratory in the city until his death.

2 Although Martineau talks up the attractions of such an industry, it was in decline for some time: 'Kelp is also an old and considerable article of trade. It is principally manufactured in Connemara, and is brought to town by sea. For some years about 4,000 tons were annually exported, a considerable portion to the northern parts of Ireland, where it was much used in the manufacture of linen, and the remainder to England and Scotland. The price and consumption of this article, however, have of late very much diminished'. James Hardiman, *The History of the Town and County of Galway* (Dublin: Folds, 1820), p. 287.

3 'Whilst the basking shark was known to frequent the shallow inshore waters of the west coast, sometimes appearing in numbers in the secluded bays in fine weather, it was realised from very early on that these fish represented only the fringe of the great shoals to be found some distance from land. Thus we are told by Whitely Stokes in 1821 that the Aran boatmen "go great distances in the Atlantic in pursuit of the basking shark, called sun-fish". K. McNally, *The Sun-Fish Hunt* (Belfast: Blackstaff, 1976), p. 15.

4 Whether the story of selling the liver oil from basking sharks as train oil is true or not, the idea that Claddagh fishermen were unaware of the manufacturing uses (and financial attractions) of such oil is nonsense: 'The oil was used by many country people for a variety of domestic purposes: in addition to the more obvious outlets such as fuel for lamps, dressing wool and preserving timber, it was applied as a soothing balm to skin burns and bruises, and esteemed as an embrocation for the relief of muscular pain. Industrially the oil was used for lighting and in certain manufacturing processes, including the hardening of cast steel. As early as 1740, and possibly much before, sun-fish oil was supplied to contractors responsible for maintaining lanthorns in the streets of Dublin'. McNally, *The Sun-Fish Hunt*, p. 9.

5 'The apparent dearth of basking sharks noted in the 1830s had marked a turning point in the fortunes of the fishery, as had to some extent the winding up of the Fisheries Board and the discontinuance of the bounty scheme some years earlier. Hitherto sun-fish oil had enjoyed a prestige in certain quarters that kept demand ahead of supply most seasons; yet by 1836 it was "scarcely to be found in the trade". Some observers attributed this decline to a lack of industry

on the part of fishermen and to ineffective equipment, rather than to any significant reduction in the numbers of fish visiting the coast, but it is likely that the run down state of the fishery also reflected the increasing availability of alternative commercial oils'. McNally, *The Sun-Fish Hunt,* p. 26.

6　The Claddagh always functioned in British travel literature as a spectacularly Irish affair. It managed to appear threatening (largely because self-governing) and exotic (mainly because of the attire of its inhabitants, their speech, and so on) at the same time. However, no visit to the west of Ireland was complete without a call to the Claddagh, and during the 1840s and 1850s it held a particular fascination for travellers, ethnologists and prosleytizing missionaries alike: 'Like the inhabitants of some of the fishing villages in Scotland, these Claddaghites seem to have acquired and retained some special usages and habits of their own. Even their Irish is said to differ from the Irish in common use. They have a nominal local government of their own, with a so-called mayor'. John Forbes, *Memorandums of a Tour in Ireland* (London, Smith, 1853), p. 222.

7　Martineau is highly selective in her descriptions of these events. Although she acknowledges the clerical status of the 'victim' of this case, her attention is more drawn towards his role as an improver of Irish manufactures, and of native Irish intransigence in the face of potential improvement. However, the subject to whom she refers, Alexander Synge, uncle of playwright John Millington Synge, was ensconced on Inis Mór, one of the three Aran Islands, in 1851 as the first permanent representative of the Church of Ireland on the islands. His job was to establish a mission on the island and to prosletyize. The flare-up to which Martineau refers may have been ostensibly over fishing rights and practices, but Synge was also identified by locals with the prosleytizing mission. Interestingly, the year after Martineau left Ireland relations between Synge and local fishermen, mainly from the Claddagh area of Galway, reached a new low. After more threatening behaviour from the fishermen, Synge decided to identify the culprits in April 1853, only to succeed in creating a riot in which a division of police, with fixed bayonets, charged his assailants and wounded several people. The matter ended up in the Galway Petty Sessions, whereupon the men involved against Synge admitted liability and asked for the mercy of the court. The rioters were discharged after Synge asked that the matter be dropped, on 30 July 1853. Synge remained on the island until 1855. His famous nephew, in *The Aran Islands*, was somewhat circumspect about the events: 'This evening an old man came to see me, and said he had known a relative of mine who passed some time on this island forty-three years ago. "I was standing under the pier-wall mending nets," he said, "when you came off the steamer, and I said to myself in that moment, if there is a man of the name of Synge left walking the world, it is that man yonder will be he"'. J. M. Synge, *The Aran Islands* (1917) (London, Penguin, 1992), p. 9. For a fuller discussion of the case, see B. and R. Ó hEithir (eds), *An Aran Reader* 1991 (Dublin, Lilliput, 1999).

8　The Irish Colleges Act of July 1845 'allowed for the establishment of one or more university college in Ireland. This college or colleges would be built by a government subvention and then supported by annual parliamentary grant. The legislation did not actually lay down where the new college or colleges would be sited but in the months that followed its passing, the locations chosen, after considerable debate and lobbying, were Galway, Cork and Belfast'. B. Walker and A. McCreary, *Degrees of Excellence: The Story of Queen's, Belfast 1845–1995* (Belfast, Institute of Irish Studies, 1994), p. 2.

9　Thomas Skilling, Professor of Agriculture, Queen's College Galway, 1849–65.

10　Since this was written, the commissioners have reported against Galway for an American packet-station. [H.M.'s endnote]

11 'Between 22 August and 10 September 1850 a Catholic synod was held at Thurles, Co. Tipperary. There the bishops agreed to strengthen their collective authority and the supremacy of the Pope; to regularise devotional practice and root out religious customs of doubtful Christian origin; to launch a counter-attack on Second Reformation missionary activity; to insist that Protestant partners marrying Catholics guarantee that all their children be brought up as Catholics; and to campaign for denominational education at every level, though the decision to oppose the non-denominational Queen's Colleges funded by the Government was arrived at only with difficulty'. Bardon, *Ulster*, pp. 344–5.

12 Very Reverend J.P. O'Toole, Vice-President, Queen's College Galway, 1850–2.

13 The Pope has compelled him to resign his office, while declaring that lay students are not forbidden to attend the colleges. [H.M.'s endnote]

LETTER TWELVE

1 Richard Martin (1754–1834). Magistrate and MP for Co. Galway, and resident of Ballinahinch Castle. Supporter of the Union, and of Catholic Emancipation. Co-founder of the Royal Society for the Prevention of Cruelty to Animals (1824).

2 Sir Charles Gavan Duffy (1816–1903). Journalist, lawyer and nationalist, he founded the *Nation* in 1842, and was active in the Young Ireland movement. Arrested in July 1848 (on the eve of the Young Ireland uprising), he was active in the land reform movement, being elected MP for New Ross in 1852. In poor health, he emigrated to Australia in 1855, and became active in both the law and politics. In 1871 he became Prime Minister of Victoria and was knighted in 1873. He retired to the south of France in 1880, where he lived until his death at the age of eighty-seven.

3 John D'Arcy (1788–1839), High Sheriff of Galway, began the construction of the town of Clifden in the early years of the nineteenth century, with particular success in the 1820s and 1830s: 'The binding together of a new community is never an easy task, but this would appear to have been carried off successfully by John D'Arcy in the case of Clifden. As Landlord, chief employer, and Magistrate for the area he carried almost unquestionable authority'. K. Villiers-Tuthill, *History of Clifden, 1810–1860* (1982) (Connacht Tribune, 1992), p. 24.

4 'On the 18th November, 1850, the town of Clifden and almost the entire Clifden, Sillery and Kylemore estates were purchased by Thomas Eyre of Pulteny Street, Bath, Somerset, England, for the sum of £21,245. The Eyre's were absentee landlords and visited the Castle for holidays only. After John Joseph Eyre's death on 15th April, 1894, the lands were held in trust until 1st May, 1931, when they were purchased by the Irish Land Commission. The Castle was abandoned some years before by the family and fell to ruin through neglect'. Villiers-Tuthill, *History of Clifden,* pp. 63–4.

5 'After the famine, attempts were made to clear the land of tenants and replace them with livestock as the income from rents were unreliable and troublesome to collect. Connemara was now almost deserted. Some townlands had only one tenth of the population it had before the famine'. K. Villiers-Tuthill, *Beyond the Twelve Bens: A History of Clifden and District 1860–1923* (1986), (Connacht Tribune, 1990), p. 20.

6 Begun in 1844, D'Arcy's statue was eventually completed in 1995 by the Clifden Heritage Group, and unveiled by Adrian Lead, a descendant of D'Arcy's.

7 'South and east of the town the old Martin Estate was almost all, in 1860, the property of the Law Life Assurance Company London'. Villiers-Tuthill, *Beyond the Bens,* p. 15.

LETTER THIRTEEN

1 The village of Salruck, where there was a church and school built by the Irish Church Mission Society. The landlord, Major-General Thomson, was a supporter of the society. I am indebted to Kathleen Villiers-Tuthill for this information.

2 'Jumpers' was an insulting term for Protestants. It seems to have originated as the name of a Welsh Methodist sect who jumped as part of their acts of worship. T. Colville-Scott, *Connemara After the Famine*, T. Robinson (ed.), (Dublin, Lilliput, 1995), p. 100.

3 'The Irish Church Mission continued its activities in the region throughout the 1850's and 1860's, although with less aggression than in earlier years. However, this particular legacy of the Famine lingered with the people of Connemara for many years. And up until the Society quit the region in the 1950's its members still managed, at certain periods in the history of the region, to incite bitterness and cause division among the people'. K. Villiers-Tuthill, *Patient Endurance: The Great Famine in Connemara* (Dublin, Connemara Girl, 1997), p. 138.

LETTER FOURTEEN

1 'Frederick Twining, a young engineer from London, was a member of the famous Twining tea family. In September 1855 he married Elizabeth Kathleen Nelson, born and brought up in Bermuda, where her father served in the Foreign Office, but whose family were originally from County Tipperary. The young couple came to Ireland where Frederick had recently purchased almost nine hundred acres of land at Cleggan Bay'. Villiers-Tuthill, *Beyond the Bens*, p. 140.

2 Thomas Butler, of Rockfield House, now known as Crocknaraw: 'We now came to a house called Rockville, a property belonging to Mr. Butler (a Protestant), from Carlow. In front of Mr. Butler's lawn and gardens was a small rocky eminence, on which from a slight flag-staff I saw revelling in pure air the British Union Jack, beneath which several children were gambolling. The young plantations were thriving very luxuriantly'. F.B. Head, *Fortnight in Ireland* (London, Murray, 1852), p. 177.

3 'In contrast to the activities of the Irish Church Mission Society was the very personal Christian mission taken by James and Mary Ellis [who], on reading the reports of their fellow Quakers on the terrible conditions in the west of Ireland, decided to uproot themselves from their comfortable surroundings in Bradford, England and take up residence in Connemara. They made the move in 1849 and for the next eight years they "spent their time and income there in trying to set an example of honest dealing and generous treatment of the poor Irish"'. Villiers-Tuthill, *Patient Endurance*, p. 138.

4 John MacHale (1791–1881). Educated at Maynooth, he became lecturer in theology there in 1814. An outspoken critic of English policy in Ireland, he wrote to Lord Grey in 1831 proposing denominational education, Repeal, abolition of tithes and Tenant Right in order to remedy the country's ills. He was made Archbishop of Tuam in 1834, and used this key position to condemn mixed schooling, at all levels. Immensely popular in Connaught, although less influential outside of the province because of the dynamic figure of Archbishop Cullen, he was one of the most vociferous opponents of the Protestant mission on Achill Island.

5 A cousin of Lord Byron, the Reverend Alexander Dallas was an influential Evangelical figure, who established missions in the Connemara region in late 1849 and 1850, and inflamed the passions of local people and clergy alike: 'As

the ICM [Irish Church Mission] established itself firmly in Connemara, the Roman Catholic Church became seriously worried about the large numbers converted to the Protestant Faith. It is difficult to ascertain the exact number of converts, however, as reports tend to be exaggerated by both sides'. Villiers-Tuthill, *History of Clifden*, p. 71.

6 'The little farm of Mr. Ellis is surrounded by moors and barren hills, and was, indeed, only four years since, nothing but a barren moor itself. By indefatigable and continuous exertions, and a great expenditure of money, Mr. Ellis has converted this wild spot, if not to a paradise, certainly to a cultivated, fertile-seeming, English-looking homestead, – a green smiling island amid the dark desert of moors and bogs around it. Even now, Mr. Ellis's works supply the staple support of the labouring class in the district, as, at this very time he constantly employs about sixty persons on his farm, and in breaking up fresh moors to add to it'. Forbes, *Memorandums*, pp. 260–1.

7 Thomas Eastwood took possession of Addergoole Farm in 1847, and lived there for eleven years. The property is now owned by the Benedictine Nuns of Kylemore Abbey.

8 Alexander Nimmo (1783–1832). Scots engineer and surveyor. Undertook an extensive survey of the bogs and coastline of Ireland and in 1822 was appointed engineer of the western district. He oversaw construction of piers, harbours, and roads, and the reclamation of wasteland: 'Alexander Nimmo, engineer to the western district, was sent to Clifden in 1822. He drew up plans for a quay at the town and various Government bodies contributed financially to its construction. Mr Nimmo was also responsible for the laying down of roads through central Connemara and along the coast, linking Clifden with Galway and Westport'. Villiers-Tuthill, *Beyond the Bens,* p. 11.

9 George John Browne, Marquis of Sligo (1820–1896). Educated at Eton and Trinity College, Cambridge, Sligo was a Liberal in his politics until 1886, at which time he declared himself Unionist. Twice widowed and married three times (his second wife died in childbirth), he nevertheless died without heirs.

10 William Pike was one of three purchasers who made up the shortfall when the Achill Mission bought the island from Sir Richard O'Donnell in 1850.

11 Edward Nangle, a young Church of Ireland minister, established a missionary settlement on Achill Island, to convert the Catholics (1834). The mission aroused intense interest in Ireland and abroad, and vigorous opposition on the part of the Catholic Church, led by Archbishop MacHale. Great success in conversions were claimed during the Famine, but the missionaries were criticized for linking relief with conversion. The venture declined in the 1880s.

LETTER FIFTEEN

1 'The people of Inishkea used to worship a stone, called Naomog; a dress of flannel was made for the stone when a "favour" was required. The local priest when he heard about it arranged for the stone to be thrown into the sea. A similar story is told about Achill, the people, according to Nangle, "worshipping a stone for their god"'. T. McDonald, *Achill. 5000 B.C. to 1900 A.D. Archaeology, History, Folklore* (1992), p. 104. For a sarcastic contemporary account of the Inishkea islanders, see Caesar Otway, *Sketches in Erris and Tyrawly* (Dublin, Curry, 1841), esp. pp. 107–9.

2 'From the 1830s onward, some attention was given by the Grand Jury of Mayo to the problems of providing a practical road system in the more forward-looking parts of the island. But, by and large, little of permanent worth was

accomplished before the end of the century. The most primitive of these "roads" were little more than single-file paths that run straight over bog and mountain with the greatest linear economy, their sole purpose being to bring the traveller to his destination within as short a walking distance as possible'. K. McNally, *Achill* (Newton Abbot, David and Charles, 1973), p. 123.

3 Reverend Nangle (above) began his Achill mission in 1834 at the village of Dugort. Amongst other things, he oversaw the construction of St Thomas's church, a farm, a post-office, and a printing office from where he produced the *Achill Missionary Herald and Western Witness*, a publication in which he 'made no pretence that the Achill Mission was anything but a proselytising station of the Second Reformation which encouraged large donations from overseas towards the upkeep of the "colony"'. Although opposed by many Catholic and Established Church members alike, Nangle's mission saw considerable success. However, when Martineau was visiting in late 1852 changes were underway: 'When the Rev. Nangle left Achill in 1852 the Mission was in decline. By 1865, the congregation had dwindled considerably and very few Achill children attended the Mission schools'. McDonald, *Achill*, pp. 78, 85.

4 'Only the name of the Mission remained in 1880, and in 1883 the schools were placed under the care of "The Irish Society for the Promotion of Education of the native Irish through the medium of their own Language". The Mission society withdrew from the island in 1885. Today, the settlement in Dugort stands witness to the endeavours of the Mission Society. The neat street plan, unlike other settlement forms on the island, testifies to its non-native origin. The Church of St. Thomas today invites all denominations to enter freely'. T. McDonald, *Achill*, p. 86.

5 'Between 1841 and 1851 the population of Achill, including the islands of Achillbeg and Inishbiggle, decreased by 906 inhabitants. This represents a population decline of approximately one-fifth, a sizeable fall by any reckoning but one which compares favourably with the county of Mayo as a whole, which lost almost one-third of its people in the same period'. McNally, *Achill*, p. 83.

6 Archbishop MacHale of Tuam, Co. Galway (above).

7 Archbishop MacHale made several efforts to stave off encroachments by Bible-readers and other evangelizing groups, particularly during the Famine years. Regarded by many as just as fanatical, he countered the Reformational zeal of individuals such as Nangle by building Catholic churches, such as the monastery at Bunacurry on Achill Island.

8 One priest has been since convicted, and fined £5. We do not know the fate of the other. [H.M.'s endnote]

9 Scalding seems a favourite idea with the priests. 'May the Almighty scald your soul, when you come to die!' is one of their imprecations: in one case used by a bishop to a convert. [H.M.'s endnote]

10 Although the inhabitants of Achill suffered tremendous hardship during the Famine, it is unclear if a settlement such as Martineau describes ever existed at Keem since transhumance (or booleying) was a regular part of island life. Caesar Otway, visiting Achill in 1839, made the following observation: 'Keem, I said, was a singular village; it is only inhabited in summer – who would suppose that the Achillians had such a superfluity of houses, that they had both their winter and summer residence. It seems the owners of the village of Keem, and the renters of the adjoining district, have other houses in a distant part of the island, where they spend winter and spring'. Caesar Otway, *A Tour in Connaught* (Dublin, Curry, 1839), p. 401.

11 '"The village of Kim [*sic*], a little to the east of the diamond (amethyst) quarry" is mentioned in the Ordnance Survey Letters (1838–40)'. Mc.Donald, *Achill*, p. 145. How active it was at the time of Martineau's visit is unclear.

LETTER SIXTEEN

1 Perhaps a few lines from the American traveller, Asenath Nicolson, might do instead: 'Well did James Tuke say, in his graphic description of Erris, that he had visited the wasted remnants of the once noble Red Man in North America, and the negro-quarter of the degraded and enslaved African; but never had he seen misery so intense, or physical degradation so complete, as among the dwellers in the bog-holes of Erris'. Asenath Nicolson, *Annals of the Famine in Ireland* (1851), M. Murphy (ed.), (Dublin, Lilliput, 1998), p. 91.

2 'At the beginning of 1849, the Boundary Commissioners made a recommendation that fifty new unions should be created. Their list was based in order of urgency, the most immediate need being in the west of the country, that is for unions to be established in Belmullet, Castletown, Berehaven and Killala'. Kinealy, *This Great Calamity*, p. 283.

3 'Our first visit was to the station for curing fish, lately established by Government, for the encouragement of the fisheries, and as a model for private enterprise, – having a parcel of fishing-tackle, from a Friend of Dublin, for the superintendent. We found this gentleman – sent for from Scotland for the purpose – intelligent and obliging, and ready with any information required. The object is to open a market for the poor fishermen'. William Bennett, *Narrative of a Recent Journey of Six Weeks in Ireland* (London, Gilpin, 1847), p. 21.

4 There would appear to be some confusion concerning this particular incident. The only curing-house that I have been able to trace suggests a somewhat different, probably Famine-related, set of reasons for its decline: 'During the 1840s, a fishing station was established in the vicinity of Belmullet. It was opened in January of 1847. The Society of Friends who were actively involved in relieving the poor and starving of the town helped finance the station. They placed a Mr. Campbell, a Methodist preacher, in charge as their agent. At the station fish were washed and cured, boats were built 'with a view to inducing the people to fish'. Unfortunately, the station was forced to close in January 1849 because the fishermen who supplied the station with fish were imprisoned for plundering a passing vessel laden with flour'. S. Noone, *Where the Sun Sets* (Naas, Leinster Leader, 1991), pp. 75–6.

LETTER SEVENTEEN

1 George Charles Bingham, 3rd Earl of Lucan (1800–1888). Elected MP for Co. Mayo in 1826, a seat he held until 1830. Had a distinguished military career, including commanding the 17th Lancers (known as Bingham's Dandies) at Balaclava.

2 Ophthalmia spread rapidly in the overcrowded workhouses during the Famine. In 1851 William Wilde (1815–1876, father of Oscar, medical commissioner of the Irish census of 1841, and probable 'eminent surgeon' referred to by Martineau) published *Epidemic Ophthalmia* which discussed the prevalence of the disease.

3 'After a good deal of unsuccessful petitioning on the part of the starving people and many delays and many unfulfilled promises on the part of the upper class, the government was moved at last to extend relief by giving employment in the shape of making "broad roads", as they were called. Government engineers were sent out at a good salary to mark out the new lines of roads, through rocks and bogs and every other impediment. The greatest engineering and ingenuity used in laying out these were to find out the most difficult routes, impossible to

make and impossible to tread'. Hugh Dorian, 'Donegal, sixty years ago' (1896) photostat copy in NLI Ms 2047, cited in N. Kissane, *The Irish Famine: A Documentary History* (Dublin, National Library of Ireland), p. 70.

4 'Here is where the government advisers dealt out the successful blow and it would appear premeditated, the great blow for slowly taking away human life, getting rid of the population and nothing else, by forcing the hungry and the half-dead men to stand out in the cold and in the sleet and rain from morn till night for the paltry reward of nine pennies per day. Had the poor pitiful creatures got this allowance, small as it was, at their homes, it would be relief, it would be charity; it would convey the impression that their benefactors meant to save life, but in the way thus given, on compulsory conditions, meant next to slow murder'. Cited in Kissane, *The Irish Famine*, p. 70.

5 'Among the greatest of [the] depopulating landlords was the earl of Lucan, who owned over 60,000 acres. Having once said that he "would not breed paupers to pay priests", Lord Lucan was as good as his word. In the parish of Ballinrobe, most of which was highly suitable for grazing sheep and cattle, he demolished over 300 cabins and evicted some 2,000 people between 1846 and 1849. In this campaign whole townlands were cleared of their occupiers. The depopulated holdings, after being consolidated, were sometimes retained and stocked by Lord Lucan himself as grazing farms and in other cases were leased as ranches to wealthy graziers'. James S. Donnelly, Junior, 'Landlords and tenants' in W.E. Vaughan (ed.), *A New History of Ireland, vol. V: Ireland Under the Union, I, 1801–70* (Oxford, Clarendon, 1989), p. 341.

6 'By the end of 1847 some 230,000 had left for the Americas and Australia, and tens of thousands more had gone to Britain. The potato failure of 1848 provoked a further mass exodus. Throngs of people again sought winter passages in 1848–9 and 1849–50, and whole districts became deserted. With larger families also cutting their losses and departing, even "clearing" landlords became alarmed at the "depopulation" of Ireland. In 1849 and 1850 the numbers leaving for America exceeded 200,000 per annum. They peaked in 1851 at just under a quarter of a million, and then began to decline'. P. Gray, *The Irish Famine* (London, Thames and Hudson, 1995), p. 100.

7 'Already in the 1830s Irish movement out of the British Isles was widely believed to be a "chain migration", whereby the selection of future emigrants lay largely with those who had gone before. Chain migration, at first serving to reassemble household units temporarily fractured by the hurried departure of "pioneers", became the main agency for trans-planting the young adults of each generation. The chain mechanism gradually broadened its function from household to communal replanting'. D. Fitzpatrick, *Irish Emigration 1801–1921* (Dublin, The Economic and Social History Society of Ireland, 1984), p. 21.

8 'The focus of evangelical missionary activity in Connaught during the early 1830s was the result of a well-defined strategy of projected advancement based on the evangelisation of the impoverished, underdeveloped, and mainly Irish-speaking counties of the Atlantic seaboard. From its origins in the late eighteenth century, and increasingly as the nineteenth century developed, the chief objective of Irish evangelicals had been the conversion of the native Catholic population to the reformed path'. I. Whelan, 'Edward Nangle and the Achill Mission, 1834–52' in R. Gillespie and G. Moran, *A Various County: Essays in Mayo History 1500–1900* (Westport, FNT, 1987), p. 114.

LETTER EIGHTEEN

1 An Irish friend protests against this statement, saying that nobody in the world ever ate raw potato. He declares it must have been Swedish turnip. All we can say is that we did not judge by the eye alone. We asked the children what raw root they were eating, and they said 'potato'. They might however be only gnawing it. [H.M.'s endnote]

2 The Quakers in Ireland, unlike many other religious groups, have been a genuinely charitable presence, especially during the Famine. In response to the deepening crisis of 1846, for example, they established the Central Relief Committee of the Society of Friends in November of that year: 'The first aim was to raise funds for places where distress was most serious and to collect information about the real needs of the starving people. Separately, Friends in London also set up a committee and immediate cooperation ensued, most of the help from Britain being distributed through the Irish committee. The most important immediate result was the visit of experienced Friends to the worst areas and their detailed reports on conditions'. M. Wigham, *The Irish Quakers: A Short History of the Religious Society of Friends in Ireland* (Dublin, Historial Committee of the Society of Friends in Ireland, 1992), p. 85.

LETTER NINETEEN

1 On 22 July 1852 soldiers of the 31st Regiment of Infantry, accompanying voters to the court house at Sixmilebridge, Lower Bunratty, Co. Clare, fired upon a crowd, killing seven men. An inquest was held at Sixmilebridge between 3 and 18 August, at which contradictory accounts were offered: the soldiers claiming that they were attacked; other witnesses claiming that they fired without provocation. Eight soldiers and a local Magistrate were found guilty of wilfully murdering the seven men. The case was referred to the Grand Jury for sentencing.

2 Lord John Russell, Marquis of Tavistock (1792–1878). Educated at Edinburgh, he was elected MP for Tavistock in 1813. Russell had a long involvement with Irish affairs, visiting his father, the Lord Lieutenant at Dublin Castle in 1807. A liberal in politics, he long advocated parliamentary reform, and was keen to see reforms initiated in the Irish Church. He supported the Catholic Relief Bill in 1829, and opposed coercive measures in Ireland. In 1835 he became Home Secretary and Leader of the House of Commons, and was associated with the promotion of radical and liberal policies in education, poor law and religion. Russell became Prime Minister in July 1846, and shortly afterwards supervised the passage of a Coercion Bill for Ireland almost identical to one he had opposed under Peel. He resigned temporarily in February 1851, and permanently in February 1852, following disagreements with Lord Palmerston.

3 In November 1850 Russell sent a letter to the Bishop of Durham (in response to a Papal Bull which created Roman Catholic Bishops in England) which was virulently anti-Catholic. Amongst other things, Russell made reference to high churchmen as 'unworthy sons of the Church' and to certain Catholic Church practices as 'the mummeries of superstition'. Although well received by staunch Protestants, it did a great deal of damage to relations between Russell and prominent Catholics: 'Seldom has a statement by a prime minister evoked such an enthusiastic response. The press applauded him. Protestant bodies throughout the realm acclaimed him. The archbishop of Canterbury, bishops, and deans showered congratulations on him. Russell had emerged as the

champion of Protestantism against insidious Romanism'. Donal Kerr, '*A Nation of Beggars'? Priests, People, and Politics in Famine Ireland, 1846–1852* (Oxford, Clarendon, 1994), p. 247.

4 The Ecclesiastical Titles Act of 1851 was a response to the restoration of the English Catholic hierarchy in 1850. It strengthened the existing prohibition against 'the assumption of territorial titles in England by Catholic prelates', and has been described as 'a measure that combined minimal effectiveness with a massive amount of offence to Catholics'. R.V. Comerford, 'Churchmen, tenants, and independent opposition, 1850–56' in W.E. Vaughan (ed.), *A New History of Ireland*, p. 401. Catholic feeling was so strong that Irish Liberals opposed the government over unrelated parliamentary issues, causing the brief resignation of Lord John Russell as Prime Minister in February 1851.

5 For a flavour of nineteenth century Irish electioneering, see K.T. Hoppen, *Elections, Politics, and Society in Ireland 1832–1885* (Oxford, Clarendon, 1984).

6 Colonel Vandeleur was on the Board of Guardians at the Kilrush Union, and Conservative candidate at the time of the Sixmilebridge affair: 'Crofton Vandeleur of Kilrush, Colonel of the Clare Militia, who "knew every part of the county, and almost every person in it". Vandeleur had unsuccessfully contested the county as a Conservative in 1841, and came from a family of paternalist and "improving" landlords who had developed Kilrush into a substantial town. Unfortunately the Famine was to demonstrate the limits to Vandeleur's paternalism, for between November 1847 and July 1850 he evicted over one thousand people from his estate and became the most notorious practitioner of what one Select Committee report described as a "wholesale system of eviction and house levelling"'. D. Fitzpatrick, 'Famine, entitlements and seduction: Captain Edmond Wynne in Ireland, 1846–1851', *English Historical Review*, 110 (June 1995), p. 602.

7 Evidence offered by James Frost, Deputy for the Sheriff and supervisor of the polling, contradicts this. He testified at the inquest that he had kept the courthouse free from supporters of either side: 'There was an equal impediment to the Liberal voters as to the others from the crowd in the passages, which I had cleared wherever I observed. The Priests did not accompany the Liberal voters to the polling place; I did not permit them to do so'. PP, vol. XCIV, p. 79.

8 John C. Delmege, JP from Whitehall, Co. Clare, and eight soldiers of Her Majesty's 31st Regiment of Infantry were charged with the deaths of James Casey, James Flaherty, Michael Coleman, Michael Connellan, Thomas Ryan, Jeremiah Trawley and Michael Moloney.

9 The petition against his return has been withdrawn. [H.M.'s endnote]

10 'The coroner's jury duly brought in verdicts of wilful murder against the men, but when the case came before the Grand Jury early the following year, the bills were ignored and the case collapsed. The regiment [however] remained branded in popular opinion'. Virginia Crossman, *Politics, Law and Order in Nineteenth-Century Ireland* (Dublin, Gill and Macmillan, 1996), p. 105.

LETTER TWENTY

1 Sidney Godolphin Osborne (1808–1889). Born in Cambridgeshire, educated at Brasenose College Oxford, Osborne was appointed Rector of Stoke-Poges in Buckinghamshire in 1832. A philanthropist, Osborne published *Gleanings in the West of Ireland* (1850), as well as a series of well-publicized letters to *The Times* on the subject of famine-stricken Ireland. See Margaret Kelleher, *The Feminization of Famine* (Cork, Cork University Press, 1997) for a discussion of Osborne's contribution to Irish Famine literature.

2 In a letter to *The Times*, dated August 1850, Osborne made several allegations regarding the state of the paupers in Kilrush Union (below), including a lack of time and attention given to each applicant for relief ('indecent hurry and noisy strife between the guardians, officers and paupers'), frequently inedible food, and high rates of ill and infirm inmates. The allegations were to have such an impact that W.H. Lucas, a Poor Law inspector and contemporary inspector in charge of Kilrush Union, had to make a defence to the Poor Law Commissioners on 14 April 1851. PP, vol. XLIX, pp. 1–7.

3 This was a common enough strategy, whereby women would admit themselves and their children as 'deserted', when in fact their husbands were working in Scotland or England. See Dymphna McLoughlin, 'Workhouses and Irish female paupers 1840–70' in M. Luddy and C. Murphy (eds.), *Women Surviving: Studies in Irish Women's History in the 19th and 20th Centuries* (Dublin, Poolbeg Press, 1989), pp. 117–47.

4 A highly dubious statement, since the majority of ophthalmic victims were children: 'In 1849 the Poor Law Commissioners were greatly alarmed by an epidemic which they described as ophthalmia in the workhouses. It was particularly rife in the overcrowded and insanitary establishments of the south and west and was especially common among children under fifteen years of age'. Margaret Crawford, 'Food and Famine' in C. Poirteir (ed.), *The Great Irish Famine* (Cork: Mercier, 1995), p. 72.

5 'The workhouse, situated about one and a half statute miles from the town of Ennistymon, was inspected. We found the houses filled with paupers, insufficiently provided with every requisite, without necessary furniture or utensils, regular food or sufficient clothing'. *Copy Report from the Vice Guardians to the Commissioners*, 21 February 1851, PP, vol. XLIX, pp. 439–40.

6 In September 1853 the number of boys and girls aged between 9 and 15 in the Ennistymon workhouse was 194 and 334 respectively. Although 199 girls were receiving instruction in embroidery, the boys, despite Martineau's impression, were not so well catered for. Only 24 boys were receiving instruction in a trade: 16 as tailors, and 8 as weavers.

7 'With total property valuation of only £59,000, even before the first failure of the potato crop in 1845, the Kilrush Union was one of the most impoverished areas of the west of Ireland. During the years of the Famine, its people suffered on a horrendous scale, and tens of thousands died from the effects of starvation and disease. The suffering of the people of Kilrush Union accelerated after the Poor Law Extension Act of 1847 placed financial and administrative responsibility for relief of distress entirely on the poor law, which could not remotely support the burden'. Clare Local Studies Project, *Kilrush Union Minute Books, 1849* (Ennis, Clasp Press, 1997), p. i.

8 'I attended the usual weekly meeting on Thursday last for the admission of paupers in the Kilrush Union. The applicants were numerous, and the majority of the applicants were in a low physical condition, and bore evident traces of great suffering and privation'. *Copy Report from Mr. Lucas, Temporary Poor Law Inspector to the Commissioners*, 7 January 1851. PP, vol. XLIX, p. 361.

9 'I regret to have to report that the pressure for relief in the Kilrush Union continues to an alarming extent, and that during the weeks ended the 4th and 11th instant, upwards of 700 paupers have been admitted into the workhouses'. *Copy Report from Mr. Lucas*, 13 January 1851. PP, vol. XLIX, p. 362.

10 'The Commissioners will observe that the mortality has been increasing for the last three weeks; this may be attributed to the very low physical state in which during that period the majority of the paupers have entered the workhouse,

many of them dying a short time subsequent to their admission'. *Copy Report from Mr. Lucas*, 3 February 1851. PP, vol. XLIX, p. 367.

11 'As in many workhouse unions, the Kilrush guardians of both kinds were for the most part not competent to the responsibilities incumbent upon them. Very few treated these responsibilities with the seriousness they required, and most in fact never even turned up for meetings on a regular basis unless for the specific reason of exercising the patronage of appointing officials or granting contracts to the union's suppliers'. Clare Project, *Kilrush Union*, p. i.

12 'The average cost of the food per inmate at this period [1850] was probably scarcely a penny a day. At any rate, a year later when the diet had improved to some extent, it was costing only 8d. per week per person. Dr. Madden commented on it at this stage: "In the Kilrush dietary, then, we look in vain for animal food, for vegetables, for milk and indeed for bread fit for the food of man"'. I. Murphy, *A People Starved: Life and Death in West Clare 1845–51* (Dublin, Irish Academic Press, 1996), p. 75.

LETTER TWENTY-ONE

1 'As landlords, both the Herberts and the Kenmares shared the same world vision. Their world was one of rank and order, a world over which they presided, bestowing patronage on those below them in a manner in which they saw fit. They came to see themselves, not merely as wealthy landowners, but more as the pre-ordained heads of society; people in whom both power and patronage had been vested for the benefit and good of all'. D. Horgan, *Echo after Echo: Killarney and Its History* (Cork, Blackface, 1988), p. 94.

2 'The line opened in 1853 and before long tourists were flocking in by train, many to stay at the celebrated Railway Hotel which is today known as the Great Southern Hotel'. Mulligan, *Irish Railways*, p. 49.

3 A variety of beet, cultivated for food for cattle. Regarded by some botanists as a hybrid between the red and the white beet.

4 Augustus Welby Northmore Pugin (1812–1852). Architect and writer, trained by his father. Published several influential architectural texts, from 1836–43. Composed detailed drawings of the Houses of Parliament for Sir Charles Barry. Confined to Bedlam as a result of overwork (1851).

5 St Mary's Cathedral, Killarney. Although the foundation stone had been laid in 1842, work ceased in 1848 due to the pressures of the Famine. Work resumed in 1853, and on 22 August 1855 it was consecrated, dedicated to the Assumption of the Virgin Mary, and declared open for divine worship.

6 Ireland was part of a general European-wide expansion of the asylum system, but the government more enthusiastically endorsed the construction of asylums in Ireland than in Britain. Throughout the nineteenth century, an extraordinary total of twenty-two district asylums were constructed, filled for the most part by patients admitted under the Dangerous Lunatics Act (1838, amended 1867). This legislation, which applied only to Ireland, made a direct association between criminality and insanity, and encouraged a perception on the part of civil authorities that asylums were adjuncts of the prison system. I wish to thank Oonagh Walsh for clarification on this point.

7 'In concluding this Report, I must again refer to the fact, that the inconveniences and evil effects resulting from the inadequate Asylum accommodation at present afforded to the Pauper Insane Classes of this country are greatly increasing, and numerous and urgent applications to the District Asylums for admission are daily refused from want of room. Most of the recent and violent cases thus thrown

back upon their own resources, are eventually committed to the County Prisons, which are now crowded with this class of patient'. *Report of the District, Local, and Private Lunatic Asylums in Ireland for 1845*, PP, vol. XXII, pp. 420–1.

8   Given the asylum context, it appears that Martineau refers here to Dean Swift's famous lines: 'He gave the little Wealth he had/To Build a House for Fools and Mad/And Shew'd by one satyric Touch/No Nation wanted it so much', *Verses on the Death of Dr Swift* (1739).

LETTER TWENTY-TWO

1   See Donald Akenson, *The Irish Education Experiment: The National System of Education in the Nineteenth Century* (London, RKP, 1970) for an assessment of what he calls, the 'ecclesiastical and administrative intrigue' (p. 225) behind nineteenth century Irish primary education.

2   'Amongst the guides and boatmen of Killarney, O'Donoghue Mor was something of a folk hero. In their minds, the spirit of this Gaelic Chieftain of old reposed in the many eerie limestone rocks and forms of Loch Lein. The associations with O'Donoghue were numerous'. Horgan, *Echo after Echo*, p. 114. For a truly exhaustive study of the legend of O'Donoghue, see T. Crofton Croker, *Killarney Legends* (London, Fisher, 1831).

LETTER TWENTY-THREE

1   Thomas Campbell Foster published, between August 1845 and January 1846, a series of Irish articles in *The Times*. They were subsequently published (like Martineau's *Letters*) as a volume entitled *Letters on the Condition of the People of Ireland*, (London, Chapman, 1847). Letter XXXI, referred to by Martineau, begins thus: 'Before I enter upon the subject of my letter today I think it necessary – due, in fact, to you – that I should briefly advert to the recent defence of Mr. Daniel O'Connell, in Conciliation-Hall, Dublin, to my charge against him, and which I now repeat – "that amongst the most neglectful landlords who are a curse to Ireland Daniel O'Connell ranks first; that on the estates of Daniel O'Connell are to be found the most wretched tenants that are to be seen in all Ireland;" and that "whenever a 'middleman' is execrated his name will not be forgotten"'. 2nd ed. (pp. 457–8).

2   'Daniel O'Connell, by the universal report of the neighbourhood, has the character of being a kind, indulgent, and improving landlord; and bad as is the condition of many of the tenantry on his estates, they would be much worse off without him; and they are, by appearances, better and more comfortably off than those on the adjoining estates of some standing very high in the government of the country'. Bennett, *Narrative*, p. 122.

3   An Augustine monastery, it was dissolved by Henry VIII. The lands of the abbey were acquired by the O'Connells in 1745, and a three storey house built by O'Connell's grandfather. Daniel O'Connell succeeded to Derrynane in 1825.

LETTER TWENTY-FOUR

1   'Smugglers and pirates frequented Valentia for centuries – pirates who were feared, smugglers whose activities might be welcomed by some of the population. Piracy continued long into the eighteenth century. In 1710 a Captain

Talbot based his privateer of six guns and eighty men in Valentia Harbour and the crew went on plundering excursions ashore'. D.C.C. Pochin Mould, *Valentia: Portrait of an Island* (Dublin, Blackwater, 1978), pp. 50–1.

2   'A manuscript in the Trinity College archives, with the first folios missing, but thought to be written about 1660, says: "About this island (Valentia) is harbour for shipping. Cromwell, the usurper, in the year 1653 built two forts in this island"'. Pochin Mould, *Valentia*, pp. 48–9.

3   Sir Peter George Fitzgerald, 19th Knight of Kerry (1808–1880). Vice-Treasurer in the last ministry of Robert Peel, he succeeded his father in 1849. He resided permanently on Valentia, and was a considerate and progressive landlord, particularly concerned with the welfare of his tenants. He was noted for his implementation of enlightened management in Valentia, and his enthusiasm for modernization ensured that the Atlantic cable terminated on his estates.

4   A reference to Glanleam House, the Fitzgerald residence on Valentia.

5   I have been unable to verify who established the fishery, or how much fishing was being conducted at the time of Martineau's visit. However, one thing is sure: within twenty years of her visit a certain finality had taken hold of Valentia fishing: 'By 1871 the population of the island had declined and with it the fishing . . . the men who carried on the pre-famine fishing had died or emigrated and the few who remained had neither boats, nor nets, nor the capital to procure them'. N. O'Cleirigh, *Valentia: A Different Irish Island* (Dublin, Portobello, 1992), p. 72.

6   The slate quarry on Valentia opened in 1816. The early working was on a small scale, although expansion occurred in 1825 when the Irish Mining Company took over. The quarry was leased in 1839 to an English company who, under the name of the Valentia Flag Company, operated it until 1877.

7   'Even though the supervisors were Welsh during most of the period when the Quarry was worked, the bulk of the workmen were local. The Welshmen associated with the Quarry were supervisors and technically qualified tradesmen, but the manager for the period of its greatest prosperity was an engineer named Bewicke Blackburn, who became quite famous as an inventor and whose daughter, Helen, became involved in the Suffragette movement'. O'Cleirigh, *Valentia*, pp. 64–5.

LETTER TWENTY-FIVE

1   After this was written, we learned more than we could have anticipated of the decay of the practice of confession among the men in Ireland. Among the women it continues; and from them, and by other means, the priest knows enough, it is believed, to stop agrarian crime, if he was bent upon it. But his knowledge of popular secrets is not what it once was. [H.M.'s endnote]

2   Nicholas Patrick Stephen Wiseman (1802–1865). Born in Seville in 1802 of Irish parentage. Ordained in 1825, he became Rector of the English College, Rome, having demonstrated great intellectual ability. In 1850 he was created a Cardinal, and as part of the Pope's restoration of the hierarchy in England, was appointed Archbishop of Westminster.

3   'In the morning I was credibly informed that nine deaths had taken place during the night, in the open streets, from sheer want and exhaustion. The poor people came in from the rural districts in such numbers, in the hopes of getting some relief, that it was utterly impossible to meet their most urgent exigencies, and therefore they came in literally to die. The town itself is overwhelmed with poverty; and the swollen limbs, emaciated countenances, and other hideous

forms of disease to be seen about, were innumerable. In no other part of Ireland had I seen people falling on their knees to beg. It was difficult to sit over breakfast after this'. Bennett, *Narrative*, p. 128.

4 Henry Petty-Fitzmaurice, 3rd Marquis of Lansdowne (1780–1863). Educated at Westminster School, Edinburgh and Cambridge. Elected MP for Calne in 1802, he became Chancellor of the Exchequer in 1805. From an early age he demonstrated a liberal attitude towards issues as diverse as Catholic Emancipation, education, and political reform. During the Famine he was instrumental in relief, introducing the Relief Bill for destitute Irish in February 1847. He withdrew from the House of Lords in 1852, but retained an active, but discreet, political profile until his death.

5 'Otherwise the bulk of assisted emigration was conducted by ten major landlords, who sent out 30,000 emigrants in batches ranging between one and six thousand per landlord. In roughly descending order of "munificence", these benefactors were as follows: Fitzwilliam (Wicklow), Wandesforde (Kilkenny), Lansdowne (Kerry and Queen's)'. Fitzpatrick, *Irish Emigration*, p. 19.

6 Robert Emmet (1778–1803). Educated privately and at Trinity College, where he became known as a political radical within the United Irishmen. He travelled extensively on the Continent, forging contacts with Tallyrand and Napoleon. He planned an Irish uprising for 1803 which took place in July, but with no foreign support quickly failed. Intending to flee to France, he travelled to Dublin to take his leave of Sarah Curran, to whom he was secretly engaged. He was arrested and found guilty of treason, making an extraordinary and moving speech in his defence before being sentenced. He was executed on 20 September 1803.

7 Sarah Curran (d. 1808). The youngest daughter of John Philpot Curran, she became secretly engagd to Robert Emmet, against her father's wishes. Following the exposure of Emmet's role in the 1803 Rising, and her father's denunciations, she left Dublin for Cork, where she met and married Captain Sturgeon in 1805. She moved with him to England where she died three years later.

8 William Smith O'Brien (1803–1864). MP for Co. Limerick (1835–48), joined the Repeal Association (1844), co-founded the Irish Confederation. Led an abortive uprising in 1848, convicted of treason, sentence of death commuted to transportation. Unconditionally pardoned, 1856.

9 Thomas Francis Meagher (1823–1867). Studied law, active in the Repeal movement, a founder of the Irish Confederation. Convicted for sedition (1848), transported to Van Diemen's Land (1849), escaped to America (1852).

10 John Mitchel (1815–1875). Solicitor, nationalist. Aided the Repeal Association, wrote for the *Nation*, established the *Weekly Irishman* (1848). Tried for sedition (1848) and transported, escaped to San Francisco, active for the Fenians in America and France. Elected MP for Tipperary (1875).

11 The last letters Emmet wrote in prison, on the night before his death, were to Sarah Curran's brother Richard, and to his own brother, Thomas Addis Emmet. Both of these describe his feelings for Sarah, and the letter to Thomas Addis asks that although their engagement was a secret, he treat Sarah as if they had been married, if she should be abandoned by her family following Robert's execution. The letters never reached the addressees, being sent to Dublin Castle instead. However the section of the letter to Thomas Addis, detailing Sarah and Robert's engagement, was sent to her father. He swiftly denounced her, and she had to leave the family home. See L. O'Broin, *The Unfortunate Mr. Robert Emmet* (Dublin, Clonmore, 1958), pp. 168–9, for extracts from the letters.

LETTER TWENTY-SIX

1 'Emigration is proposed as a remedy. So long as there is land that would repay
the expense of labour lying unreclaimed, and much more land only half
cultivated, it is opposed to every mercantile principle to send that labour away.
We have in Ireland the two great elements that lie at the foundation of all
national and individual wealth, – land and labour. We have them both in
superabundance . . . Place these three or four million Irish in a fair position,
enable them to earn the necessities and decencies of life, and we have a finer
market opened at home than any of our hard-earned and expensively
maintained possessions abroad: and Ireland is capable of maintaining several
times its present amount of population. At the best, emigration can only be like
the medical man's remedy of bleeding, which can but be done at the expense of
the constitution'. Bennett, *Narrative*, p. 140.

2 On the same subject, only seven years later, Martineau had this to say: 'The
impression left by a historical survey of Irish educational endowments is, that
there has been abundant anxiety, from Henry the Eighth's time downwards, to
win over the Irish, and render the possession of their country secure, by giving
them, early in life, English ideas, desires, and associations. After the long series
of efforts which has been detailed, what has been the result?' H. Martineau,
Endowed Schools of Ireland (London, Smith, 1859), p. 30.

3 Although Martineau discusses the social effects of emigration on both those who
are left behind, as well as those who must depart, emigration is never spoken of
as the result of mass evictions. Bardon describes John Mitchel's *The Last
Conquest of Ireland*, particularly in its assessment of the extent of pre-Famine
evictions, as 'propagandist exaggeration'; nevertheless, Bardon does go on to
argue that Mitchel's 'description could be applied accurately to the six-year
period between 1849 and 1854 when forty-nine thousand families – amounting
to almost one quarter of a million persons throughout Ireland – were
permanently dispossessed in the post-Famine clearances. These figures do not
include the evictions between 1846 and 1848, before the constabulary began
making returns, when dispossession seems to have been particularly relentless
in the counties of Armagh, Antrim and Monaghan'. Bardon, *Ulster*, p. 312.

4 John Henry Ashworth was one of the better-known settlers to the West. In 1852
he published a travel-cum-promotional narrative which captured much of the
potential referred to by Martineau: 'From hence, too, we could distinctly mark
the line of communication which is to unite these two large lakes; and gazing as
we did upon a vast extent of country below us, the mind could not but speculate
upon the rapid changes which must soon come over this fertile, but hitherto
almost unknown region. A more delightful location for a settler than this I can
scarcely conceive'. J.H. Ashworth, *The Saxon in Ireland: or, The Rambles of an
Englishman in Search of a Settlement in the West of Ireland* (London, John
Murray, 1852), pp. 71–2.

5 Theobald Mathew (1790–1856). Catholic priest and temperance advocate.
Signed a total abstinence pledge (1838); travelled extensively through Ireland,
England and the United States preaching the temperance gospel. A charismatic
speaker, he persuaded thousands to join his temperance crusade. Assisted with
relief work during the Famine.

6 A reference to Holy Trinity Church, Cork. Work started on the church in 1832
and, with the exception of the spire, was completed in 1850. The spire and
façade were not added until 1890.

7 'Only with the coming of Father Mathew's crusade after 1838 is it possible to
detect a significant impact on drink consumption itself. While economic factors,

such as excise duty and grain prices, had some influence on the dramatic falls in consumption that occurred around 1840, there seems little doubt that the teetotal crusade was the major factor involved. It has been commonly assumed, however, that the effects of Father Mathew's crusade were temporary and that it had virtually no lasting significance'. E. Malcolm, *Ireland Sober, Ireland Free: Drink and Temperance in Nineteenth-Century Ireland* (Dublin, Gill and Macmillan, 1986), p. 329.

LETTER TWENTY-SEVEN

1   The Church of Ireland was actually disestablished by the Irish Church Act of 26 July 1869. Originally intended as part of a package of measures by Gladstone, it finally stood alone as a key piece of legislation. The Act '[broke] absolutely the legal connection between church and state'. Lyons, *Ireland Since the Famine,* p. 144.

Index